GENESIS OF INDIGENOUS CHAKMA BUDDHISTS AND THEIR PULVERIZATION WORLDWIDE

GENESIS OF INDIGENOUS CHAKMA BUDDHISTS AND THEIR PULVERIZATION WORLDWIDE

S.P. Talukdar

KALPAZ

Published by

Kalpaz Publications
C-30, Satyawati Nagar,
Delhi – 110052
Ph.: 011-47034999, 9811692060
www.kalpazpublications.com
E-mail: kalpaz@hotmail.com

Distribution Network
gyanbooks.com
India, USA, Canada, UK, Australia, France

ISBN: 978-93-5722-388-1 (PB)

First Published, 2024

Printed at: Gyan Press, Delhi.

Genesis of Indigenous Chakma Budhist and their Pulverization Worldwide

Author: S.P. Talukdar

Dedicated to

Indigenous Tribal peoples
and those protecting their lives,
lands and human rights

Some Clippings (Epitoms)

"Wonder is the foundation of all Philosophy,
enquiry the progress. Ignorance the end."
—Michel DE Montaigne (1533-1592), French Philosopher

"There are only two lasting bequests we can
give our children… one is roots,
the other wings"
—Stephen Covey

"Time is a certain part of eternity".
—Marcus Tullius Cicero (106-43 B.C.)
Latin writer, statesman

"To know, is to know that you know nothing,
that is the meaning for true knowledge."
—Confucius (C. 551-479 B.C.), Chinese Philosopher

"A reasonable man adapts himself to the world;
the unreasonable one persists in trying to adapt
the world to himself. Therefore, all progress
depends on the unreasonable man."

—George Bernard Shaw

Contents

Preface

In the present world, there is stiff struggle for strategic power amongst nations for control over one another. Such is the case of the indigenous the Buddhist Chakmas too, of Chittagong Hill Tract in the hinterland of the sea port, Chittagong in Bangladesh. They are now in the holocaust of winter, fractionally divided into a number of countries, but their mind fighting always that they are the broken part of Sakyan race, behind time, whose wheel of fate has fallen differently in the vast changing world of the present day. Once a venturesome tribe now in decline dissemination and in reality they are the disperies popoulation in different circumstances and yet united as a community. A water shade in the life of the indigenous tribal people in CHT who changed forever at the time when Hindus and Muslims were awarded their homelands. In 1947, the transfer of power of the British Colonial Govt. to India and Pakistan on the basis of division of boundary commission resulted in ramifications for Buddhists as CHT was clandestinely added to East Pakistan in violation of the partition rules of colonial India. I have to thankfully acknowledge the kind help received from Srimati Anjali Dewan, Supriya Talukdar, Rabindra Lal Chakma, A.K. Dev Barman and Dr. R.S. Dewan scientist, Dr. David Brazier, founder and head of Amida Trust, London, Ven (Dr.) Bhikkhu Pragya Lankar, Ven. Bhikkhu Priya Pal and Ven Bhikkhu Anomodharshi in preparing this book. I would also like to express my gratitude to Gautam Talukdar, Mrs. Manisha Dev Barman, Nihar Kanti Chakma for their contribution in contingencies defraying much expenses in to the on encomposing all the relevent materials and miscellaneous items on this book. My thanks also goes to R. Excelicia Cunville for translating rendering the Bengali poems of a most estimed Chakma poet, writer Pran Hari

Talukdar's writing into English inessence. Last but not the least my thanks goes to Ven. Bhikkhu Sasana Kitti alter ego Hye Dahl for his contribution of an article 'The ways of Enlightenment'. Kindly pardon me, if I have inadvertently omitted some names. I received from many handsome tips, glean datas and ideas. Please know, how much I appreciate your kind help. Most of all, I would like to express my gratitude to Rohit Talukdar, my nephew without his support this book would not have seen the light of the day. The materialisation of the book could not have taken place.

S.P. Talukdar

Introduction

The book testifies to the fact that there are reasons to believe Chakmas belong to the original Buddhist race in India. They are being maligned by intransigent powerful rulers. They are mired in sufferings for government's subservient policies to them. Thus, they lost their native homeland and became landless and going through a tormented era. In the past, they had a major role in history being the offshoots of Sakyan progeny which had out worn and it could be seen, if we turn to their intrinsic historical past with studying their language, culture, civilization, religion and other aspects. All this has been dredged up in this book of original Buddhists who had been the victims of de-civilization in the modern era being mired in ignorance and getting into the swing of obliviousness, squarely divided in many dominions, and states. When, more than a decade ago, my previous publication was "*The Chakmas Life and Struggle*", I thought, I was summing up things of intellectual enquiry of loss of a sense of identity of Buddhist Chakmas reviewing the origin of their crestfallen era. But, as a matter of fact, I was repressive of my mind as a wage earner at that time and many facts remained unquoted and remained unsubstantiated. Its review was done by *The Hindustan Times* dated 2nd October, 1988 by Kalyan Mukherjee[1] and next was done by P.C. Biaksiama[2] former Dy. Finance Advisor, N.E. Council, Govt. of India, Shillong that was broadcasted AIR (NES) Shillong in Dec. 1996. The social physics of the problem is multilateral and multifarious, which has been dealt in this book, putting up on more backups and esoteric, informations on Chakmas having picked up the thread where I left off in my previous book which had set my mind thinking of many under-covered facts of the Buddhist civilization on the nodal point in Indian sub-continent. The book review understood my innate interest and intentions of my people who were at the receiving end since the independence, 1947. They mentioned in the hindsight, "History Past and Present", of the beleaguered Buddhist Tribe, ousted from their home land CHT now in Bangladesh, which became a sanctuary for insurgents of Muslim fundamentalists and its breeding grounds in this region, they overran the whole area of CHT and carried out an onslaught and outnumbered the locals (tribal). One of the greatest tragedy befalling the contemporary world is the human tragedy, that is the problem of unwanted people, a mismatching community in a Muslim state with aberrated belief (or a way of life) like the Buddhist Chakmas in Bangaladesh. Chakmas Buddhist persuasion has remained a total perfidious act. This has been cited with transparent evidences, and categorically explained in this book. At the highest political level the aim has been to get the Buddhist into the swing of things and in the fullness of time they will be getting into oblivion. This has held back their progress and now at the bottom level of world grouping of classification of people. A renowned Buddhist scholar from Bengal, Pandit Atisa Dipankara, said that giving compassionate love to the helpless and the poor is as important as meditating on emptiness. This virtue of compassion is the principal foundation stone of Mahayana Buddhism.

References

1. *The Chakmas Life and Struggle* by S.P. Talukdar, review of the book by Kalyan Mukherjee.
2. *The Chakmas Life and Struggle* by S.P. Talukdar, review of the book by P.C. Biaksiama.

Prologue

Mr. Rigoberta Menchu Tum[1] recipient of the Noble prize for peace and goodwill Ambassador for 1993, had advocated for the right of world's 300 million indigenous people writing on them is a very finicky job as nothing much is known about them. Many micro indigenous tribes had already been written off or have already lost their original identity in the majority culture with telling effect. Behind the veil they can only raise their voice. In the global scenario their need for social justice and more democratic right and freedom, protecting them equally against sinful activities of the authorities and who can pull powers. This book is in the light of an ever shifting fabric of events resulting in the stratification of Chakmas (Changma as they pronounce themselves) far and wide from their own homeland in the last 50 years. In 1947, the representatives of India and Pakistan (our national leaders) at that time made an infamy ray decision on the acceptance of the British boundary commission's report on Bengal by Sir. Cyril Rad cliffe reading an inflationary spiril in the situation of the future Buddhist Chakmas to their identity unfixing as they had to forgo their geographical area in the burgain of Hindu and Muslim interest with an striking deal of transfer of power for freedom. It was the externalization of quagmire of Chakmas. From the historical perspective once upon a time Indian sub-continent was known to be Buddhist India, when Saka Tribe in which Sakya muni Gautama Buddha was born and they seem to be magnate at many places in smaller and bigger powerful ways like kushan empire who was termed saka or seythian tribe, entered India over 60,000 years B.C. through different routes by Hindukush ranges (Iran) and the Himalayan ranges (Nepal, Tibet and the river valleys (Brahmaputra known to be Tsangpho in Tibet).

In Asoka's time there used to be a friendly relation with yun-nan (China) through Shan states (Myanmar) and the local Buddhist traditions still alive and it seems they belong to the same stock of people, like. Singpho (India), Jampho (China). Khamte, Tai-Phake, Nam-Phake, Tai-Khamyang of one group of people. Chakmas (India, Bangladesh) Daingnak and other denominations inMyanmar of the same stock of people. Some believe Chakmas were in Brahmaputra valley in Assam before their migration to CHT, as their traditional, cultural, physical and linguistic affinities are very common to the Ahom people in Assam. They all grew up in Buddhist ways/ideas. In Hiousen-Tsang's memorial it is written there were eighty-eight thousand stupas from east to west from kingdom Tamralipta to the border of Sindh. There used to be a lot of Stupas in Manipur. The impact of Buddhim is still stongly visible in them which had a tie with Dhanyabati (Dha-ngya-wati) ruled by Sankyan of the same progeny of Gautama Buddha of Kapilavastu (now in Nepal) and moved out after the massacre during Buddha's life time and established kingdom in Myanmar (Burma) and as time rolled in Sakyan's rule was established at Dha-ngya-wati (Arakan). According to Arakan history Gautama Buddha visited Arakan and in his honour a Mahamuni Monastery was established there. Around 7-8 A.D. there used to be a Buddhist learning centre in Vikramsila in Champa kingdom on the bank of the Ganges from where there used to be a direct communication link to Arakan by river and sea route. The site of Vikramsila has remained untraceable by archeologists and the real history has remained unknown. This is the short form of their history upto 1947 this is based on the analysis of certain section of the human geneme-such as the y-chromosome in men or mitochondrial DNA in women—that helped to determine the human migratory pattern. After having moved out of their ancestral home place Chittagong Hill Tracts, now in Bangladesh and their deliquescence can be seen world-wide. The homeland has become a living space for others compelling them to flee away from there, and it has become a trouble torn area. Having no role in the modern events of history they are being defaced. They are in a land not dovetailed with them and are being faced with inveterate perpetual provoking and being defaced inwards and outwards disasters. Only peace can recreate the golden era that has put the time backward. Let me now digress for a moment and explain the events of history from ages back. The term Chakma is the integral part of the people and can have variant spelling T-Sak-Ma (T-silent, Sakma), Chakma, Thet-Ma, etc. in phonological terms in different parts of human geography. Ethnographically, they belong to T-Sak, Thet (k) tribe. The word T-Sak witnesses the meaning of the people Sak or Chak. Historically a clear meaningful understanding of the two identical words. The T-Sak originated from Central Asia[2]. In the olden days they were known to be Scythians. Historigraphically the father of historial Hirodotus says: Persians and other peoples in it as referred to the Scythians living in Asia as Sakas. Hirodotus describes them as Scythians, although they figure under different names: Indo-Scythians and invasion of India by Scythians tribes: Sakas[3] receive numerous mention in Indian text, including the Puranas, the *Manusmriti*, the *Ramayana*, the *Mahabharata*, the *Mahabhasaya of Patanjali*, the *Baharat Samhita of Vraha Mihira*, the *Kavyamimasa*, the Baharat-Katha-Manjari and the Katha-Saritasagara. In India they were called Saka (Shakas). As History writes although the Sakas had a reputation of peace and war like, one of the greatest sages the Buddha descended from this tribe: he had the title Shakyamuni which means 'Shaka monk, The root of Sak: wanderer. They have been stratified throughout the history but there are still substantive identities to be carried out of them. A circumscription of Sakyan from ancient time to the present day is a history of interpersonal, speculation between people as no serious study has yet been worked out. The Chakma (T-Sakma) the name evolved in the tribes of Brahamputra valley in Assam which is known as

(T-Sangpho in Tibet). In 1947, at the time of decolonization monstrosity on dividing British India on the basis of two nation theory for creating homeland for the Hindus and the Muslims, the CHT changed hands which was originally to remain with India, but finally it was gifted to Pakistan violating the norms on which India was divided CHT 98 P.C. Buddhist inhabited area from the very ancient time (in the erstwhile East Pakistan) was exchanged with Ferozpur (Sikh dominated Hindu area) in West Pakistan by the National Leaders at the top (Nothing specific is known about the bartering behind the scene or the under hand plot) and thus the life of the Chakmas changed forever, the last remnants of Indian Buddhist in partisan way. The ethos of the Chakmas was under threat and became obsure. The wheel of fate of Indigenous Chakmas berated and became the victims of Human rights violations since then. The tragic incidents of their life has become a routine feature. They are facing tyrannical oppressiveness, exploitations (Genocide) by the majority from the very inception. The social and cultural milieu reached the apex of unacceptability and finally they began fleeing their ancestral homeland since 1964, after the construction of a Hydro Electric Kaptai Dam on the river Karnaphuli inundating 40 per cent of the best agricultural land[4]. This resulted in Chakma exodus from their ancestral homeland in perpetuity. It was an excruciatingly painful situation when many outsiders from plains began pouring in crushing their powers. Since dispersion is one of the topics in the epics of Asian history. History reaps on them driven from their natural home. Their mental disposition began to wane in various ways in complex environmental surroundings, milieu of culture and political interest. The actions and utterance of the power behind the scene was to bring them into the fold of Islam. But they have diverse ideas of their commemoration of a flourishing city 'Champa' (indicating their name Chakma), their original homeland, which remained unearthed till today. Their many places by the name Champa which are follows:

Champa-Sak, is the name of a town in Laos, close to Thailand border. It was the name of a Kingdom where eastern boundary was formed by the sea of China and the west from the valley of Mekong river. Chakmas' estimation of their old memory has been fictionalized, believing that they were from Dinnawadi, Champa Kingdom from where traders sailed to Suvarnabhumi, Danyaboti now Arakan in Myanmar, in the trans-Gangetic region. The Gangetic valley was occupied by the Mongoloid (Turanian, Myanmar Origin) in the olden era. Probably they were of Sakyan lineage. The Tibetan and the Burmese races have a common origin and have now obtained universal acceptance having moved westwards from starting point to find ultimate resting place in Tibet, N.E. (India) and finally CHT. The location of Champa was just off to Mithali now in Bihar, India. Champa is referred to as one of the six principal cities of ancient India in 6th B.C., presently Champa Nagar a village near south Bhagalpur. Champa was a kingdom comprising of Monghyr, Santhal Parganas, Birbhum whose capital was Odantapuri (till unexcavated). There was a great centre of learning Vikramsila[7]. Vikramsila monastry (still unexcavated fully) (probably at Anthichak – Paharghata near Colgong, District – Bhagal Pur, Bihar. It was built by Dharama Pala, Odantapuri – Maha Vihara (cited at Bihar Sarif near Nalanda and Jagaddala – Mahavihara established by Ramapala in Varendri (north Bengal) won international fame. Some Buddhist luminaries of these monasteries including Dipankar Srijana Atisa (AD 980 –1053) head of the Vimkramsila establishment went to Tibet. Buddhism was discouraged[8] in 9th Century onwards and finally it was massacred by Muslim invaders in 12 A. D. There was old river Koratoya[9] between Bengal and Assam, where Buddhism flourished at one time. T-Champa is referred to a place in Shan Kingdom. The Shans (Yunnan in China and on the western part of MeKong river swamped over Burma.

They over populated the earliest indigenous Shakyans all over. The first came, Tibeto-Burman race, the second came, Mon–Kamer race and the third came, Tai-Chinese race. The word Sakas has been written off in the ever-changing scenario of racial dominance with its neighbours blend with. Sakyans (Chakmas) belonging to Tibeto-Burman race, whose great numbers are seen in this region. T-Sanpay Nago like the name Champak Nagar has been referred in the Hill tracts between Assam and Burma and on the upper Brahamaputra by Lt. R. Wilcox, (1825): which *reads as* under:

> "Old T-Sampaynago Myo is situated at the mouth of a small river flows from Mogout and Kyatpan, and falls into the Irrawaddy immediately opposite the modern choki of that name. No foreigners says Captain Hannay, except the Chinese are allowed to navigate the Irrawaddy above the choki of Tsanpaynago, situated about seventy miles above Ava, and no native of the country even is permitted to proceed above that post, excepting under a special license from the Government. The trade to the north of Ava is entirely in the hands of the Chinese and the individuals of that nation residing at Ava have always been vigilant in trying to prevent any interference with their monopoly."

Strategically, there is too much at stake in this trouble torn region till today and their history remains to be written. Their dreadful struggle is at bay long since the moral responsibility of safeguarding the innocent people has become far beyond recognition by international community till today. It makes nothing for rich and powerful communities in the present world this is the chief worry for the indigenous people all is over the world, where it is worthwhile to know something of Chakmas, whose fortune is overcast in darkness. The storm remained unending over their head in the brevity of worldly life, who are innately born. But under the present nuclear world everything is value based.

Therefore, their value must be enshrined in the judgement of Human Rights, so that they play a roll in the progress of human endeavour.

Sakas

Asians, especially Persians, knew the Scythians in Asia as Sakas. The Indo-Scythians had the name "Shaka" in South Asia, an extension on the name "Saka". Herodotus describes them as Scythians, called by a different name:

> "The Sacae, or Scyths, were clad in trousers, and had on their heads tall stiff caps rising to a point. They bore the bow of their country and the dagger; besides which they carried the battle-axe, or *sagaris*. They were in truth Amyrgian (Western) Scythians, but the Persians called them Sacae, since that is the name which they gave to all Scythians." (Herodotus VII. 64)

Shakas receive numerous mentions in texts like the Puranas, the Manusmriti, the Ramayana, the Mahabharata, the Mahabhasiya of Patanjali, the Brhat Samhita of Vraha Mihira, the Kavyamimamsa, the Brihat-katha-Manjari, the Katha-Saritsagara and several other old texts. The accounts typically group Scythians as part of an amalgam of other war-like tribes from the northwest.

Although the Shakas had a reputation as fierce and war-like, one of the greatest sages of peace, the Buddha, descended from this tribe: he had the title *Shakyamuni* which means "Shaka monk".

Indo-Scythians

The Indo-Scythians, a branch of the Scythians, migrated into Bactria, Sogdiana, Arachosia, Gandhara, Kashmir, and finally into the Punjab and the northwest of the Indian subcontinent, between the middle of the 2nd century BC and the 1st century BC.

The "king of the Sakas" (*compare with the Greeks' King Omarg / Amorg*), driven out of Farghana, transferred his headquarters to the south across the Hanging Passage leading to Jibin. His retreat from Farghana took place in the mid-second century BCE, and by approximately the mid-first century BCE Saka kings appear in India. It is significant that the first Saka king known in India (*Maues on coins: Moga in epigraphic evidence*) had the same name as the king of the Amyrgian Sakas (*Mavakes*) during the time of Alexander II of Macedonia. Apparently this king figures in Chinese sources as Yinmofu, the ruler of Jibin. It is not by chance that Ptolemy records the Kaspirs (= *Jibin*) as occupying a vast territory from the Bidaspes (Jhelum) River to the mountain of Quindion (*Vindhya*), including the town of Modura (*Mathura*) (*7.1.47*); this evidently reflects the situation during the early period of Saka dominion in India when Kashmir was still regarded as the center of the kingdom. Apparently the king's horde, drawing after them the rest of the Amyrginas, moved from Farghana and the Alai valley, at first through areas where the Amyrginas were already assimilated, via Qarategin, Darvaz, and the western Pamirs, and then through the passes of the Hindu Kush. Individual groups of the Amyrgians might have taken routes farther to the west (although still within the limits of the eastern, mountainous area of Central Asia). In this way, the ancestors of the Munjans penetrated into the Gbkcha valley and Badakhshan. It is also possible that the Parsii mentioned in Classical sources ended up in the Bamiyan region, and the Parsyetae, the ancestors of the Afghans, on the upper Kurram. Thus, one may conclude that the Sakas who appeared in India and the eastern part of the Iranian plateau in the second-first centuries BCE were Amyrginas from Farghana and that they migrated across the western Pamirs and adjoining western mountainous area, rather than, as is commonly assumed, through the eastern Pamirs.

Route from Central Asia to India, the ethnic of the Sakas (Scythians) – I. P'iankov, the free encyclopaedia.

Some British writer believe earlier Koch kingdom in north Bengal and Chakmas in CHT were Scythian origin.

An account of Chittagong Hill Tracts R.H. Hutchinson "The chieftainess rendered the Government a certain amount of aid in the dark days of the Indian Mutiny. She secured and delivered up some of the Sepoys of the native regiments that mutinied at Chittagong and had be taken themselves to the Hills to avoid retribution, otherwise, for forty years she proved a thorn in the side of the Government, she was an exceedingly able woman, and, having surrounded herself, with Bengali Lawyers from the Chittagong, fought very hard to avoid meeting her obligation, and put forward all sorts of real and imaginary, claims to land settlements in the Chittagong District itself. She exercised a very great influence, over her tribe and was generally feared —An Account of Chittagong Hill Tracts – R.H. Hutchinson –p. 94.

Destruction of Champa (South of Bhagalpur)

In Hiouen-Tsang time (7 AD) north Bihar was divided into Vreji to the north and Vaisali to the south, both countries stretching east wards to the Mahananda. South of the Ganges were Hiranya Parvana (Monghyr) and Champa (south of Bhagalpur the Santal Parganas and Bhirbhum). The rulers of both these kingdoms were probably Scythian of Mal origin. In the ninth century the Buddhist dynasty founded by Gopal included Bihar in its dominies. The last of this line was defeated in 1197 by Muhammad-i-Bakhtyar-Khilji, whose soldiers destroyed the capital of Odantapuri and massacared the Buddhist monks assembled there.

Imperial Gazetteer of India Vol. XV, p. 24.

It is recorded Bengal may be radically divided into two great stocks, the Negrite or Dravidian with its nucleus in Chutia, Nagpur, extending over the whole of south Bihar, western Bengal Orissa and large part of north Bihar, and the Mongoloid or Lohitic which includes eastern and northern Bengal with off-shoots into North Bihar, and which was divided probably by the great river Koratoya into two groups, of which the southern was coterminous with Bengal or the Barendra Desh and was peopled by chandals, while the northern, known as the Matsya Desh, the land of fish, was the home of the Kochh. The Koratoya flowed east of Pabna, but south of Dacca, and the Kochh-Mandi, still found in latter district, are probably the remnants of the earliest inhabitants. It is singular fact that the Tibetan traditions place one of the capitals of Sakyas or Scythian on the bank of Bhagirathi, a fact that could probably point of Turanian Sovereign resident at Gaur before the ancient capital had become Hindu metropolis.

References

1. Freedom for indigenous people by Rigoberta Menchu Tum.
2. Route from Central Asia to India, the ethnic of the Sakas (Scythians) –I. P'iankov, *The Free Encyclopaedia.*
3. Sakas and Indo-Scythians.
4. An extract from the book *Chittagong Hill Tracts* by R.H. Sneyd Hutchinson.
5. Destruction of Champa (south of Bhagalpur) *Imperial Gazetteer of India*, Vol. XV, p. 24.
6. *Ibid.*
7. Vikramsila Monastery (University).
8. Buddhism Discouraged, Imperial Gazetteer Vol. VII, p. 210.
9. Karotoya, Imperial Gazetteer of India, Vol. XV, p. 24.
10. The two great ethnic stocks of Bengal (Census of India, 1891 Vol. III, p. 262 by C.R. O'Donnell).

1

Progenetory

History

There is no semantic or syntactic informations evidences of the origin of Chakmas, who identify themselves to be Changma claiming to have originated from Sakya (Sakyan race in which Sakamuni Gautama Buddha was born in Saka race in Nepal. History is displaced, as history really is, when we breathe into it, such is the case of the Buddhist Chakma tribe of Chittagong Hill Tracts now in Bangladesh. Their perpetuity in Buddhism originated from very ancient times when the realm of Buddhism reached its culmination in Burma now Myanmar. From the facts of history we know, Abhiraja[1] alongwith Sakyan clansmen came from Kapilavastu (The little village of Pipprahwa 93 kms from Lumbini via Sonauli), the capital of Sakyas, where Buddha spent the first 30 years of his life. If Lumbini is remote then Kapilavastu seems to be caught in a time wrap in India (now Nepal) and founded Kingdom at Tagaung (850 BC) in Burma and Arakan (825 BC). Down in the line of descendency, there was Binnakya Raja (523 BC) of Burma whose contemporary was Dhaza Raja of Kapilavastu. During his period Sakyans were massacred in Nepal. He with his followers fled to Male (Burma) and married Binmakya Raja's widow being of the same Sakyan clan. From historical information it is known that Sakya King Dhaza Raja passed through Manipur on way to Kubo valley in Myanmar where he established his kingdom.

The Sakyan in Manipur were uprooted by Meitheis from Shan of Yunnan, China (Kubo valley changed hands in 1834

AD, the British gifted it to Myanmar and later became a part of India, but again in 1953 AD India ceded it to Myanmar). Before British colonial rule the India's Eastern frontier was in Burma. By the treaty of Yandaboo ratified in 1826 the Burmese were forced to cede Arakan and the strip of Tenasserim coast as well as Assam and Manipur to the British, thus securing India's north eastern frontier zone. Finally, in 1862 these areas were amalgamated to form British Burma and made a province of the Indian empire.

They were all living in peace and harmony, since the earliest time: the homeland of T-sak ma (Chakma) the land of Mongolian people (If Champa of 6th AD is T-champas or Shans whose jurisdiction was from Mekong China-Thailand, then the T-sak-ma (Chakma) might have closeness to Shans. Tagaung was overthrown by Chinese Shans in about 600 B.C. and Sakyan moved out and founded kingdom at old Pagan and went further to Prome. Dhaza Raja's dynasty, a line of 17 Kings ruled at Tagaung (old Pagan) until, within one generation posterior to the year 568 A.D., it was displaced by Hkum – Long who installed his eldest son Ai – Hkum – Long on the throne of that kingdom. In this connection it may be noted that there is a significant mention of a revolt of 12 villages in the *Tagaung Chronicle* with the result that Tagaung became subservient to the Shan Chinese. This undoubtedly refers to the first success of the Shans under Hkum – Long's generalship in ousting the Indian Sakya dynasty from Tagaung kingdom. From historical information we have the knowledge of ramification of Sakya race throughout Burma in the space of time. The earliest indigenous 'Sak' people in Burma are known as 'Thet' pronounced 'Sak' who inhabited in Cak – Htaung in Myanmar.

The name Brahmaputra river in Assam is known to be T-sanpho in Tibet which enters at a confluence estuary called Dihing in the north-east region in India. The inhabitants on both sides of the river Dihing are now known to be by different names like Abors, Miris (Mishing), Padam-Mishing, Adi, Nishi and others. They worship nature, while those who came into plains lost their identity in Hinduism. But their counterparts in Tibet and Burma are Buddhists. There has been a variation in their identities, language, and culture in different countries in the space of time. The Ahom Shan kings of Assam continued the custom at least as late as the seventh century, and would even bury one of the slaves alive to look after a lamp in the tomb, until the English compelled them to abandon slave holding. It is notionally believed that Chakmas have genealogical link with Arakanese for the reason that those who inhabited in the Chittagong hill tracts are known to be Annakya Chakmas and those who were in Arakan (Mayanmar) are called Doingnak Chakma and Tangchangya Chakma (they moved into Chittagong hill Tracts around 1819 AD). They use Chakma as surname. Arakan was known as Rowyangya and some of them are called Rowyangya Chakma. In 1582 AD Chittagong was annexed to British company during the reign of Todar Mal (Mughal).

Mughal Rule

The Mughal dominated period continued from 1526 – 1803 AD. In 1712 AD, there were several encounters between the forces of Chakma King and the Mughal Governor of Chittagong of a border dispute and the Chakma chief captured two canons, which are known as 'Kalu Khan' and 'Fatheh Khan'. However, 1713 AD the Chakma king, Fateh Khan made peace with the Mughals and obtained permission from the Mughal emperor, Farruk Shiyar to allow traders to trade with hill cultivators on payment of 11 mounds of cotton which was largely grown in the hills and transported through the river Karnaphuli. It also gave access of hill cultivators to Chittagong for buying their necessities, i.e. salt, dry fish, etc. There had been no external interference by any outside power in the affairs of the CHT until 1787 when an agreement was signed with the British and the British colonization started since 1860 during the reign of Queen Kalindi Rani (Chakma Queen). So the Kings of CHT reigned independently during the whole pre-British era.

Jhuming Forest Hill Tract

The status of CHT was as hill cultivation tract/Jhoom tract. Slash and burning of forest continued even after British Company took over from the Mughals, and was administered by a superintendent whose official designation was raised to Deputy Commissioner in 1860. The first D.C. Lt. Col. T.H. Lewin whose headquarter was at Rangamati. A CHT Police force was raised with indigenous hill people and its effectiveness was well recognized. The same is the case of many indigenous tribes was broken up in space and time but their moral ethics and culture remained unaltered. Their mainstay in Jhuming (Forest slash and burning), was in Arakan Yoma (Bhootidong, Rothidong, Dinnawadi), Matamuri river valley, Karnaphuli river valley in Bangladesh, Thega river valley, Tuichong, river valley and Sajek (Khawthiangtuipui) river valley in Mizoram, India. In time and space they swamped over and spread over in this geographical region which is abundantly seen. These areas are the outlying parts of CHT, now divided into different states and number of countries.

Groups and Sub-groups

One such is the case of a tribe of Arunachal Pradesh in India. This tribe is known to be Singphos who are known as T-Sangpho in Tibet, Jimpho in China and Kachin in Myanmar. Interestingly, the single fact is that they are of one group of people under different names in different countries. As gleaned in history Mongolian hords passing southward from Tibet in successive waves towards the sea doubtlessly populated the valleys of Burma and Arakan and bordered with CHT a successive group of hill tribes. There are clear evidences that Sakyan Chakmas have undergone changes at different places at different times since ages. Much the same is the case of the Chakmas of Chittagong hill tracts and Tunkhungya of Ahom in Assam who are Tangchangya chronologically from Burma (Myanmar) at one stage of time. Its name from the village Tungkhung in upper Assam where they had ancestral residences. Similarly a group of Ahom people who are called Chakmai, who knows, what kinship they had with Chakmas of CHT, whose association with Brahmaputra river valley is supposed to have come from the foothills of the Himalayan ranges at one stage of time, that has been passover. The historical information says the Burmese invaded Assam in 1817 AD and took possession from 1819 to 1825. It suggest that Tangchangya (Tungjainya) from 1817 had mixed with Chakmas (Changma) in CHT and became its sub-groups while Tunkhungia mixed with Hindu natives in Assam (Tai-Shan Race). Chakmas in CHT are fluvial on the bank of the river Karnaphuli. Earlier they were known to be Khyengtha (Arakanese word) signifies people or nation leaving near water. In Burmese pronounciation Khy-chaw i.e. Khyeng-Tha/Chaweng-Tha means Changma. In the written language it has become Chakma, now in the midst of which a vast water reservoir of Kaptai Hydo–electric project. A legendary history of Chakmas suggest that an unseated royal family member of Sakyas was leading a novish Buddhist Monk's life; Moisang raj (Moisang means a novitiate in religious order) on the river valley Matamuri in the South of CHT, near Arakan. A fictionalized song of Chakmas reflecting it in their Genkhuli songs.

> *"Aa-long Moisang lalach nei*
> *Na aa-long Moisang lalach nei*
> *Chal bap bei chal jai champak nagar pheri jai*
> (English translation)
> No more eagerness whether Moisang raj
> returns or not.
> Brothers and sisters! Let us return to Champak Nagar

There is a discrete history of Chakmas (originally from the word Chaws of only few families) Sakya race who lived in Dinnwavati suggest that they had a very sophisticated society of old families of respectability who were continually attached to the spot from local association. It remains unknown to the modern world. It was noted by the famous British scholar R. Beileu Pemberton in his report on the eastern frontier of British India in the *Imperial Gazetteer*. At Dinnwadi there was an immense master piece Buddha shrine dated back to early British era. It was taken to Mandalay in 1785. It is indicative that Buddhism entered much earlier and has deep relevance to Myanmar history. The natives of this area are deeply consumed by the passion and reverence to the image of the living Buddha (Mahamuni). The prowess of Buddhism entered interior Myanmar through this route of interactions. Risley in his book *'Tribes and Caste of Bengal'* published in 1891 described the Chakmas as a Lohitic Tribe of CHT. In trying to examine the basis of their being called Lohitic, Fridrich Miller and other German anthropologists hold that the term Lohotic applies to the Chakmas because of their association with Brahmaputra river to the bank from which they are supposed to have come from the foothills of the Himalayas region which has been departed from mind, but it is still stored in the brain in a subjective manner. Chakmas bear a distinct Mongolian spot, a deep pigment commonly present in the sacral region which generally disappears soon after birth. Also, a fold of skin often called 'Mongoloid fold' extending from the eye lid over the inner cantus of the eye. The actual barometer of their oneness is to be seem in their physiognomic features and other characteristics which enshrine in their tradition and linguistic similarity of Burmese (Myanmar), Cambodian, Laos, Thailand and Shans (state in China). Their past is enshrined in the present perceptions which corresponds in the Chakmas. The present is the continuation of the past. It can be distinctively seen in the religious practices and syndrome of the Chakmas. They all preserve Buddhism in inter-subjected world of many nations. In this region there was no such rigid outline of nations since the ancient times of Buddha'a era (560–480 BC). People moved freely which is fictionalized in their memories. In a sense people were living in a heterogeneous society in different group's very peacefully. Categorically they all belong to the Sakya genealogy. In historical and cultural realities Sakyans are the people whose ardent faith was in Buddhism. In its present configuration its true reflection is being diluted. The aspiration of the indigenous Buddhist in this region is to bring Buddhism through enlightened interactions internationally. In India Buddhist means they are out of power poor and in misery. Giving compassionate love is the foundation stone of Buddhism.

Erection of Stupa over Buddha's Remains

As gleaned from the Mahaparinibbana Sutta, as it transcendents, the actual events surrounding the death of the Buddha are remarkable. The Sutta concludes with an account of an elaborate funeral and the distribution of the bones and ashes of the Buddha to the nine (9) influential Buddha clans and individuals (Buddha's time), who vow to erect monuments (stupa) over the remains. The erection of stupa is religiously a very notable worthy task but too expensive for poorer communities/nations. Resourceful people in the world are lending their hand for it to many disadvantaged Buddhist communities/nations with love and compassion. Needless to say that the Chakmas are in an impoverished condition and hard up, but yet many of them are in absorbed in spreading the message of Matriya (friendship) the distinctive novelty of Buddhism. (Keeping one's nose clean).

Holistic World

The greatest God is love and compassion power of regions and the path to reach through the Union of mind with the whole nature, holistic world. It is being influenced by self interested people in ambiguous ways and world peace is being devastated bringing ill fate to human being. In spite of the fact human beings originated from nature, we deliberately take no notice of it. Life is an evolution, "it is continuous adjustment of internal relation to external relations." Synchronization of the holistic world where everything has some intrinsic value.

Chakma Rajas

The list of Chakma Rajas is as under :

1.	Raja Bijoygiri of Chakmas	Legendary history
2.	Jabbar Khan	1686 AD
3.	Jallal Khan	1706 AD
4.	Fateh Khan	1713 AD
5.	Shermust	1731 AD
6.	Sher Daulat Khan II	1758 AD
7.	Ramu Khan	1773 AD
8.	Jan Baksh Khan	1782 AD
9.	Dharm Baksh Khan	1818 AD
10.	Kalindi Rani	1855 AD
11.	Bhuban Mohon Roy	1876-1934 AD
12.	Nalinaksh	1902-1951 AD
13.	Tridiv Roy now in Pakistan	1933
14.	Devasish Roy (notionally chieftain Bangladesh)	1959

Genealogy

They have been claiming substantively from history to Sakya genealogy. Genetic research in modern population reveals that the same paternal Y-Chromosome (hereditary structure in living cells) haplo group represents a genetic linage currently found in central western and South Asia and in Slavic population of Europe. The simplest explanation of this distribution involves this Y-Chromosome mutation originating in people of the Kurgan – building culture of prehistoric Scythia. Scythians were a nomadic tribe in central Asia in the olden age. Recent genetic mapping of the Indian population suggest that the ancient Vedic may well tell an accurate tale of an indigenous Indian (Dravidian) population conquered by invading tribes from Central Asia who became the high caste Brahmans. The Brahmans, some recent studies suggest, carry genetic marks closer to those of Central Asia and Asia Minor (Anatolia) than of Southern India. In Tamil language the world Pariah and Sakya are synonyms meaning untouchable caste. The author of the famous classic book *The Thirukural* was a Pariah and the book is an epitome of *Tripitaka* sacred religious book of Theravada Buddhism. People in the Indian sub-continent had intermingled and become varied identities (Bahujan), many of them claiming to be from Sakya line. During the Mughal period, Jadu, son of Raja Kans (Khan), the only Hindu king in Bengal embraced the Muhammadan religion in order to be allowed to succeed his father. In Bengal many Hindus became Muslims after Maghs (Arakanese) passed through their homes and so caused them to be outcasted. Chakmas adopted Khan Title to get favour from ruling powers. The title Khan means the head of a tribal group of people (feudal) similar to Chenghis Khan in China. In the past, Rajnagar was the capital of the Chakma King now in Chittagong district. The British authorities put them on the sential guards on the distant hills to face the brunt of barbarous attacks of fierce tribes on the British subjects.

"The principal creek near Babootoung hills throw off two branches which run through and are crossed by lofty wooden bridges; a good deal out of repair. On the southern side of the principal street which runs east and west, are the ruins of the ancient palace and fort, consisting of the triple square enclosure of stone and brick wall, connected with lime; the stone having apparently been originally employed in the construction and the subsequent repair effected with bricks and the work altogether is of considerable extent, and the labour bestowed in connecting the different detached hills by curtain of stones and brick walls must have been immense. They are now in a dilapidated state and as sites more favourably situated have been selected for occupation by the civil and military authorities of the province, it can never be an object of importance to repair these works. The inhabitants of the town may be estimated at from eight to ten thousand, and they consist principally of old families of respectability who are continuously attached to the spot from local association."

The Chaws were consisting of only a few families. All the tribes were divided into separate clans, often at deadly feud with each other.

British Burma and its People by Capt CJFS Forbes (1878) published by John Murray, London.

From the Commissioner of 16th Division
and Sudder Board

The Collector of Chittagong

Sir,

I hope the honour to acknowledge the receipt of your letter of the 24th instant together with copy of the order of the civil court called for by my letter of the 22nd instant No. 789.

(2) It appears that on the death of the late Raja Dharam- bux Khan in 1832 the civil court recognized the succession of Ranee Kalindee to his lands and possession and

on the 27th March 1833, the Colletor recommended "that she should be left in charge of the Property" and that the estates should be recorded in "her name". The Commissioner doubted her capacity to manage the property, but it appears her incapacity was considered established because she refused to engage for some No-abad lands the justness of the essessment of which she denied.

(3) In all parts of India these Jungles Rajahs are exempt from devision under the Hindu law of succession, and it appears to me in every account desirable that the integrity of the Raja should be preserved and opportunities embraced of strange-thening the hands of these border Rajahs instead of weakening their authority. We can only rule in the hills by their means and they can be of use only when strong.

I have the honour to be

Commissioner Office
Chittagong
The 26th August 1842

Sir

S/d Henry Ricketts.
Commissioner and Revenue Sudder Board

CHT Lineage from Champanagar Bihar

The tribe consider themselves descendants of emigrants from Bihar who settled in the Chittagong District in the days of the Arakanese kings. The assistance of Brahmans has been invoked and the following history compiled. Some centuries ago there reigned at a place called Champanagar in Bihar a Kshatriya King of the Surjya or Sun race. He had two sons, Bijoygiri and Samagiri. Bijoygiri at the head of an army started forth to conquer new worlds, and crossing the river Meghna, which is described as a sea, he marched against the Arakanese forces and defeated them. Bijoygiri now prepared to return home, but news reached him that his father had died, and that his younger brother Samagiri had usurped the throne. In consequence Bijoy made terms with the Arakanese kings and settled down in the neighbourhood of the Naaf river to the south of the Chittagong District. His people intermarried with the Arakanese and gradually became converts to Buddhism. They subsequently migrated to the valley of the Matamuri river, where traces of their occupancy in the shape of thanks and ruined buildings still exist. Here Bijoygiri raised four of his Captains by name Dhurjiya, Phurjiya, Dhabana and Piabhanga to the rank of Diwans or managers to assist him in ruling the country. The last of the Champanagar line of chiefs was Sher Daulat, nicknamed the "Pagla" or madman. He was credited with supernatural powers and was supposed to purify himself from sin, by removing his inside, washing and replacing the same. The curiosity of his wife was aroused, and when spying upon him she was discovered by the Chief, who in his rage slew her and the whole of his family. His eccentricities and tyranny grew so great that his people finally assassinated him, and fearing the consequences removed themselves further north and settled in the neighbourhood of Rangonea on the Karnaphuli river.

Chittagong Hill Tracts page 22—R.H. Sneyd Hutchinson, Indian Police (1978), Vivek Publishing Company, Delhi

Study on the Lost Sakya Tribe

A study is being carried out on the origin of Sakya people who claim a common heritage going back to the times of Gautama Buddha himself. This hypothesis is being studied using genetic variation on the Y-chromosome and other disciplines of knowledge like archaeology, history, genetic anthropology and that might open up light on this study. This is being carried out under the leadership of Dr. Mark,

University College, London. This research study is approved by the joint university college of London/University college London Hospital committees on the Ethics of Human research (study number 99/0196).

As you will know, the Sakya people claim a common heritage going back to the times of Buddha himself. We would like to test this hypothesis using genetic variation on the Y-chromosome. The Y-chromosome is only present in males and as such, is only passed on from father to son. Because changes occasionally occur in the Y-chromosome when it is passed on from father to son, the Y-chromosomes of men often differ. However, these changes are very rare. Consequently, if two men share a recent common ancestor through the male line, then we would expect their Y-chromosomes to be either identical or very similar. The same logic can be applied to whole populations (of men). If two populations are descended from one original source population, then we would expect that the distribution of different Y-chromosome types in the two descendent populations to be very similar. Furthermore, we would expect that the distribution of different Y-chromosome types would be more different the longer ago two populations share a common ancestral population.

In the case of the Sakya, if their beliefs about a common origin are true, then we would expect the Y-chromosomes of different Sakya populations to be more similar to one another that they are to their non-Sakya neighbours. Thus to test the hypothesis, it is essential that we have samples not only from Sakya but also from non-Sakya people who live near the Sakya people.

We have already looked at a number of Sakya and non-Sakya populations in India and the general picture that emerges is that the Sakya people are indeed more similar to one another than are to their non-Sakya neighbours.

As information received on 17.10.07 from Dr. Mark Thomas CVL, one post doctoral fellow had joined in analysing the genetic data for some years. This study is not guaranted but is encouraging.

The famous British scholar R. Beileau Pemberton in his report on the Eastern Frontier of British India had acknowledged that near the ancient capital Dhanyavati, there stood at the head of inferior branch of the Gat-shaha or Kolodyne about 50 miles from Akyab a principal city known as Babootoung.

Abhiraja with his Sakyan clanmen came from Kapilavastu in India founded Tagaung 850 BC and Kyaukpadaung in Arakan 825 BC. Tagaung was overthrown by the Chinese about 600 BC, and its people then founded old Pagan; they went further south also, founded in 443 B.C., Prome, a glorious city which, under the great king Duttapaung 443-373 B.C. contained a splendid court and 3,000 Buddhist monks. Meanwhile Buddha himself had visited Legaing and Shwesettaw (in Minbu district), as is borne out by the existence of Kyaungdawaya pagoda, and of his two footprints, each three cubits long, at Shwesettaw; on his way back he passed by Prome—witness the Po-u-daung pagoda there, and look at the very hill where he stopped, Tankyidaung (to be distinguished from its namesake opposite Pagan).

History of Burma—G.E. Harvey Frank Cass & Co. Ltd. 1967 page 307.

References

1. Abhiraja Sakyan king, *History of Burma* by G.E. Harvey, Frank Cass and Company Ltd., 1967.
2. *Dhanyavati in Myanmar in Arakan* by R. Beileau Pemberton.
3. A Study on the Lost Sakya Tribe in the Department of Biology, University College, London.

For further informations please contact :

Dr. Mark G. Thomas

Department of Biology

University College London

Wolfson House

4 Stephenson Way

London

NW12HE

Tel : ++44(0) 207 679 7418 (int. 2-7418)

Fax : ++44 (0) 207 6795052

Mobile : 07973 725955

Email : m.thomas@ucl.ac.uk

Web:ww.ucl.ac.uk/tcga/

4. Buddhist India by T.W. Rhys Davids.

2

Sprinking of Chakmas

Back in the early times Chakmas lived at Alikadam in the south of CHT near the mountain stream, Matamuri[1], surrounded by a cluster of champa trees- a kind of flowering tree (botanical name: Michelia Champaca Linn). They moved it up at a place in Rangoonia (Rajnagar, Sakyapur) around 16th century A.D. at a time, when Chittagong was a battle place of struggle of supremacy in Bengal between the raja of Arakan and Bengal rulers. For administrative convenience when the British took over, they shifted Chakmas at Rangamati, the last sentinel border post in this region to protect the British civilians from attack of distant tribes (the area beyond this was unknown at that time). Among the Chakma rulers, the most spirited Chakma queen was Kalindi Rani[2] whose incure impression at (1844-1873). She stood by the side of the British government during the sepoy mutiny[3]. The British government had a great admiration of her abilities. In 1857, she delivered up some of the sepoys, of the native regiment that mutinied at Chittagong and had taken themselves to the hills to avoid retribution, otherwise, for forty years she proved a thorn in the side of the government. She exercised a very great influence over her tribe and was greatly feared[4]. During her reign she drove away Rouli system corrupt, fictitious Buddhist religious practices and brought home Therovada Buddhism which enshrine in their traditions with grand patronage during her period. Much changeability had taken place during her reign, which is enormously visible in the modern times. It caused quite a stir in the community. In

1860 AD, the Chakma Kingdom[5,6] was divided into two halves: I. Chittagong II. Hill tracts of Chittagong (CHT). The former part was included into Bengal as a regulated district, while the later part was retained as non-regulated district (CHT) comprises a total of 5,093 sq. miles (13,189 km.) which is about 1/10th of the total area of Bangladesh with over 1.325 million population (1,700 million indigenous people and 0.625 million permanent Bengali Muslims, infiltrated and politically transmigrated Bengali Muslims settlers). It shares borders with Myanmar on the south and southeast. India on the north and northeast and Chittagong district on the west. It is completely different in physical features, agriculture practices and soil conditions from the rest of the countries with mountains and beautiful landscapes. CHT is located between 21°-40′ degrees and 23°-47′ degrees north latitude and 91°-41′ degrees and 92°-42′ degrees east longitude. It is a unique territory with mountains and beautiful landscapes and socio-economically and culturally completely different from the rest of the Bangladesh. It roughly runs from north to south for 280 kms. From time immemorial the CHT has been the home to eleven indigenous ethnic peoples. They collectively identify themselves as the Jumma people (High landers), the first people of the CHT. They are the Chakma, Marma, Tripura, Tanchangya, Murung, Lushai, Khumi, Chak, Khyang, Bawn, and Pankhua. Beside, a very small numbers of descendents of Assamese and Gorkhas also lived in there. The Jumma people are distinct and different from the majority Bengali people of Bangladesh in respect of race, language, culture, heritage and religion.

In 1892, the Chakma Chief divided CHT into 9 (nine) circles, 33 blocks (Taluks) and a number of Mouzas (taxation areas), as below :

Sl.No.	*Name of circle*	*Head of circle*
1.	Kachalong	Indrajoy Dewan
2.	Chengi	Nila Chandra Dewan
3.	Mahaphrum	Raj Chandra Dewan

4.	Satta	Kamalakha Chaudhury
5.	Ichamati	Sarat Chandra Roangza
6.	Rangamati	Krishna Chandra Dewan
7.	Subalong	Trilochan Dewan
8.	Barkal	Kumar Romani Mohan Dewan
9.	Khas Rajar Area	Raja Bhuban Mohan

The head of each 'Taluk' was designated as Talukdar, in the pass over era. During the 2nd World War, the eastern war front was in Burma. For the Logistical support in the war front, the British government maintained a track called Lunglei to Haka (now Mizoram to Myanmar) whose supporting base was through Demagiri, now Tlabung in Mizoram and Rangamati now in Bangladesh which strengthened the defence at this region a strategic spot in the war.

Allocation of CHT to Pakistan

CHT was clandestinely gifted to Pakistan as, it was the outcome of negotiations on 16th August 1947 between two just downed dominiom governments of India and Pakistan exchanging Sikh dominated area Zira and Ferozpur of Punjab to CHT (indigenous Buddhist area) of the erstwhile East Bengal and it was declared on 17th August on 12th August 1947, Sir Cyril Radcliffe's Bengal Award contined the allocation of CHT to Pakistan Mr. Vallabh Bhai Patel, Indian National leader sensed it and said any award against weight of local opinion and terms of reference should be considered a collusive or partisan award and will have to be repudiated. On 16th August 1947, Pandit Nehru said he had never considered that alloction of CHT to East Bengal (Pakistan) was possible under the terms of refence of the Boundary Commission. He and his colleagues had assured the local chief and leaders of CHT that there was no question of CHT being included in Pakistan, the reason being CHT's population was 97 per cent Buddhist and Hindus. On religious and cultural grounds CHT should form part of India. But later, on the ground that the whole economic life of the people of CHT depends upon East Bengal and it would be disastrous for the people themselves to be cut off from East Bengal. But infact it was externalization of quagmire of Chakmas. Victim of portion see page 235. In a sance, Chittagong, the only port of East Bengal also depends upon CHT. Finally, Mountbatten said "I assume that the fate of Hill Tracts would be a matter for negation between two dominion govt's or there constituent Assemblies and not for decision of Boundary Commission". It was a very sinking feeling news for the Buddhist as it was against the norms of partition of Indian sub-continent, that Chakmas could never buoy up. The detailed text of the constitutional relations between Britain and India (transfer of power edited by Pendemal Moon, Her Majestic's stationary office, Vol. no. IX, XI and XI, full text are given in the accompanying enclosure[7]. page 98-127 The original Buddhists of India were caught in the cross-fire between the larger religious communities Hindu and Muslims and their fate was crushed between the hammer and anvil by then the tallest leaders of India and Pakistan and that the trauma of the Buddhist seems to be never ending on the insinuating feeling of politicians.

Erstwhile Pakistani Rule

The Pakistani government was inclined to suspect from its very birth the indigenous Chakmas with an eye of mistrust as anti-Pakistani as well anti-Islamic. They became waring, wide awake when CHT police force was disbanded and the native offices were transferred to different places outside CHT, wheareas more Bengali Muslim officers were brought in with spurious motives. This facilitated enticement to large number of Muslim infiltration. This needed amendment of CHT regulations of 1900 A.D. It was passed against the will of the indigenous people. Tribal

Nationals through abrogation of "Excluded the Area" status act of CHT in 1963. The indigenous tribals lost their ancestral land and right privileges that were granted to them. In the final outcome, the indigenous people's homeland became the living space for Muslims from the plains. The tribals are now outnumbered with the influx from the plains and paving the road for many under the patronage of the government. In August, 1947, when India was partitioned the tribal population of the district was 97.5 per cent and the Bengalis 2.5 per cent as per 1941 census. At present the tribal population is 4,98,595 and the Bengali population is 4,68,825 i.e. percentage of tribal population is 51.5% while the percentage of Bengali population is 48.5% (CHT area 13,181 sq. km. population 9,67,420 as per census 1991). During the last fifty years, the tribal population has not doubled, whereas during the same period Bengali population increased by 68.22 times. The reaction of the people of CHT against the nefarious policy of Pakistan was alarming. As a result of repressive measures followed by Pakistan government, discontentment and resentment was simmering throughout CHT. In 1964, CHT was placed under the direct administration of central (west) Pakistan, vesting more powers to the Muslim bureaucrat. Not only that, they started interfering with the inner domestic and local matters of the tribals, but also began acting behind the scene. At one instance while Raja Tridiv Roy[8], was exercising his justice in his local court (Raj-darbur), he was interfered with by the hooliganist Bengalist. It was due to the timely action by then British Dy. Commissioner Angus Hume of CHT, he was saved and it turned to be a big issue in the government. A Hume had to resign from his service for protecting the Chakma chief. There was another incident. In 1970, when some ten thousand Tribals were evicted from Reing Khyong Reserve forest and nearby areas, as the area was fixed for the Mizo rebels, who used the area to develop massive guerilla training bases for them and other insurgent groups from north-east India. This eviction of the tribal people created bitterness between the Chakma Chief Tridiv Roy and the then Deputy Commissioner, CHT. There was no motherly feelings for too the natives in the government. Western educated Islamic people, with modern political consciousness and thinking had thought of ways of withstanding the repressive policy of Pakistan government. There was nothing common of Chakmas with the rest of West and East Pakistan in language, religion, culture, nor psychological makeup. Their question was how to overturn the situation and what to do at the ground site. The government decided to inundate the area in the pretext of modernization of erstwhile East Pakistan by power generation at Kaptai at the cost of sacrificing the safety and welfare of the ethnic Buddhist. In the name of so called industrial development, government of Pakistan built the Kaptai Hydro Electric Project on the Karnaphulli river in the heartland of indigenous Chakmas which flooded 1.036 km of land and submerged 54% (54,000 acres) of agricultural land and also displaced about 100,000 (one hundred thousand) people from their ancestral hearth and homes for good. Many animals rapidly depleted as reservoir caused serious damage to the ecosystem of CHT resulting in effacement who failed to grow to the environment. Many fled to India and Myanmar. Those disposed of who had migrated to Arunachal Pradesh (in India), are yet to be treated at par with the natives in receiving benefits from the government, as they are not yet granted full citizenship[9,10] rights in India. They seem to belong to another era. India government could have taken up the issue to set the record straight of CHT at the time of liberation of erstwhile East-Bengal now Bangladesh in 1971. It has just abandoned ethnic Buddhist hill tribe, as the victim of silence[11].

Manobendra Narayan Larma (1939-83) President and founder of the Parbatya Chattagram Jana Samhati Samiti

(PCJSS), was a student leader in early sixties. He was the torch bearer of the Chakmas of CHT and rated a notch above the rest of notables till the present day. In an instance the PCJSS movement instilled confidence in all the ranks of the group, but following the release of Shantu Larma from army captivity, as it shaked some of its ranks of their position. On 10th November, 1983 Manobendra Narayan Larma met his end in a shoot out overstrife in his party over some disillusionment muttering threats at the commanders' level when Mr. Larma wanted to purge the top cops. The internal conflict situation reached to a point extreme gravity at a sanctuary which hugs on the borders of Tripura with Bangladesh. The overall development of the indigeous people had no place in the mind of Bangladesh national leaders. In order to materialise its evil design and breaking down the economic backbone of CHT.

Bangla Rule (Liberation War of East Pakistan)

M.N. Larma awakened the political awareness among the indigenous tribes in CHT. In 1970, he was elected in the East Pakistan Provincial Assembly (MPA). The Chakma Chief, Tridiv Roy also contested the election of Pakistan National Assembly as independent held in 1969 and was elected as member of National Assembly (MNA). The Indo-Pakistan War started on 3rd December, 1971 and on 4th December Pakistani army was withdrawn from Pansuri area of CHT. On 5th December Bangladesh forces (Mukti Bahani) entered Pansuri and stormed and ransacked the whole area when the locals came out to welcome the Bengali forces. They slashed to earth with their big *daos* eighteen (18) tribals before their eyes in broad daylight. The women could get no safe place to escape from rape. It was a dreadful situation with the arrival of Mukti Bahini. On 14th December, they unleashed another wave of killing, looting, arson on their way to Khagarachari (killing 22 tribals including women and children and burnt down atleast 176 houses). A number of young males were shot dead on the ground of their allegation that they supported Pakistani soldiers and some were beaten to death. (CHT Hill people were branded as pro- Pakistani). The matter continued to worsen unabated in the CHT. At Rangamati the Chakma Raj family was saved only by the timely intervention of the Indian Army. Earlier Tridiv Roy had moved to Pakistan before the defeat of Pakistan Army in the east. As the situation deteriorated of inhuman atrocities incomprehensible sufferings many fled from CHT at the cost of lives. They were on the horns of dilemma as the horror of liberation was beyond description.

Bangladesh emerged as an independent state on 16th December 1971. The victorious Mukti Bahini (Freedom-Fighter) entered into CHT with vengeance and communal hatred, creating a thorny situation region throughout CHT. The Mukti Bahini fell upon the innocent Jumma people, killing, arsoning and raping women, burning house and villages, victimizing and terrorising the inhabitants who were forced to take refuge in the woods. In 1973, after the Ist general election results in favour of Awami League under the leadership of seikh Mujibur Rahman in the newly liberated Bangladesh, he was of the belief of in a unified political system called BAKSHAL (Bangladesh Krishak Sramik Awami League) that divided the whole Territory into 64 administrative divisions under which CHT was divided into three Hill districts with H.Q. at Rangamali, Khagarachari and Bandarban, unfortunately, it created a strong tirade against government, consequence to this an Army uprising took place on 15th August, 1975, that massacred the whole family of Sheikh Mujibur Rahman (except the daughters who were abroad). The indigenous people have been a fractured group in CHT, with despondency and dependency. In 1972, two delegations of indigenous tribal groups from CHT met the President, the

Prime Minister, Bangabandhu Sheikh Mujibur Rahman and submitted a memorandum with four demands :

(1) Provincial Autonomy for CHT with legislature of its own;

(2) Retention of CHT regulation of 1900 in the Bangladesh constitution;

(3) Retention of Tribal chief's office;

(4) Constitutional provisions restricting the amendment of the 1900 regulation and imposition of a ban on the influx of non-tribal people into CHT.

The delegates returned with worry on the back of their mind as their demands were rejected. Prior to it, Bangabandhu on his return from Pakistani jail, sent Rajmata Benita Roy to New York to bring back her son Tridiv Roy (at that time he was chief deligate of Pakistan in the U.N. Assembly) to Bangladesh but the latter refused to come back. At that time the newly liberated Bangladesh was under the protege of the government of India, which is known for its Hindu characteristics. They do not consider Buddhism in the same equity with them as Gautama Buddha had *insulatd* denying the authority of Vedas-Indo Aryan Vedic scriptures/religion, Vedas classification of people. It was scrupulously seen, how the Government of India exchanged CHT with Zira and Ferozpur in Punjab in Pakistan, despite repeated assurance given to the people of CHT by the Hindu Leaders that their homeland will be in the fold of India. So, the Chakma chief was reminiscing the past and therefore, not inclined to return to Bangladesh/India as happened in 1947. Tridiv Roy was not likely to be off to Bangladesh, as he was reckoning treachery and was not deflected by promises and perfidiousness. He kept his name on the side of Z.A. Bhutto as he was friends with him. But unfortunately, he came to an end stroke of ill lucks enforced by the military rulers. Had it not taken place the fate of Chakmas would have much brighter at this period of time, where life is now at their peril. When the constitutional movement ended in failure to safeguard the national interest of the people of CHT and became the victims of step motherly treatment. Under the leadership of M.N. Larma (PCJSS), "a parallel administration" (insurgency militancy movement tactic) was set up in CHT and the movement took new shape and dimensions. The government took a strong arm policy to deal with insurgents with vigorousness in killing and brutality on the pretext that "enemies can not be seen in the operation". The new nation Bangladesh sank in soul-subduing situation after the assassination of Banga Bandhu Sheikh Mujibur Rahman with his family members in August, 1975. In November, Chief Justice Abusadat Mohammad Sayam became President and Chief Martial Law Administrator and Mrs. Binita Roy, Mother of Tridiv Roy (Chakma Chief) was made advisor to the President Sayam for up beating a good feelings and to ward off political waywardness and volatility, but on the reverse government put the cart before the horse by fortification of security forces and BDR Posts. The police station were many folded and Armed Police and Ansars were posted, while armed licences from the tribals were withdrawn and their arms were seized. Bengali families from the plains were brought in and set against the tribals in CHT. Henceforth, occasional skirmishes took place between the forces and the Shanti Bahini (peaceforce) armed wing of PCJSS. Several representations were made to successive administrator (rulers) of the country, but it ended unsuccessful. In 1980 the government of Ziaur Rahman was approached for the basic demands of CHT, but it again ended without result. Since, 1979, the Bangladesh government started to settle Bengali Muslims from the plain districts into CHT. Their total number rose to 80,000 families with a population of 4 lakhs with the outnumbering of indigenous Jumma people with the objective for using them as human shield. The government declared that each settler family will be given 5 acres of hilly land, 4 acres of plain and bumpy land and 2.5 acres of paddy land and rations for unlimited period. The CHT covers 5,093 sq. miles or about 10 per cent of land area of Bangladesh. The categories of which can be classified as under :

(1) land suitable for rice cultivation – 77,00 acres 2%.

(2) land suitable for horticulture – 6,70,000 acres 21%.

(3) land suitable for forest only – 16,00,000 acres 51%.

(4) Reserved forest – 8,00,000 acres 26%.

Thus, if all the cultivable lands of the tribal people were taken over, it would fail to meet the demand. So government created a grim death situation over the possession of land, as the new Muslim settlers were given only paper documents against the land that were already cultivated by indigenous people. So the settlers started to forcibly occupy the indigenous Jumma peoples' land under protection of powerful authorities in the government. In May 1985, Survival International cited notes on genocide in CHT with new evidence – Human Rights violation on women, old and children. In April 1992, the Logang massacre in which a few hundred Jumma people were held by security forces and Bengali settlers. And again in November 1993 at Naniachari similar massacre had taken place.

The international work group for indigenous affairs, Denmark cited notes below (extract) :

Women

"There are some pretty girls there."
"Then tribal women very beautiful and they are freez."

These were remarks by military officers. Tribal women are especially attractive and exotic to them. They move around more freely and are not bound by the same cultural and religious impositions that restrict the freedom of movement of Muslims women. These culture differences combined with the military presence and the increasing domination of Bengali Muslim culture in the CHT have made the tribal women more exposed to sexual predatory and insidious attacks. They were perpetually on the age of brutality, impetuousness.

Rape

A woman who is now in Tripura told the Commission: About 50 army personnel came in the night and rounded up the whole village and gathered us in one place. In the morning all the men were arrested. I was tied up hands and legs, naked. They raped me. There were three women there. They raped me in front of my father-in-law. After that we were tied up together, naked facing each other. Then they left. Three other girls were raped in front of me. This happened in the month of Ashar (June/July) of 1985. One pathetic tale of Kalpana Chakma women student leader as cited below. On the night of 11th to 12th June, 1996, Organizing Secretary of the Hill women Federation, Kalpana Chakma (23) was abducted from her home in Lallyagona Village, in Rangamati District by a group of armed plain clothed security personnel till date she remains untraced.

The growth rate of population and household in CHT as cited by Arun Shourie in his book 'A Secular Agenda' as under.

Demographic Profile

The demographic picture in the three districts of the CHT is different from national spectrum. The following statistics from 1991 census of Bangladesh throws significant light.

National Growth of population 2.02%

National Growth of households 2.09%

Growth Rate of Population and Households (1991 Census)

District	*Growth in*	
	Population	*Households*
Khagrachari	2.2%	4.5%
Rangamati	4.1%	5.3%
Banderban	3.6%	4.3%

The higher growth rates of both population and households in Rangamati and Banderban Districts are due to settlement of Bengali Muslims from plains districts. The lower growth rate in Khagrachari district is due to presence of nearly 56,000 Chakma refugees in Tripura since 1986. The higher growth of households in this district only underscores settlement of Muslims from outside which is fast reducing the majority of Non-Muslim tribals in the CHTs. This has heightened insecurity of the tribals fueling Chakma insurgency over the years. The successive government had dialogue with the PCJSS for resolving the CHT problem through political means, but it ended in failure, as the envision was of dominance on the indigenous Jhummas and there was no dealing of accelerated progress and self right towards equality. In June 1996, Sheikh Hasina became the Prime Minister of the country. A 12-member National Committee on CHT Affairs headed by the Chief Whip of the Parliament was formed entering into a political fray with purposeful manner. On 2nd December, 1997, the CHT Peace Accord was signed between the government and the PCJSS ending more than two decades of old armed struggle of Self determination, but it led to a worsening of the situation. It has created a creamy-layer of one Minister, two Dy. Ministers and four public representatives equivalent to Dy. Ministers for the upliftment of CHT and to delieever goods to the needy. It is now the job of elected leaders to prune the whole matter in a skillful way. But there has been no honest delivery of re-settlement scheme of Shanti Bahini who had laid down arms, rather it has created flawed administration in the hands of manipulative leaders that created a dreadful impact.

Taking the leaf from Indian constitutional provision for setting up Autonomous council for reflection of internal freedom for ethnic minorities, the Bangladesh government established three councils in the CHT. But the contention of it remained unmaterialized till date. Till recently, there was no elected government in Bangladesh, the president was functioning on the advisory committee of all the ministeries whose Chief advisor was Dr. Fakiruddin Ahmed. Mr. Devasish Roy, notionally the Chakma Chief was the special advisor to the chief advisore Dr. Fakiruddin Ahmed on CHT ministry, comprised of the following :

1. Chairman, CHT Regional Council
2. Chairman Khagarachari Hill District Council
3. Chairman Rangamati Hill District Council
4. Chairman, Bandarkan Hill District Council
5. Chairman, CHT Development Board

In addition to it, there are 6 (six) leading professionals/ personalities in the committee. The government machineries successfully created internecine between the members of PCJSS and spliting it into 2 (two) factions—1. Lamba and 2. Badi (factive meaning freedom on long wend policy and short wend policy) groups disalliance of a faction which is now known to be united peoples democratic form (UPDF), under the leadership of Prasit Bikash Khisha, the follower of rival groups. It is believed they have undergone a change of hearts and now on the verge of group mass slaughter.

Revolution is an ambiguous thing. The success is generally proportionate to the power of adoptation and to the re-adoptation within then of what they rebelled against. The situation of Chakmas in CHT, undermines the problem of the indigineous Communities all over. Will there be any realistic solution in hand of radicals? Will they ever find solution ? For it these might have lot of fronts.

MIZORAM

A chip of Chakmas have been living in the erstwhile Mizo District (now Mizoram) that abuts on the south- western part of CHT since ages. This now constitutes a part of the region of North-East India, which has amalgamated to then Assam province for administrative conveniences by the British colonial rules, while CHT was in the Bengal province, till 1954 AD, these were pre-dominance of Chakmas in the area. It is recorded that a person by name Labamoni Chakma was the chief of Lokhisury under the acquisition of chief right's let of Assam, he lost the land ownership right by receiving a compensation of Rs. 3,840.[12]

The word meaning Mizo (Highlander) and Ram meaning land; Mizoram (land for Highlanders). On this analogy Chakmas fall in the terminology of Mizo. But they are the religious linguistic minority constituting 10 per cent of the total population of Mizoram. Historically, they are connected with this land by the pathway of their habitual living. Mizos are moved with pre-conceived notion of a Mosaical or Jewish origin that induces greater strength in them of unification with western culture and civilization. While Chakmas of Mizoram are economically ethnologically at the backyard of modern civilization with sub-standard level of education and poor economic condition. For Mizos, it helps them to draw the attention of the world community and the Central Government of India in their favour.

Since 1972 AD Chakmas of Mizoram have been divided into two groups: (one) in the area of the autonomous Chakma district council which include 30 per cent of them and the remaining 70 per cent are left outside the area of the ACDC. Several economic, political, environmental and social factors are influencing their economic hardships and backwardness. They are most disadvantaged group of people in Mizoram. They get disillusioned of their fate when they turn their eyes their brethren in ACDC and see the vasts difference of the standard of living between the two communities (Mizos and Chakmas). The material wealth enjoyed by them has an ocean of difference. This is the result of the progress Central aid to the State Government There is no pro-poor delivery policy. There has been a growing demand for inclusion of all the Chakma areas of Mizoram into ACDC and to upgrade the status of ACDC to the union territory, as their has been a vast growth of population in the ACDC area for factors already mentioned; no absolute worry for survival in ACDC. They need a new solution to their problem catching in the services of big powers. The social pathway of Mizos is community based organization who are devoted for the upliftment of the whole community under a centralised body of religious ethos. There is no success organization for the social upliftment of the Chakmas. There are no such promotional activities for them.

A social perspective *"neither here nor their"*[13] by Rosenmary Zoramchani which was published in the *North East Telegraph* on Monday 29th September, 1997 throws some light on the detrimental conditions of the Chakmas in Mizoram.

The Chakma demand for a separate Union Territory has precipitated a socio-political crisis in Mizoram, says **Rosenmary Zoramchanil.**

I need land. I am a farmer, but I do not have any land to feed my family and earn my livelihood," says 48 year-old Binoy Kumar Chakma, surviving on odd jobs and small-scale trading activities.

Binoy, a father of four, came to Mizoram in 1966 as a refugee from the neighbouring Chittagong Hill Tracts of erstwhile East Pakistan, married and settled down to life in penury. His eldest son, however, is a government employee, although Binoy is yet to be granted Indian citizenship.

Development has taken a backseat in the areas under the Chakma Autonomous District Council (CADC) which has an annual budget of Rs. 6 crore to develop its areas as a substantial portion of the funds are siphoned off by the ruling clique of the council.

After a recent visit to the Chakma areas, the committee on petitions of the Rajya Sabha has made recommendations to the Centre, which if implemented, may alter the lives of the inhabitants of Mizoram. The committee has recommended that "Chakmas should be treated differently from other refugees, with sympathy and on humanitarian basis."

The committee has reasoned that according to the policy formulated at the time of Partition, since the Chakma population in the Chittagong Hill Tracts was more than 98 given to India and the Chakmas should have been Indian citizens.

Bankim Chakma, leader of the Committee for Citizenship Rights to Chakmas of Arunachal Pradesh, argues that as far back as 1946 the Chakmas had made formal representations to the interim Indian government to make the Chittagong Hill Tracts a part of India. "We do not know why India did not accept our proposal but were compelled to become part of East Pakistan."

The formula for division of the subcontinent stipulated that the newly-created Pakistan would comprise only the

Muslim-dominated areas while the non-Muslim ones would be part of India.

The historical blunder of the founding fathers of independent India has resulted in compounding the ethnic and other problems of the northeastern region. Valtea, a member of the Mizo Zirlai Pawl, argues: "The Centre should open discussions with its Bangladesh counterpart to hand over Chittagong Hill Tracts to India so that the Chakmas may get back their land and even become a state of the Indian Union."

Valtea's views are echoed by the Chakmas, who have expressed their wish to become a part of India than even present-day Bangladesh. "We would not have to seek land in Mizoram or Arunachal Pradesh if we could get back our land in the Chittagong Hill Tracts."

"Like the Jews in the first half of the century, the Chakmas have also been deprived of their land and were forced to disperse to various states in the northeastern region," says Parimal Chakma, claiming that "There are about one lakh Chakmas in Arunachal Pradesh being victimised by (the Arunachal Pradesh Chief Minister) Gegong Apang, while about 1.5 lakh-Chakmas are facing the wrath of Mizos in Mizoram.

Parimal Chakma, a student, claims he belongs to Mizoram and even has a certificate to prove it. His friends, however, say he hails from Arunachal Pradesh and had to fake his father's name to get admission in a college in Assam. *For all anyone knows he could be from Tripura, where a large number of Chakmas have also entered the college based on fake credentials even as* the state government looked the other way on "humanitarian" grounds.

However, the governments of Tripura, Arunachal Pradesh and Mizoram are perturbed over the issue of Chakma citizenship for various reasons. The Chakmas in

Tripura were systematically hemmed in by state administrations to ensure that they could be easily identified by the dominant community of migrants from erstwhile East Bengal.

It has been relatively easier for Tripura to deport the Chakmas to Bangladesh unlike the two tribal states. Unlike the Arunachal Pradesh, the erstwhile Lushai hills had a few hundred families of the Chakmas residing in the mountains adjoining the CHT, making it difficult for the Mizoram government to evict the hapless tribal community. But the Mizoram chief minister, Mr. Lalthanhawla, is peeved at the Centre's attempts to absorb the ever-increasing number of Chakmas migrating to the state from Bangladesh, Tripura and Arunachal Pradesh, on humanitarian grounds.

Lalthanhawla has publicly stated that he is amenable to the granting of citizenship to the Chakmas who came to India prior to the Indira-Mujib Pact, 1972, which laid down the cut-off date for acceptance of all refugees from Bangladesh who came on or before March 25, 1971.

However, Pu Lalthanhawla has refused to expand the jurisdiction of the Chakma Autonomous District Council. Mizoram is a bit larger than neighbouring Tripura with a total of 21,000 square km of surface area and 98 per cent Mizo population amounting to nearly 9 lakh.

The Mizoram chief minister has pointed out that Chakmas originally resident in Mizoram and their descendants also are legitimately entitled to reside in the state and avail of facilities provided by the state and district council administrations.

The Mizo Zirlai Pawl, the student body of Mizoram, visited the Chakma areas for a head count and also to look into the antecedents of those claiming to be the original residents. The figures were so shocking that the state government was forced to legitimize its findings through its own officials.

The body found out that there were legitimately only about 40,000 legally acceptable Chakmas, while the rest were "infiltrators."

The Mizoram finance minister, Lal Sangzuala, even went on record saying any Chakma, influential or otherwise, would be proceeded against as per the law. Among the most shocking disclosures by the students' body was that the Congress legislator and minister in the Lalthanhawla ministry, Nirupam Chakma, was also a "foreigner."

Significantly, Nirupam Chakma has also been suspected of fomenting the move for a separate Union Territory status to Chakma-inhabited areas, including the council areas. The committee has upheld this demand.

Looking Beyond?

"Parliament should consider expansion of the Chakma Autonomous District Council area considering the population density, percentage of Chakmas in those areas and their overall conditions. The council should be put under direct control of the Centre till living conditions are at par with the rest of the state."

The council was primarily created alongwith the Laiu Autonomous District Council to provide the minority tribes in Mizoram the right to self-governance and the right to develop their lands and their people.

The Centre by an amendment to the Sixth Schedule of the Constitution on December 6, 1988, provided that funds meant for the district councils should be administered through the Governor's office. The deputy commissioner would be giving the funds on behalf of the governor on the basis of utilisation certificate issued by the district council.

The fact that these funds were siphoned off by the respective district council's executive members is well-known.

The former Assam chief minister, Hiteswar Saikia, in his capacity as the governor of Mizoram had permitted profligacy and even institutionalised it as he prepared Mizoram for elections to the 40-member Legislative Assembly in January 1989 after a six month's spell.

His successor, Capt. Williamson Sangma, had little time for the district councils and it was left to Swaraj Kaushal, to delve into the corruption charges for political reasons.

He initiated the development process by the district councils and brought to light the massive fraud perpetuated by the councils administration. The amendment of the Sixth Schedule of the Constitution was primarily to ensure that the state government did not siphon off funds meant for the district councils.

The increasing number of Chakma migrants from various places outside Mizoram has therefore made the Rs. 6 crore budget for the 40,000 minority tribals look like a drop in the ocean. The committee has recommended that "since the ratio of Chakmas in Mizoram is 1:10 in comparison to other communities, the council should be allocated funds on a prorata basis. If the committee recommendation is implemented, the council should get Rs. 60 crore out of the Rs. 600 crore state budget. It would raise the per capita expenditure on the 40,000 Chakmas to Rs. 15,000 per annum, a dream even for the 9 lakh majority Mizos on whom the per capita expense at present amounts to Rs. 6,666 only.

Significantly, the Chakmas are the only minority group demanding a separate Union Territory as a prelude to full-fledged statehood within the Indian Union. Chakma families have begun to fan from the council areas towards Tripura along the Mizoram border with the Chittagong Hill Tracts in Bangladesh.

The Congress legislators and prominent ministers in the state Cabinet like Mr. Saikapthianga, Mr. Liasuamar are worried over the slow steady infiltration of the Chakmas to swamp the areas bordering India and Bangladesh to demand a state carved out of Mizoram in lieu of the Chittagong Hill Tracts.

With the state preparing for Assembly polls scheduled in December 1998, the issue of Chakma citizenship and demand for a Union Territory status are tailormade for the Mizo National Front, the main Opposition party in the state and the Congress which has a stranglehold over the Chakma hill areas to encash on.

Though Lalthanhawla has agreed to grant citizenship to the Chakmas, who came prior to March 25, 1971, the Mizo are still perturbed by the recommendations of the committee that those born in India should also be granted Indian citizenship. Given the sympathetic attitude of the Chakma Autonomous District Council authorities, acquiring a certificate of birth in Mizoram for the right price is no big deal. However, the Mizoram government has not been allowed to treat illegal migrants as refugees with the Centre providing financial and essential commodities, like that of Tripura. The illegal migrants are a drain on the funds of both the state and council respectively, but the committee has made no recommendation in this regard to the Parliament.

Before the Flood – When the Chakma People were Happy writes Adam Curle

From 1956 to 1959, Adam Curle was an advisor to the Pakistan Planning Commission. My responsibilities spread to East Pakistan, which is now Bangladesh and included the remote area beyond the Bay of Bengal, which was the homeland of the Chakmas, the largest of several tribal groups in the Chittagong Hill Tracts. One of my main responsibilities was to look into particular problems, such as tribal conflict, famines, epidemics and so on.

Early in 1957 there were rumours in Karachi (then the federal capital of Pakistan where the Planning Commission was located) that a dam was to be built in the CHT which might flood out a few hundred tribal people living in the steep valleys behind the dam. But nobody knew much more. A couple of colleagues and I decided to go and assess the situation. We flew to Dacca (now Dhaka), on to Chittagong, then up to Rangamati the chief town of the CHT by jeep, and after that further travel was also by elephant, country boat, or foot through beautiful wooded hills and steep valleys.

The local people knew something alarming was in the air, but were not sure what. They told us, they said, they had seen men painting lines on trees, but didn't know what they signified. I was captivated by the Chakmas. Rangamati and the area up stream from town were predominantly populated by these delightful Buddhist people. They were artistic, cheerful, hospitable. They lived in houses perched on top of stilts which, if overcrowded, tended to sway. Wherever we went we were offered hospitality. On one occasion, when a large group had come to visit and drink rice wine, the sway was too much for the stilts and the whole structure sank gently to the ground. We felt, in a silly western way, guilty for this, but the Chakmas laughed and said it was an old house and was bound to collapse soon anyway.

Children played in the bright waters of innumerable streams. Old men pottered round with hoes. The valleys were fertile and it seemed no one was undernourished or hungry. Beautiful girls wove the clothes with which they sometimes covered their breasts. For several days we traveled with the uncle of the young head of the Chakma nation, the Chakma Rai. The situation gradually became clearer. Yes, the dam was going to be built, indeed was already *being* built, as we saw with our own eyes on the journey back – a great gash through the forest, hundreds of men shifting buckets of soil, a hostel for the foreign engineers where, feeling like traitors, we were given eggs and sausages for breakfast.

The dam would be completed. No doubt of that, powerful American firms had already spent millions on it. The backed up waters would flood the fruitful valleys. What then? The people would be displaced – driven up into the inhospitable hills or to the alien and non-Buddhist coastal areas. This gentle and creative civilization would disappear. In the last phase of our journey, the unhappy face of the future became increasingly clear to us and our Chakma friends. It was miserably sad. And justifiably, for the nightmares soon became the reality. Ironically, too, for in most respects the dam was a failure, particularly as a generator of energy,

I returned to Karachi and did what I could, but the dam construction could not be reversed. We persuaded the government to set up an organisation to mitigate the hardships that the Chakmas would inevitably suffer. There were schemes to develop agriculture round the shores of the lake, to populate it with fishes, and to build up fishing industry. Experts on terracing were brought in from Indonesia to show how the hitherto wild hillsides could be cultivated to replace (partially) the valleys. There were plans to educate young Chakmas in skills appropriate to their changed circumstances. But none of these measures had any chance of fulfilment. History saw to that.

In 1971 the Bengali people of East Pakistan protested against the tyranny of the drunken Pakistani President, Yahya Khan. He at once unleashed a vicious campaign of almost genocidal repression. India then intervened and the Pakistan army, a thousand miles from its base, could only surrender. Thus Bangladesh was born.

But history is replete with examples of how people, freed from oppression themselves, proceed to subjugate and repress minority groups within their own borders. The new order of Bangladesh had no sympathy with the harmless Buddhist people of the CHT. It cast envious eyes on the territory of this negligible minority and encouraged the increasingly violent incursion of settlers, most of whom would stick at nothing to establish themselves in this delightful country and have only contempt for its age-long inhabitants.

A few of these remain, but as a whole the Chakmas are a sadly damaged and scattered people.

Chakma Descent

According to the traditional source in history, Chakmas lived on the river valley Brahmaputra in the olden days around 6th - 7th AD. At that time they were termed 'Tsak-ma' and after having gone to the Karnaphuli range they became known by the term 'Chakma'. With the turn up in history the number of Sub-tribe or sect (Gozas) in them were as under :

Name of Tribe	*Name of Sect*	*Personal Name*	*Remarks*
T-sak-ma	Phwa-ho	A-on-chi-a	
OR	Tai-yo	Dzu-ro-dhan	Dhurjodhan
Chak-ma	Ang-ngu		
	Bor-ua-Kwzu	Ison-na-dhan	Sona-dhan
	Bung-ngu-	O-ri-nat	
	Zotia	Me-go-nat	Meghanat
	Bung-ngu-solichia	Kho-leng-nga	
	Bar-se-ke	Go-zai-ya	
	Undo-talao		
	Ang-ngu	Sur-ja-dhan	Surja-dhan

Extract: *The Tribes of Brahmaputra Valley* (1901:18) by L.A Waddel
Publication: Sanskaran Prakashan, New Delhi.

The original personal name's tone was in the form of Burmese or Arkanese and later in Sanskrit. It is to be noted that the only final consonant sound that Burmese possess are particularly four (k, t, n and ng), that the two first are almost undistinguishable that all four exist only in combination with certain vowel sounds, and, except in Arakanese, there is no 'r' sound at all and that the alphabet lacks both 'f' and 'v'. It is obvious that the scope of variety in the rendering of words like Pariah, Rangrez, Bhumiji and Vannan (to take a few of many instances) is enormous. There has been a big propagation in the number of septs in them (four times), as recorded by Sir H.H. Risley in his report 'The Tribes and Castes of Bengal' (1891). They must have reached Brahmaputra river valley from top of the Himalayan Mountain Ranges or from below the valleys. It makes one think - are they Indian- Sakyan (Scythian), like Koch, who were most dominant group of people before the British era in this region? The British rulers bisected the Koch Kingdom, one part in Bengal and the other part in Assam. They are the last remnants of Tibetan traditions. The main question is: where did they come from? The universal acceptance is that they belong to Mongoloid race of Tibets-Burman group originating from Central Asia. Historically, Tsak, Sak and Thet originated from South China. They spread over Myanmar, Arakan and adjoining areas in India and Bangladesh. Ethnographically they have affinities with Laos, Cambodians and Thais. They might be known by different names in different areas (countries), but have the same origin, like Singpho (India), Jimpho (China), Karen (Myanmar) originating from Hukong valley in China. The theory that the Tibetan and Myanmaries have a common origin has obtained universal acceptance.

From historical information we know that the Tibeto-Burman race moved eastwards in a comparatively recent era towards the head waters of the Irrawadi and Chindwin (both in Myanmar), and then divided up into separate branches, some of which maintained their westerly course, to find an ultimate resting place in Tibet and portions of Assam, while the others either worked southwards into what is now Myanmar or remained to people the country in the neighbourhood. They are now divided more than 100 sub-groups. The Myanmar (Burmese) claim descent from Gautama and the Sakya race; the derivation of the word Burma. The Sakyan King Abhi Raja and Binnaka Raja and their sons established Kingdoms in Kubo Valley, Burma and Arakan near the Karnaphulli range. Therefore, Chakmas of CHT bears a great similarity with Sakyan race – in a way it might prove of their having descended from Gautama and the Sakyan race. Their legendary remembrance of Agar Tara, Alim Tara etc and Gogen Supreme truth Lama corresponds to Tibetan faith. Tara or Arya Tara is a female Buddha[14] typically associated with Buddhist tantra practices as preserved in Tibetan Buddhism. At one time, Chakmas religious belief was in Tara, one of various expression of building society but it has dried out and the direction of their religious belief has changed to other set of Buddhism which has now become their driving force. The control mechanism view of culture begins with the assumptions that human thoughts are basically both social and public – the daily life. The common language one speaks, the way one's habit, religious faith and degree of thinking in human life. For orientation of community social life is subject to geographical surroundings, such is the case with Chakmas their forest living (jhuming) in the mountain/river valleys their concrete pattern mode of life. Many have gradually moved out from clustered surroundings, adopting rural urban livelihood.

Tibetan Goddess Tara

Tara means Tibetan Goddess, or the generic name for a set of Buddhas or Bodhisattva of similar aspect and often considered metaphoric for Buddhist virtues. The most widely known form of Taras are :

1. Green Tara, known as the Buddha of enlightened activity.
2. White Tara, also known for compassion, long life, healing and serenity; also known as the wishfuling wheel, or cintachakra.
3. Red Tara, of fierce aspect associated with magnetizing all good things.
4. Black Tara, associated with power.

5. Yellow Tara, associated with wealth and prosperity.
6. Blue Tara, associated with transmutation of anger.
7. Cittamani Tara, a form of Tara widely practiced at the level of Highest Yoga Tantra in the Gelung school of Tibetan Buddhism, portrayed as green and often confused with Green Tara.
8. Khadiravani Tara (Tara of the teak forest), who appeared to Nagarjuna in the Khadiravani forest of South India and who is sometimes referred to as the "22nd Tara". There are 5 (five) Tibetan groups : 1. Sera, 2. Nima, 3. Sakya, 4. Kajni, 5. Pembo.

Tibet has been the source of Taras (female saviour of Mahayana traditions). One of the deities adored by Ahoms in Assam is called "Phura Tara" and in its Burmese form Bura or Bhura meaning the Buddha (or rather Bodhisattva) and his female counterpart 'Tara'. Chakmas recount their *Taras*, as follows :

1. Agar Tara
2. Malem Tara
3. Sadenggiri Tara
4. Annicha Tara
5. See Moga Tara
6. Doso Parami Tara
7. Trikunda Tara
8. Bora Kuruk and Choto Kuruk Tara
9. Talik Shastra Tara
10. Aritama Tara
11. Raken Ful Tara
12. Sahas Ful Tara
13. Arinamma Tara
14. Jyon Dharma Tara
15. Anjina Tara
16. Pudam Ful Tara

17. Fudam Ful Tara
18. Sava Diba Tara
19. Cherak Ful Tara
20. Chaneng Ful Tara
21. Buddha Ful Tara
22. Sak Suttan Tara
23. Raja Hara Tara
24. Sarak Dan Tara
25. Suba Dijiya Tara
26. Sakya Tara
27. Fakiri Tara
28. Angara Tara
29. Arya Tara (immortal Bodhisattva a personification of Nirvana who is identified with Shakti or the female principle. Tara is the female Buddha typically associated with Buddhist Tantra practice as preserved in Tibetan Buddhism. The ancient wisdom of Chakmas might proclaim a lineage to tibetan religious belief in Tara whose spectra of authority was in Vikramsila university. The codes of Chakma Taras are not found in original form albeit in Chakma and Bangali scripts, the grandeur part of Chakma Mahayana had been lost in the racy human history and the wheel of future of them had turned bacakward. Chakmas were believer of 'Shamanism' : a kind of premitive biligious belief in which Gods, spirits and demons influencing all human life and Buddhist Monks protect the human into their abode by chanting sutras. They seck to occure merit and avert misfortune by paying homage to Buddhist monks. The term Tara is the generic name of the sect of Bodhisattvas which is very common to Chakma Buddhism.

The corridor of Chittagong Hill Tracts was the frontier guarding wall to protect Buddhism from the outside aggression - at that time it was Mughals and Hindus casteism, working against Sakyans. The Parsian historian gave the term Hindustan to the dwellers from the Indus Valley in Central India to the western bank of the Ganges, implying many caste men were those beyond this. The casteism (caste system) had never been able to gain foothold the time when the Tsakyans were in Brahmaputra valley; there was no caste system in this region. (There are records of their living conditions at that time), and highlighting the link of this region with South West Asia. After their migration in the Karnaphuli valley at the backyard of Chittagong province their subsistence was Jhuming (shifting cultivation) or *Choomeas*. It is mentioned by John Macrae, Esq, in his report on 'Account of the Kookies' (1808) published in *Asiatic Researches* Vol. 7, that they possessed some sort of inscription which he could not decipher. As he says, one of them however, is partly legible and it appears to be in the Hindustani language. It contains the name of Sultan Ibrahim and wishes to him for a long life. He further writes that the "Choomeas" are the inhabitants of the first range of hill bordering on the plains to the north and the east tributary. Their villages are called Chooma. Some British writers mentioned the Chuk-ma whose legendary remembrances are connected with Champa – a flourishing city in ancient India in 6th B.C. It still exists near Bhagalpur (in Bihar) by the name Champa Nagar. It can be seen as a link of Chakmas with Laotians of South-East Asia, formerly a part of French Indo-China in their physical feature, ancient customs and norms and written scripts. The Laotians allied to Saks (Thets of Barma) in the Irrawady Valley and some of those are supposed to have travelled in the South-westerly direction into Arakan and crossed mountainous tracts of the country. There is a place called Champasak in Laos. Chakmas are all fair-skinned. Chakmas have some esoteric social habits which are incomprehensible by others like the lulling sound of child to sleep. It is called "Oli- Oli" (the sound to send to sleep). They have esoteric foundling with children tending the nose, while in western countries kissing on cheeks or hands. They have some esoteric food habits which are in decadence line eating raw egg, some items that are fading away. Jhdiginous plants in their cultivable lands like "Saw tree" (soft fibre tree) for vegetable items.

The Shrine on the Hill they simply belong to by Raja Tridir Roy, former Chakma Chief

Alikadam, in the south of Hill Tracts, was one of the ancient capitals of the Chakma Kings. There are still vestiges of ruined palaces, temples and ponds. An occasional coin of those bygone days still forms a part of a young girl's necklace. A hill is even today known as Pagla Mura, after the "Pagla Raja" Shatua. Near the confluence of the Matamuri and the Toin there once stood a shrine on the hill – surrounded by a cluster of champa trees. It is said that on certain nights a blue luminescence could be discerned around the shrine which, however, vanished at human approach; but not the lingering fragrance of incense and sandalwood...

The King's favourite horse was a chestnut bay that was not born in the royal stables but under a champa tree. One day as Shatua, in his pre-dawn ride, cantered past the forest of champas he heard the pitiful neighing of a horse in pain. The King, ever sensitive to the sufferings of others, turned back, dismounted and raced up the knoll. And there he discovered the new born foal which he named Champa...

Champa is dead. The King has not the heart to ride another horse. It is not yet dawn. He saunters out of the palace gates and ambles about dispiritedly. An unseen force seems to draw him toward the cluster on the hill where years ago Champa first stood on shaky, new found, legs.

In the faint morning light he perceives, under the self-same tree, a monk in yellow robes meditating in the lotus posture. He appears to be in a trance, his body rigid, his eyes fixed, unblinking. Shatua, sensing that intrusion would be unwelcome, retires behind a tree and observes the mendicant in enthralled silence.

Presently, a blue green glow seems to emanate from the monk and still in the same posture, he is elevated gently as though by some invisible hand. The sitting figure floats about, then remains immobile, suspended in mid air, his unseeing eyes still riveted on the tip of his nose.

The monk gradually floats down to earth. The glow grows faint, then vanishes. The rigidity is gone and he seems to breathe. His eye-lids stir and he blinks. He is normal again, a man sitting under a tree, relaxed, serene.

Shatua had heard of Yogis and Tantrics but had ever been sceptical of their prowess in the occult, dismissing most of the accounts as exaggerated hearsay. Now he is astounded at seeing a man actually levitate before his very eyes. He goes forward and bows.

"Holy One, I am amazed at what I have witnessed. Are you an Arahat?"

"No, son, still a seeker."

"Do you follow the esoteric doctrine handed down through Kasyapa the Elder?"

"The Guru did not specify. He said the Tathagata showed the way."

"Holy one, if I become your chela will you teach me levitation and the power to read minds and look into past lives?"

The monk smiles. "An Ekachari does not accept chelas, son. He sojourns alone. He can merely give guidance to one who seeks. He has achieved Jatiswar knowledge and a little of levitation but cannot read minds – not all minds."

"Tell me, then, what must I do?"

"You must vow not to speak of the powers you may gain except only to him whom you may teach. And you may teach only to those with the capacity to learn."

"But how will I determine that?"

"You will be told. You must also vow never to use your powers for evil."

"I vow."

"To observe these conditions until death?"

"Yes, Holy One."

"Remember that mind controls matter and will controls mind. Learn to view all phenomena through knowledge, not through the senses. Consider the faculty of sight. Every impression – every image that the eye conveys to the brain is the inferior image – the image of limited truth. The mind must superimpose the true image, in all its perspective, in its entirety. Now, a word about breathing"...

The King has had a shrine built on the knoll of champas. Unfailingly, every Tuesday and Saturday he retires there and remains alone from midnight to sunrise. No one, on pain of death, is permitted within a radius of two hundred cubits of the shrine. There are whispers that the King undertakes strange activities there. Some say he hangs head down like a bat, changes form, that he practices suspended animation.

One evening, at the palace, when the King has retired to his bed chamber, he hears a knock.

"Who is it?"

"My Lord, it is I."

Shatua opens the door to let in Amangali, his Chief Queen. Her mind has been poisoned by certain courtiers, whose insidious promptings insists that the King has entered into evil ways, and that only she can set things aright before it is too late. These Cassandras had predicted depletion of the royal coffers long ago, yet, despite the King's charitable exuberance the royal treasury is fuller than ever and the people more prosperous.

"My Lord, why do you prevaricate? Is it evil – what you do in the shrine?"

"No, Amangali, there is no evil involved. I have told you so before. Why do you persist in this matter?"

"People speak of strange going-on. And there is a great change in you. You do not delight in our company any longer. Is it a fancy for some new woman?"

Shatua laughs, "Women do not delight me any more, Amangali; nor I them, I dare say. I cannot feel any passion for them, for I see beyond the externals – I perceive the defilements they are composed of."

"Are we then repulsive to you – even the beautiful Damayanti, whose society you could not have enough of before this change in you?"

"No, they do not repulse me – it is that they do not attract me either."

"Damayanti is pining for you, though pride makes her hide her heart."

"And what makes you hide yours, Amangali?"

"I ? But... my head... I feel weak." She faints, Shatua sighs, "Poor misguided woman. Yet what is fated has to be."

He restores her, then goes to the chamber of Damayanti, his youngest wife. At his approach she rushes forward to greet him and then abruptly draws back recoiling at her own rebounding passion that could not penetrate the King's aura. She blinks back her tears, uncomprehending, hurt.

"Forgive me, Little One, I should have warned you. Believe me, I would speak, were it possible."

Damayanti looks at him through her tears. The Kings sits on a low stool by the window across the room.

"Do you still love me, Little One?"

Damayanti nods, "Yes, more than ever. But my Lord's love has dried up-like a marsh in summer heat."

The scent of jasmines wafts in through the open window. Through a pause in the northern flight of clouds the full moon is visible again in its splenderous isolation. The King turns from the window and looks at her. There is a wistful smile in his eyes.

"It has not dried up, Little One, only changed form."

The plaintive note of a distant flute lends the night an added poignancy.

"Now, listen. My end is drawing near—a violent end."

"No, never. I shall not let it happen. Who dares hurt my noble King?"

"There is greed and hatred and delusion around us. The die has been cast. And my former Karma impels me toward such an end." He looks at the Matamuri flowing on in its silent, incessant, continuity.

"I shall take form only once more, if you help."

"I ?"

"Yes, Little One. I cannot rely on any one else. May I ask this favour of You? A difficult one, though."

She looks at her Lord and is stricken at the expression of infinite sadness and hope. "Anything, my heart, anything."

He sighs and turns to gaze at the moon-bathed Matamuri and ponders its illusion of permanency, of immutability. Yet it is in a state of perpetual flux, not a drop remaining in one spot for even a moment on its journey to the sea. But then what is a river without its banks or a Being without its Name and Form? Perhaps its essential no-self, no longer a part of the Whole, but the Whole itself.

"After I am killed, before the rise of the seventh day sun you must cremate me, you with one trusted maid alone. Could you, would you, Little One? Then collect the ashes and release them where the Toin joins the Matamuri."

The Queen is speechless.

"It is either yes or no. I give you my word that what you do is to prevent the recurrence of evil, the evil in me, the last vestige of it."

The young Queen bites her lips to smother the swelling tears. "Yes, my lord, I shall do as you bid."

"Do you give your solemn word—no matter what I—or any one else says or does—that you shall do exactly as I have said?"

"I do."

"May all accumulated merits of my myriad existences surround you in blessing. Now, the time is nigh, I must go away. Grieve not, Little One, all things pass away. Remember evil can never be cured by evil but by love alone. This is an eternal verity."

It is past midnight. Amangali creeps out of the palace gates and stealthily proceeds toward the shrine. She peers through the peephole she had had gouged out in the wall earlier. All is darkness within save for winking green-blue glow-worms—or so they appear to her. She watches spellbound. The King, in rapt concentration, is washing his heart and entrails. Amangali shrieks at the sight—again and again.

Shatua hastily completes his ritual ablutions and rushes out. But by then she has made good her escape. Some feel that the rude disturbance in the midst of such a psychically delicate operation deterred him from re-inserting his vital organs properly. Others are of the view that he was then in some sort of suspended animation and his real psyche could not re-enter his body. The surmises are many. It is given out that the King's mental equilibrium is affected. And thenceforth he is known as the Mad King—the Pagla Raja.

People are immensely saddened at this tragic development and begin to murmur at the apathy in the palace, for no physicians or witch doctors are permitted to see the King. Some say that he is seized with deep melancholia and is confined to a room where he paces ceaselessly and mutters to himself. Some whisper that there is a conspiracy to murder the King and that in fact he is perfectly sane. One day this is what happens :

Knowing the King's pet avertion to elephants, someone raises an alarm that an elephant has gone berserk. Shatua thrusts out his head through the window to see for himself. Amangali's father severs it with a single blow of the axe. The head, however, does not fall on the ground. Unaccountably it vanishes. The conspirators quietly secret the body out of the palace and bury it near the shrine. They dare not announce the King's death for people would demand to see his body; and a headless one would not be acceptable, if for no other reason, as clear evidence of foulplay. As the King is childless Amangali takes the reign of Government in her hands. People hear garbled accounts of the assassination and clamour for justice, and for a proper cremation. Amangali acquires the appellation, "Daughter of the Regicide."

But the head cannot be found and this cannot be divulged. While public clamour mounts, Damayanti dreams. In her dream the King implores her to open his grave on the seventh day but not to cremtate him, so that he may come back to life by his magic powers and avenge himself. The dream recurs again and again.

Before the dawn of the seventh day Damayanti, accompanied by a maid, visits the grave which her trusted scouts had located earlier. They find the necessary implements, as instructed, and begin to dig. Damayanti finds the King whole, the severed head miraculously conjoined with the body, and the body warm with reviving life.

There is a tremendous struggle within her, a temptation to slink away and do nothing—and let the King come back to life and punish the perpetrators of this fulsome perfidy. But again and again the King's voice and the infinite sadness and hope in his eyes come back to mind—and her pledge—and his words :

> "Evil can never be cured by evil but by love alone. This is an eternal verity."

She grits her teeth and with every fibre crying out against it, she yet carries out her King's last behest, and with her own hand ignites the incense strewn pyre of sandalwood.

The blushing eastern sky shyly awaits the appearance of her lord, the sun. Damayanti places the ashes in an ivory casket and wearily wends her way down to the confluence of the rivers. Tears coursing down her face, her heart breaking with anguish, she gently lowers the King's last remains into the river. Ever slowly, the casket sinks. The ripples widen in concentric circles, then vanish.

Agreement between the National Committee on CHT affairs formed by the government of the People's Republic of Bangladesh and the Parbattya Chattagram

Jana Samhati Samiti

Under the framework of the constitution of Bangladesh and having fullest and firm confidence in the sovereignty and integrity of Bangladesh the National Committee on CHT Affairs, on behalf of the government of the People's Republic of Bangladesh and the Parbattya Chattagram Jana Samhati Samiti, on behalf of the inhabitants of the Chittagong Hill Tracts, with an objective of elevate political, social, cultural, educational and financial rights and to expedite socio-economic development process of all citizens in CHT, arrived at an agreement described in four parts as below:

(A) General

1. Both sides, considering CHT as Tribal Populated Region, recognized the necessity for protection of the character of this region and for overall development of it.

2. Both sides, in accordance with the decisions and responsibilities stated in these paragraphs under this agreement, determined to make, change, amend and add concerned rules and procedures as per laws/rules.

3. With an aim to observe the implementation process of this agreement an Implementation Committee shall be formed with the persons stated below :

(*a*) A member to be nominated by the Prime Minister ———————— Convenor

(*b*) Chairman of the Task Force formed under this agreement ———————— Member

(*c*) President of the Parbattya Chattagram Jana Samhati Samiti ———————— Member

4. This agreement shall be in force from the date of signing the agreement. This agreement shall remain in force until all steps and measures According to this agreement are completed by both sides.

(3) HILL DISTRICT LOCAL GOVT. COUNCIL/ HILL DISTRICT COUNCILS

Both sides agreed to change, amend, add and repeal the Hill District Local Government Council Acts, 1989. (Rangamati Hill District Local Government-Council Act, 1989, Bandarban Hill District Local Government Council Act, 1989 and Khagrachari Hill District Local Government Council Act, 1989) and its various sections described as below :

1. The term 'Upajati' shall be in force.
2. The name of the *Hill* District Local Government Council shall be Hill District Council.
3. Who is not a tribal and possesses land legally in the Hill District and generally lives at a certain address in the Hill District he shall be meant 'non-tribal permanent resident'.
4. (*a*) There shall be 3 (three) seats for women in every Hill District Council. There shall be one-third of the said seat for non-tribal women.

   (*b*) Sub-section (1), (2), (3) and (4) of section 4 of the original rule shall exist.

   (*c*) The words "Deputy Commissioner" and "of the Deputy Commissioner" placed in the second line of sub-section (5) of the section 4 shall be replaced with the words "Circle Chief" and "of the Circle Chief respectively.

   (*d*) Following sub-section shall be added in the section 4:

   Whether a person is a non-tribal shall be determined, along with the identity of non-tribal to which he belongs, by the concerned Circle Chief on the provision of submission of certificate from concerned Headman/Pourasabha Chairman/Union Parishad Chairman and no person can be a candidate for the office of the non-tribal member without a certificate from the concerned Circle Chief in this behalf.

5. It is narrated in the section 7 that a person elected chairman and member shall make an oath or announce confirmation before Divisional Commissioner of Chittagong. By amendment of it there shall be added the portion that the members shall make oath or announce confirmation before "Justice of High Court Division" in lieu of "Divisional Commissioner of Chittagong".
6. In lieu of the words "Divisional Commissioner of Chittagong" shall be placed the words "as per election procedure" in the fourth line of section 8.
7. The words "three years" placed in the second line of section 10 shall be replaced with the words "five years".
8. There shall be a provision in the section 14 that—

If the office of the Chairman falls vacant and in absence of the Chairman a tribal member elected by other members of the Council shall preside and perform other responsibilities.

The existing section 17 shall be replaced with the sentences mentioned as below:

A person shall, under the Act, be elligible to be enrolled in the electoral roll, if

(1) he is a citizen of Bangladesh;

(2) his age is not less than 18 years;

(3) he is not declared mentally unsound by any competent court;

(4) he is a permanent resident of Hill District.

The words "determination of electoral constituency" shall be added in the sub-section (2) of section 20.

1. There shall be a provision in the sub-section (2) of section 25 :

   The chairman and in absence of him a tribal member elected by other members shall preside over all the meeting of the Council.

2. As all the area of Khagrachari District is not included in the Mong Circle, so the words "Mong Circle Chief and Chakma Circle Chief" shall be placed in lieu of the words "Mong Chief of Khagrachari" in the section 26 of the Khagrachari Hill District Council Act. Similarly facility of attending the meetings of the Rangamati Hill District Council by Bohmong Circle Chief also shall be maintained. In the sameway, there shall be a provision of attending the meetings of the Bandarban Hill District Council by Bohmong Circle Chief.

3. There shall be provision in the sub-sections (1) and (2) of section 31 that—

   There shall be a Chief Executive Officer as secretary in the Council. Tribal Officers shall be given priority in this post.

4. (*a*) There shall be a provision in the sub-section (1) of section 32 that—

   For the proper conduct of its affairs the Council may with the approval of the government, create posts of various categaries of officers and employees.

   (*b*) The sub-section (2) of section 32 shall, by amendment, be made as follows :

   The Council may, in accordance with regulations, appoint, transfer, suspend, dismiss, remove class three and class four employees and inflict any other punishment on them.

Provided that, priority to the tribals is maintained in the matter of the said appointment.

(*c*) There shall be provision in the sub-section (3) of section 32 that —

The government in consultation with the Council may, as per regulation, appoint, transfer, suspend, dismiss, remove or inflict any other punishment on other officers of the Council.

15. In the sub-section (3) of section 33 shall be mentioned "as per regulation".

16. The words "or any other way determined by the government" placed in the third line of sub-section (1) of section 36 shall be omitted.

17. The original rule shall be in force in the fourth of sub-section (1) of section 37.

18. Sub-section (3) of section 38 shall be repealed and by amendment the sub-section (4) shall be framed as follows :

At any time before the expiry of the financial year, if deemed necessary, budget may be framed and sanctioned.

19. In the section 42 the following sub-section shall be added—

The Council with the fund received from the government shall formulate, initiate and implement development projects on the subjects transferred and all the development works initiated at the national level shall be implemented by the concerned ministry/department through the Council.

20. The word "government" placed in the second line of sub-section (2) of section 45 shall be replaced with the word "Council".

21. By amendment of rules of sections 50, 51 and 52 the following section shall be made—

"The government, if deemed necessary, may advice or order the Council, in order to ensure conformity with the purpose of the Act. If the govt. is satisfied that anything done or intended to be done by the Council or on behalf of the Council is not conformity with law or contrary to public interest the government may seek information and clarification and give advice or instruction to the Council on concerned matters in writing".

22. The words "if the period of supersession is completed" shall be repealed and in lieu of them shall be added "within ninety days of supersession" before the words "this Act".

23. The words "of the government" in the third and fourth lines of section 61 shall be replaced with the words "of the ministry".

(*a*) By amendment of sub-section (1) of section 62– this section shall be made as follows :

"Notwithstanding anything contained in any Act for the time-being in force, all members of the rank of Sub-Inspector and below of Hill District Police shall be appointed by the Council in manner laid down by regulations and the Council may transfer and take disciplinary action against them as per procedure laid down by regulation:

Provided that in the matter of such appointment tribals shall be given priority".

(b) By repealmant of the words "on the provision of all other laws for the time-being in force" placed in the second line of sub-section (3) of section 62 shall be placed the words "as per rule and regulation".

25. The words "giving assistance" placed in the third line of the section 63 shall be in force.

26. By amendment of the section 64 the following sub-sections shall be made—

(1) Notwithstanding anything contained in any law for the time-being in force, no land within the boundaries of Hill District shall be given in

settlement, purchased, sold and transferred including giving lease without prior approval of the Council :

Provided that this provision shall not be applicable in case of areas within the reserved forests, Kaptai Hydro-electricity Project, Betbunia Earth Satellite Station, State-owned industries and factories and lands recorded in the name of government.

(2) Notwithstanding anything contained in any law for the time-being in force, no lands, hills and forests within the boundaries of the Hill District shall be acquired and transferred by the government without consultation and consent of the Hill District Council.

(3) The Council may supervise and control functions of Headman, Chairman, Amin, Surveyor, Kanungo and Assistant Commissioner (land).

(4) Fringe land in Kaptai Lake shall be given in settlement on priority basis to original owners.

7. By amendment of section 65 this section shall be framed as follows :

Notwithstanding anything contained in any other law for the time-being in force, responsibility of collecting land development tax shall be entrusted in the Council and the said tax collected in the District shall be credited to the Council Fund.

28. By amendment of section 67 it shall be made as follows- "If deemed necessary for co-ordination of activities between the Council and govt. authorities, government or the Council shall put proposal on certain matter(s)".

29. By amendment of sub-section (1) it shall be made as follows- "The government having discussion with the Council may, by notification in the official gazette, make rules for carrying out the purposes of this Act and even after having rules made the Council shall have special right to file petition for reconsideration of the said rules".

30. (*a*) By omission of the words "with the prior approval of the government" placed in the first and second line of the sub-section (1) of section 69 and to add the following portion after the words "may"–

> "provided that if the government differs with any part of the regulation made by the Hill District Council then the government shall give advice or instruction for amendment of the said regulation"

(*b*) The words mentioned in the (h) of sub-section (2) of section 69 "transfer of power of Chairman to any officer" shall be omitted.

31. Section 70 shall be omitted.

32. By amendment of section 79 it shall be made as follows- "If any law by the Jatiyo Sangsad or any other authority, applicable to Hill District, is found to be hurtful to the District or objectionable to the tribal people in the opinion of the Council, it may file a petition in writing to the government stating the reasons of its being hurtful or objectionable for the purpose of amending or relaxing its application and the govt. shall, in the light of the petition, adopt necessary measures".

33. (a) The word "supervision" shall be added after the word "order" in the No. 1 of the function of the Council of the first schedule.

(b) The following subjects shall be added in the No. 3 of the function of the Council—

(1) Vocational training;

(2) Primary education in mother tongue;

(3) Secondary education.

(c) The words "or protected" placed in sub-section 6(b) of the function of the Council in the first schedule shall be omitted.

34. The following subjects shall be added in the functions and responsibilities of the Hill District Council :

(*a*) Land and land management
(*b*) Police (local)
(*c*) Tribal law and social justice
(*d*) Youth welfare
(*e*) Environment preservation and development
(*f*) Local tourism
(*g*) Improvement trust and other local govt organisations except Pourasabha and Union Councils
(*h*) Licencing for local trade and business
(*i*) Proper utilisation of water resources of rivulets, canals, ponds except Kaptai lake and irrigation
(*j*) Preservation of death and birth and others statics
(*k*) Money lending and trade
(*l*) Jhum cultivation.

35. The following sectors and sources shall be included in the taxes, rates, tolls and fees to be imposed by the Council as stated in the second schedule :

(*a*) Registration fee from non-mechanical transports
(*b*) Tax on sale and purchase of goods
(*c*) Holding tax from land and buildings
(*d*) Tax from sale of domestic animals
(*e*) Fees from cases of social justice
(*f*) Holding tax on government and non-government industries
(*g*) Part of royalty from forest resources
(*h*) Suplementary tax from cinema, theatre and circus etc.
(*i*) Part of royalty from licence or lease for exploration and extraction of mineral resources given by the government
(*j*) Tax from business
(*k*) Tax from lottery
(*l*) Tax from fishing.

(C) CHITTAGONG HILL TRACTS REGIONAL COUNCIL

1. A Regional Council shall be formed in co-ordination with the 3 Hill District Local Government Council provided that various sections of the Hill District Local Government Council Act, 1989 (Act No. 19, 20 and 21 of 1989) shall be amended with an aim to make the 3 Hill District Local Government Councils more powerful and effective.

2. Chairman of this Council shall be elected indirectly by the elected members of the Hill District Councils where status shall be equivalent to a State Minister and he must be a Jumma.

3. The Council shall be formed with 22 (twenty two) members including the Chairman. Two-third of the members shall be elected from among the tribals. The Council shall determine its procedure of functioning.

Composition of the Council shall be as follows :-

Chairman	1
Members Tribal (men)	12
Members Tribal (women)	2
Members non-tribal (men)	6
Members non-tribal (women)	1

Among the tribal men members 5 persons shall be elected from among the Chakma tribe, 3 persons from the Marma tribe, 2 persons from the Tripura tribe, 1 person from the Murung and Tanchongya tribes and 1 person from the Lusai, Bawm, Pankho, Khumi, Chak and Khiyang tribes.

Among the non-tribal men members 2 persons shall be elected from each district. Among the tribal women members 1 woman shall be elected from the Chakma tribe and 1 woman from other tribes.

4. 3 (three) seats shall be reserved for women in the Council. One-third shall be non-tribals.

5. The members of the Council shall be elected indirectly by the elected members of the Hill District Councils. Chairman of three Hill District Councils shall be ex-officio members of the Council and they shall have voting rights.

Eligibility and non-eligibility of the members of the Council shall be similar to that of the Hill District Council.

6. The term of the Council shall be 5 (five) years.

7. There shall be a chief executive officer in the Council equivalent to a Joint Secretary and priority to a tribal candidate shall be given in appointment to this post.

8. (*a*) If the office of the Chairman of the Council falls vacant then a Chairman shall be elected from among the tribal members for an interim period by the members of Hill District Councils.

(*b*) If any office of a member of the Council falls vacant on any reason then that shall be filled through by-election.

9. (*a*) The Council shall supervise and co-ordinate the subjects vested under the Hill District Councils including co-ordination of all development activities conducted under the three Hill District Councils. Besides these, if there is found any lack of co-ordination and inconsistency among the three Hill District Councils in discharging their responsibilities the decision of the Regional Council shall be taken as final.

(*b*) The Council shall supervise and co-ordinate local councils including the municipalities.

(*c*) Regional Council may co-ordinate and supervise in the matters of general administration, law and order and development of the three Hill Districts.

(*d*) The Council may co-ordinate the activities of the NGOs along with conducting of management of calamities and relief works.

(*e*) Tribal laws and social justice shall be under the control of the Council.

(f) The Council may issue licence for heavy industry.

10. The CHT Development Board shall discharge its responsibilities under general and overall supervision of the Council. In case of appointment of Chairman of the Development Board competent tribal candidate shall be given priority.

11. If the Regional Council finds any rule of the 1900 CHT Regulation and other related laws, rules and ordinances contradictory to the 1989 Hill District Council Acts then the govt. shall remove that inconsistency by law according to recommendation of and in consultation with the Regional Council.

12. Untill and unless Regional Council is constituted through direct and indirect election the government may, by constituting an interim Regional Council, entrust the responsibilities of the Council.

13. If the govt. makes any law on CHT it shall be in having discussion and in consultation with the Regional Council. If there arises the necessity to amend any such law or to make any new law which may be harmful for development of the 3 Hill District or the welfare of the tribals, the Council may file a petition or put recommendation to the govt.

14. The fund of the Council shall be created from the following sources :

(*a*) fund received from the Hill District Councils' fund

(*b*) money or profits from all properties vested in and managed by the Regional Council

(*c*) grant and loan from the govt. or any other authority

(*d*) grant from any institution or individual

(*e*) profit accruing from investment by the Regional Council;

(*f*) any other moneys received by the Regional Council

(*g*) money received from such sources of incomes as the govt. may direct to be placed at the disposal of the Regional Council.

(D) REHABILITATION, GENERAL AMNESTY AND OTHER MATTERS

1. An agreement has been signed between the govt. and the refugee leaders on March 9, 1997 with an aim to take back the tribal refugees from India's Tripura State based on the 20-Point Facilities Package. In accordance with the said agreement repatriation of the refugees started since March 28, 1997. This process shall continue and with this in view, the JSS shall provide all kinds of possible co-operation. The internal tribal evacuees of 3 districts shall, after determination, be rehabilitated by the Task Force.

2. After signing agreement between the govt. and the JSS and implementation of it as well as after rehabilitation of the tribal refugees and internal tribal evacuees the govt. shall start survey of land in CHT as soon as possible and after proper inquires ownership of land shall be recorded and ensured.

3. The govt. shall ensure providing two acres of lands to each landless family and the family who possesses less than 2 acres of lands, provided lands were available in the local areas. If requisite lands are not available then grove land shall be provided.

4. A commission (land commission) headed by a retired justice shall be formed for settling land disputes. This commission, in addition to settle disputes of lands of the rehabilitated tribal refugees, shall have fullest power for cancellation of ownership of those lands and hills which have been so far illegally settled and occupied. No appeal can be made against the Judgement of this commission and decision of this commission shall be final. This (arrangement) shall be applicable in case of fringe land also.

5. This commission shall be set up with the following members :

(*a*) Retired justice;

(*b*) Circle Chief (concerned);

(*c*) Chairman of the Regional Council/representative;

(*d*) Divisional Commissioner/Additional Commissioner;

(*e*) Hill District Council Chairman (concerned).

(*a*) The term of the commission shall be three years. But the term of it can be extended in consultation with the Regional Council.

(*b*) Commission shall settle disputes according to the existing rules, customs and usages of Chittagong Hill Tracts.

The tribal refugees who received loan from the govt. but could not use them properly due to conflicting situation shall be exempted with the interests.

Allotment of lands for rubber plantation and other purposes: All the non-tribals and non-locals who were given in settlement of lands for rubber plantation and other purposes but had not implemented any projects within the past 10 years or had not utilised their lands properly, settlement of these lands shall be cancelled.

The govt. shall allot additional fund, on priority basis, with an aim to implement more number of projects in CHT. New projects formulated with an aim of making necessary superstructures for development in the area, shall be implemented on priority basis and the govt. shall provide fund for these purposes. The govt. shall, having consideration about the environment in the region, encourage to develop tourism for tourists from the country and abroad.

Quota reservation and scholarships:- Until development equal to other region of the country the govt. shall continue reservation of quota system in govt. services and educational institutions for the tribals. With an aim to this purpose, the govt. shall grant more scholarships for the tribal students in the educational institution. The govt. shall provide necessary scholarships for research works and receiving higher education in abroad.

The govt. and elected representative shall make efforts to maintain seperate culture and tradition of the tribals.

The govt. in order to develop the tribal cultural activities at the national level it shall provide necessary patronisation and assistance.

12. The Jana Samhati Samiti shall submit to the govt. the lists of its all members including the armed ones and the arms and ammunition under its possession and control within 45 days of signing this agreement.

13. The government and the Jana Samhati Samiti jointly shall determine the date and place for depositing arms within the 45 days of signing this agreement. After determination of date and place for depositing arms by the members included in the list of the Jana Samhati Samiti the govt. shall ensure security for return of JSS members and their family members to normal life.

14. The govt. shall declare amnesty for the members who shall deposit their arms and ammunition on the scheduled date. The govt. shall withdraw the cases against whom cases have been lodged.

15. If anyone fails to deposit arms on the scheduled date the govt. shall take lawful measures against him.

16. After the return of all JSS members to normal life general amnesty shall be given to them and the permanent residents who were involved in the activities of the JSS.

(*a*) In order to providing rehabilitation to all returnee JSS members a lump sum of Taka 50,000/- shall be given to each family.

(*b*) All the JSS members including the armed ones against whom cases have been lodged, warrant of arrest and police circular for apprehension issued and punishment has been sentenced/inflicted in the absence, after surrendering of arms and return to normal life all the cases, warrants of arrest, police circulars and punishment sentenced in the absence against them shall be exempted as soon as possible. If JSS members are detained in the jails they also shall be released.

(*c*) Similarly after surrendering of arms and return to normal life no cases can be lodged, warrant issued and punishment inflicted against anyone only for the reason that he was a JSS member.

(*d*) All the members of the JSS who took loans from various banks and organisations of the govt. but could not utilise them properly those loans including the interests shall be exempted.

(*e*) The JSS members who were posted in the services of the govt. or govt. institutions they shall be reinstated in their own posts and services and the JSS members and their family members shall be given appointment in accordance with their competence. In this case, the rule of the govt. for relaxation of age shall be followed.

(*f*) The JSS members shall be provided bank loans on easier terms and conditions to give assistance for cottage industry, horticulture etc. self-employment activities.

(*g*) The children of JSS members shall be provided educational facilities and their certificates received from foreign educational Boards and institutions shall be taken as valid.

After signing the agreement between the government and the Jana Samhati Samiti and immediately after the return of the JSS members to normal life all the temporary camps of military, Ansar and Village Defence Party shall be taken back to permanent installations except the Border Security Force (BDR) and permanent cantonments (3 at the 3 District Hqs. and Alikadam, Ruma and Dighinala) by phases and with this in view, time-limit shall be determined. In case of deterioration of law and order situation, natural calamity and such other works the army can be deployed under the civil administration like all other parts in the country as per necessary laws and rules. In this case, Regional Council may, according to necessity or time, request the proper authority for the purpose of getting assistance.

Permanent residents of CHT, on priority basis to the tribals, shall be appointed to all posts of officers and employees at all levels of govt, semi-govt, council offices and autonomous bodies in CHT.

Provided that in case of non-availability of qualified candidate among the permanent residents of CHT for a particular post, appointment in that post may be made on deputation from the govt for a term of certain period,

A ministry on Chittagong Hill Tracts Affairs shall be established by appointing a Minister from among the tribals. An Advisory Council shall be formed to assist this ministry with the persons stated below —

(1) Minister on CHT Affairs

(2) Chairman/representative, Regional Council

(3) Chairman/representative, Rangamati Hill District Council

(4) Chairman/representative, Bandarban Hill District Council

(5) Chairman/representative, Khagrachari Hill District Council

(6) Member of Parliament, Rangamati

(7) Member of Parliament, Khagrachari

(8) Member of Parliament, Bandarban

(9) Chakma Raja

(10) Bohmong Raja

(11) Mong Raja

(12) Three members from non-tribal permanent residents of Hilly areas nominated by the government from three Hill Districts.

This agreement is framed as above in Bengali language and is done and signed in Dhaka on the date of 02 December, 1997 as per 18 Agrahayan, 1404 Bengali year.

On behalf of the inhabitants of Chittagong Hill Tracts	on behalf of the government of the People's Republic of Bangladesh
SD/-	SD/-
(Jyotirindra Bodhipriya Larma) President	(Abul Hasanat Abdullah) Convenor
Parbattya Chattagram Jana Samhati Samiti	National Committee on Chittagong Hill Tracts Affairs, government of Bangladesh

(Sent by the Jana Samhati Samiti on December 10, 1997)

Militarization and the Chittagong Hill Tracts

INDIGENOUS AFFAIRS, IWGIA, 2/01, PAGES 14-19 INTERNATIONAL WORK GROUP FOR INDIGENOUS AFFAIRS CLASSENSGADE 11 E, DK-2100, COPENHAGEN, DENMARK.

An international fact-finding mission to the Chittagong Hill Tracts in 1991 described it as an area under occupation. Ten years later, the presence of the army in the region is as evident as ever. A peace accord, which was agreed in 1997 between the Govern-ment of Bangladesh and the Parbattya Chattagram Jana Samhati Samity, the indigenous party fighting for autonomy and self-rule in the CHT, has not resulted in the withdrawal of the army from the Hill Tracts. The Peace Agreement stipulates that only permanent camps are to remain, for the ostensible purposes of security and territorial integrity - and yet, the armed forces remain firmly entrenched in the region. The question therefore remains as to why?

Background

The Chittagong Hill Tracts covers a land area of about 13,189 sq. kms. (5,089 sq. miles), and is the traditional homeland of an estimated 600,000 indigenous people from among 13 different ethnic groups including the Bawm, Chakma, Khyang, Lushai, Marma and Tripura, among others. It enjoyed independent status until 1860 when it was annexed by the British colonialist powers in India. When India was partitioned in 1947, the CHT was awarded to East Pakistan, contrary of the express de-mands of the indigenous people, who believed it more expedient to be included within secular India. From 1947 to 1971, the CHT was part of what was then East Pakistan and, with the creation of Bangladesh in 1971 after a bloody civil war, the CHT became a part of this successor State. Whereas religion had formed the basis for the creation of a separate states for the Muslim population of India (East and West Pakistan), the 1971 independence war signified a shift in policies and, with the creation of Bangladesh, Bengali nationalism was born. The first constitution of Bangladesh, drafted in 1972, reflects this and denies the cultural diversity of the country. Manabendra N. Larma, the founder of the PCJSS (popularly known as the JSS)) and a member of Parliament (CHTNorth) refused to endorse the new Constitution:

> *"This Constitution does not recognize the existence of other national communities in Bangladesh. ...It makes nomention about the CHT. The British had given recognition to our separateness, the 1962 Constitution of Pakistan duly recognized our separate status. ...the framers of the Constitution have forgotten my land, my people ...We have been deprived of our rights, the country has become independent, but we continue to have a cursed life..."* (Parliament Debates 25.10.1972:292-295).

Since its creation, Bangladeshi politics have been dominated by the army, and a number of coups and counter-coups have taken place during the country's brief turbulent history as an independent nation. Two of its presidents, Zia-ur-Rahman (1975-1981) and his successor, General Ershad (1981-1990) rose up from the army corps and took power in violent take-overs. With the restoration of democracy by a mass movement in December 1990, the Bangladesh army has reverted to its traditional role as defenders of the realm, with one major exception - in the Chittagong Hill Tracts. In this region, in south-eastern Bangladesh, bordering India and Myanmar (Burma), the military remains very much in power, not just as a visible presence with surveillance posts on strategic hilltops but also in civilian matters ranging from the CHT Development Board to the requirement of a no objection-certificate (NOC) from the commanding officer for entrance to higher educational institutions.

Militarization

The presence of the army in CHT affairs has its roots in Bengali hegemony predicated on the creation of Bangladesh as a separate homeland for the Bengalis. The existence of indigenous peoples in the territorial framework of the Bangladeshi State, with their own identity, cultures and traditions, is a challenge to the concept of a homogenous state. The demands of the indigenous people for autonomy and the right to their own cultural identity were translated as being secessionist, and integration and assimilation became the fundamental pillars of the Government's policy in the CHT, with the army as its main instrument in this process. As a result, since 1972, the army has been in control of the CHT: "*Consequently, the entire region of CHT has undergone full scale militarisation and the military has been given total control of the administration of the CHT. More importantly, in the name of counter-insurgency gross violations of human rights have been committed in the area by the military.*"

Although it is difficult to estimate exactly how many troops are deployed in the CHT, a rough estimate puts the figure somewhere between 35,000 and 114,500. Military officials attest to the fact that one-third of the entire Bang-ladesh army is deployed in the CHT, an area which accounts for one-tenth of the total territory of the country. With the indigenous people numbering approximately 600,000 this is an excessive amount, by any standard, especially in a country that is not at war, and at peace with its neighbours:

> *"The CHT has been turned into an army camp. The 24th Infantry Division of Chittagong Division is in charge. The overall command for the CHT is with the GOC of the* 24th *Division. The army has four Brigade Head Quarters in the CHT: Rangamati, Khagrachari and Dighinala in the north, and Banderban in the south. There are garrisons in Ruma and Alikadam in the south and there are army base camps in each Upazilla (sub-district) Head Quarters in the CHT as well as in various villages. There are also several army camps on the roads (The CHT Commission 1991:39). At Kaptai, there is a naval base with three gunboats (Ahmed, A. 1993:46). There is also an anti-guerilla training centre at Mahalchari in the CHT (Mey 1984:147). The state does not reveal the exact number of military personnel deployed in the CHT. But from military sources it could be gathered there are 19 Infantry battalions, 11 Bangladesh Rifles [BDR] battalions, three Artillery battalions, one Engineer battalion, 18 Ansar battalions and four battalions of armed police. The military is spread out all over the area. It has five Regional Head Quarters situated in Khagrachari, Rangamati, Kaptai, Banderban and Guimara. Under these five Head Quarters there are 26 zones, 23 are with the army and three with BDR; BDR zones are located in Kaptai, Bolipara and Naikhongchari. There are over 230 army camps, more than 100 BDR camps and over 80 police*

camps in the area (CHT Commission 1991:40). The total number of men is a matter of conjecture with the figures varying between 114,500 (CHT Commission 1991:41, Mey 1984:147) to 30-35,000 (CHT Commission 1992:4). However, military officials are of the opinion that Bangladesh has deployed one third of its total army in the CHT2, which suggests that the latter figures are more accurate. The current total strength of the Bangladesh armed forces is 115,500, while the BDR (30,000), armed police (5000) and Ansars (20,000) to-gether form 55,000 (IISS 1994:152-153)." 3

A retired army officer who served as an infantry brigade and region commander in the CHT from 1989 to 1991 confirms that over 500 camps have been established and maintained by the security forces in the last 25 years[4].

Counter-insurgency

The initial reason for the deployment of the troops in the CHT was "national security" and justified on the ground that the CHT was in a geographically strategic area bordering the Indian states of Assam, Manipur, Mizoram and Tripura and the Rakhine and Chin states of Myanmar, most of which have ongoing ethnic struggles. However, the deployment of such a large proportion of the Bangladesh army in the CHT signalled the beginning of a relationship founded on hostility and antagonism; the indigenous peoples realized that the Government viewed them as "insurgents" and a threat to national security.

This conviction gained ground when the Government initiated a Settlement Programme (1979-84). Impoverished families from other parts of Bangladesh were given incentives including land, money and food rations, to come and live in the CHT. The settler families were allocated lands legally belonging to the indigenous peoples, either individually or collectively. Although approximately 54,000 acres of agricultural land had been submerged by the

Kaptai Hydroelectric-power plant created in 1960, the settlers were promised 11.5 acres of land, including 2.5 acres of paddylands (wet rice growing fields).

Since most of the CHT lands were already under cultivation or use by the indigenous peoples, measures had to be taken to ensure the settler families received the promised allotments. To this end, the armed forces included another element within their "counter-insurgency" strategy whereby indigenous people were forced to relocate to what were termed Cluster Villages where they were under strict army surveillance, with strict time schedules for free movement and labour. This also had the end result of freeing up their lands, which could then be used for the settlement programme. Through this programme, some 450,000 persons were settled in the Hill Tracts[5].

At approximately 600,000, with an estimated 450,000 settlers and nearly one-third of the Bangladesh army in the CHT, the indigenous people felt outnumbered and vulnerable.

The actions of the army did nothing to allay their concerns, as the army and para-military forces actively assisted the settler families in divesting the indigenous peoples of their lands and homes, and often taking their lives as well.

In this environment, the relationship between the indigenous peoples and the Government, which was already antagonistic and mistrustful, degenerated rapidly. The indigenous peoples felt betrayed and isolated, and began to seriously consider their alternatives in a nation-state that did not recognize their existence, or their identity. A movement for recognition of the rights of the indigenous peoples to exist as a separate people with the CHT defined as an autonomous area gathered momentum and the Parbattya Chattagram Jana Samhati Samity (JSS) was formed in 1972. In response to the increased militarization and State violence, the armed wing of the JSS, the Shanti Bahini (Peace Corps) began operations in the mid-1970s. The resulting civil war continued for two decades, culminating in the Peace Accord signed on 2 December 1997.

Human Rights Violations

The human rights abuses committed by the armed forces, often in collaboration with the settlers who had been provided with arms by the government, has been reported extensively including by the UN, the International Labour Organization (which monitors the situation of the indigenous peoples in Bangladesh by virtue of a treaty to which Bangladesh is a signatory - Convention No. 107 on Indigenous and Tribal Populations, 1957), as well as by international NGOs including Amnesty International and Anti-Slavery International.

Rape, torture and massacres of innocent indigenous villagers by the armed forces in cooperation with the settlers have all been well documented. In its most recent report on the CHT, Amnesty International included a list of year by year accounts of human rights abuses (see *Bangladesh: Human rights in the Chittagong Hill Tracts,* ASA 13/001/2000 of 2 February, 2000 for details). The following are noteworthy:

Kaukhali-Kalampati (15/03/1980): 50 indigenous persons were gunned down by the army when attending a meeting called by the military to discuss the reconstruction of a desecrated Buddhist temple;

Barkal (31/05/1984): 110 indigenous persons, including women and children, were killed by the 305 Brigade of 26 Bengal Regiment and 17 Battalion of BDR, in collaboration with the settlers. Many of the women were gang raped and later shot dead;

Panchari (01/05/1986): The army, and the settlers, killed hundreds of indigenous people (actual numbers are unavailable). Their houses were burnt down and thousands fled across the border and took refuge in camps in Tripura, India;

Matiranga (1-7/05/1986): About 70 indigenous men were killed by the army;

Comillatilla-Taindong (18-19/05/1986): A group of 200 Tripuras fleeing to India were intercepted by the BDR and gunned down;

Longadu (04/05/1989): The army, Village Defence Party (VDP, a para-military force) and settlers carried out what has been termed "a human carnage". More than 30 indigenous people were killed, their houses burnt and temples destroyed;

Malya (02/02/1992): Two bombs exploded on a passenger launch. The launch was carrying a deputation of indigenous people who were travelling to Rangamati and Dhaka to protest against army atrocities in the area. Survivors swam ashore but were attacked by armed settlers who were waiting for them; about 30 were killed (CHT Commission 1994:17); and

Logang (10/04/1992): Another component of the Government's CHT strategy was the forcible settlement of indigenous people in Cluster Villages, ostensibly for their protection, but in practice so they could be under strict surveillance and their movements curtailed. A settler cowherd had attempted to rape an indigenous woman, and when others came to her aid, he was injured. In a reprisal attack led by the settlers with members of the BDR, VDP, and armed police, many indigenous people were killed, although it is difficult to estimate the exact number, which varies from JSS estimates of 138 to the Government figure of 12. It is reported that the village was sealed off and the houses set alight.

There are also many incidents of rape, many of which never come to public attention. Army personnel stationed in the CHT were encouraged to target indigenous women. This led to many rapes, forced conversions and forced marriages. One well-known case is that of Kalpana Chakma, the organizing secretary of the Hill Women's Federation, who was allegedly abducted from her home in June 1996 by army personnel in civilian attire. Her whereabouts is still unknown. Reports continue of discrimination and violence against indigenous Jumma women, often young girls, on the part of the armed forces.

An element common to all the human rights violations that have occurred, and continue to occur, in the CHT is that those responsible are seldom if ever held accountable for their actions. As Amnesty International reports on the current environment:" *It is further marked by the failure of the Bangladeshi Government to bring to justice those responsible for these human rights violations. Past incidents of gross human rights violations have rarely been investigated. In a few cases when official commissions of inquiry have been set up [e.g. Logang Inquiry Commission] and responsibility for violations believed to be established, the reports were not made public and no action was taken against any army personnel involved.*" (Amnesty International 2000:12).

This is a significant factor in the continuing violation of human rights abuses, which have abated somewhat following the Accord but continue nevertheless. Section 132 of the Bangladesh Code of Criminal Procedure states that no magistrate, police, civil or military officer or any inferior officer, or soldier or volunteer, doing any act in obedience to any order which he was bound to obey, shall be deemed to have thereby committed an offence. (Amnesty International 1993:30). This provides the legal basis for the impunity enjoyed by the armed forces and others in the CHT.

According to Government figures, over 8,500 civilians, soldiers and "insurgents" (alleged Shanti Bahini) have been killed during the two decades of civil war in the CHT, of which 2,500 were civilians. However, the indigenous people believe the actual number of civilians killed by the armed forces is much higher. Human rights violations continue to be reported despite the Peace Accord and, in a recent incident on 18 May 2001, Bengali settlers, in collaboration with the armed forces and police ransacked three villages in the Dighinala area, and set the houses on fire. The Jumma villagers were physically assaulted, many of them seriously, including women and children. What is of even graver concern is that this incident reportedly occurred in the presence of the commanding officer of the Dighinala cantonment and the officer in charge of the police station, neither of whom made any effort to halt the arson or looting.

Civil Administration

The armed forces play a key role in the civil affairs of the CHT, and their power and influence is pervasive. For instance, the CHT Development Board was established in 1976 by an ordinance passed by then president General Zia:

> *"That the CHTDB was created to counter the insurgency became evident when the General Commanding Officer* (GOC) *of the 24th Infantry Division, Chittagong was appointed as its ex-officio chairman in 1982 by General Ershad ...The CHTDB has implemented projects and programs for construction of roads, telecommunication, electrification, and moving the hill people into the 'model' or 'cluster' villages. Although the stated goal of the CHTDB is the welfare of the hill people, in reality, most villages in the hills do not have telephones or electricity. Although the roads have been beneficial for transporting produce to markets, they have first been very useful for fast military movement. Roads expanded the mobility of the military to combat the Shanti Bahini and helped the businessmen most of whom were Bengalis."*[6]

It is only recently that the GOC has been relieved of his post as chairperson of the CHTDB; however, the armed forces continue to play a role in development issues in the CHT. Another area where the role of the armed forces is evident is land administration. As mentioned earlier, they played a key role in facilitating the settlement of the plains (Bengali) families in the CHT, with the related land losses for the indigenous peoples, many of who were either forced to move into cluster villages, or to flee to India. The third alternative was to join thousands of other dispossessed people as internally displaced.

A related effect of the militarisation of the CHT, and one which is often overlooked, is that the army camps, cantonments and other installations are created on lands belonging to the indigenous peoples. Many indigenous people have been forced to vacate their lands for military purposes, without any compensation whatsoever. This has been a major factor in the current crisis of displacement and landlessness facing the indigenous Jummas. This practice continues, and the military has plans to acquire 30,444 acres of lands in Bandarban to set up an artillery training centre. This will displace some 25,000 indigenous people and, with the loss of their lands, which are the basis for their economic and cultural survival, the indigenous peoples will be further marginalized. There are also plans to acquire another 184 acres to expand the brigade headquarters. This indicates that the army has long term plans in the CHT with no immediate plans for withdrawal, as required under the provisions of the 1997 Peace Accord.

Conclusion

Bangladesh is one of the poorest countries in the world with a population of nearly 129 million, of which 35.6% live below the poverty line. It is a major recipient of foreign aid with an external debt of US$16.5 billion (1998). The UNDP human development indicators (HDI), which are calculated on the basis of infant mortality rates, literacy, health, education etc. placed Bangladesh as 143rd in 1997,147th in 1998 and 150th in 1999, the lowest in South Asia. In contrast, the defence expenditure has steadily increased from 1% and now accounts for between 1.5 and 1.7% of GDP.

The defence budget for 2000 was 7% higher than the previous year, and Taka 32 billion has been earmarked for defence as revenue expenditure-and an additional Taka 720 million for other defence expenditures (CHT Commission 2000:20). In stark contrast, although Bangladesh has the highest infant mortality and the lowest life expectancy in the world, 2% is allocated for health and social welfare. To maintain the army in the CHT, it is estimated that the Government has to spend approximately US$125 million annually, with a daily expenditure amounting to Taka 1.5 crore[7] daily (CHT Commission 1994:2). With a Peace Accord in place in the CHT and peaceful relations with its neighbours, it is questionable whether this huge outlay on defence-related spending in a poverty stricken country like Bangladesh can be justifiable. The presence of the military in the CHT only serves to perpetuate the isolation and marginalization of the indigenous people.

The Peace Accord stipulates that all temporary army camps, Village Defence Parties (VDPs) and Ansars are to be withdrawn from the CHT and that only the border security force (BDR) and permanent army camps at the three district headquarters and at Alikadam, Ruma and Dighinala are to remain. However; three years on, there are no signs of the 500 camps of Ansars and VDPs have so far been dismantled (Report on the Implementation of the CHT Agreement, JSS, September 2000). In addition, the 1973 executive order imposing military rule in the CHT remains in force, thereby legalising the presence of the army in the area.

President Zia, who was instrumental in initiating the militarisation of the Hill Tracts, is reported to have had his doubts regarding this policy: "We *are doing some mistakes there. We are being unfair to the tribes. It is a political problem that is being dealt with by police and army action.* Yet it *can be settled very easily. We have no basis for taking over these lands and pushing these peoples into a corner. We should at least call a meeting of these tribal leaders and ask them their demands." (The Guardian,* London, 29 July 1980 as reported in Philip Gain 2000: 115).

For Bangladesh to progress as a nation, it has to address the CHT issue in a much more concerted manner. Sheikh Hasina has recognized the existence of the indigenous peoples in the CHT, and been awarded the UNESCO peace prize for her role in finalizing the 1997 Peace Accord. Yet, unless the military is withdrawn from the CHT, and the Peace Accord implemented in its entirety with the indigenous peoples given the opportunity to decide their own future themselves, peace in the CHT will remain an elusive dream.

NOTES

1. *The Politics of Nationalism: The Case of the Chittagong Hill Tracts, Bangladesh,* Amena Mohsin, University Press Limited, Dhaka, 1997.
2. "This was stated to the author by military officers (1993-1994) who had served in the CHT. They further posed the question that, if the army has to be withdrawn from CHT then where will they be stationed?"
3. Amena Mohsin 1997:171-172.
4. *Allowing Peace in* CHT *a Chance,* by Brigadier M. Sakhawat Hussain ndc, psc, (Retd), The Independent, Internet Edition, 15.11.2000.
5. For a detailed analysis of the Settlement Progamme, see *Land Rights of the Indigenous Peoples of the*

CHT, *Bangladesh,* by Rajkumari Chandra Roy, IWGIA Document No. 99, 2000 pp. 110-122.

6. *Life and Nature at Risk,* by Philip Gain, in *The Chittagong Hill Tracts: Life and Nature at Risk,* edited by Philip Gain, Society for Environment and Human Development (SEHD), July 2000, p. 34.

7. One crore = 10.000.000

Chandra Roy is an indigenous Jumma from the Chittagong Hill Tracts in Bangladesh. She is a lawyer by training with an LL.M. in international law. The focus of her work is on human rights, discrimination, indigenous rights, gender and development. Chandra Roy has worked for many years at the Standards Department of the International Labour Office, most recently on a project on indigenous peoples. She has many years experience working in the field of international law, including at the UN. She was also involved in establishing the Unrepresented Nations and Peoples Organization (UNPO) to give a voice to indigenous peoples, minorities and nations. She has written several publications on the legal rights of the indigenous peoples of the Chittagong Hill Tracts, and is now working independently on international legal issues.

Raja Tridiv Roy was born in Rangamati on 14th of May, 1933. He was the Chief (ruler) of the indigenous Chakma Tribe, which lived in the Chittagong Hill Tracts. He studied in India and in 1951, he qualified to join in Lincoln's inn, London, but on his father's death, it prevented could not be materialized and become the new chief in 1953. The Pakistan government conferred him Honorary title captain of the pakistan Army. He had won a seat in Pakistan's first democratically elected parliament in 1970 election. He was most trustful to the Prime Minister Zulfiqur Ali Bhutto, who deputed him as the Chief deligate of Pakistan in the U.N.'s general assembly in 1972 to discuss the application for entry into the U.N. and the accolade won by him from Bhutto in appreciation of his successful lobbying for stalling the admission of Bangladesh. He had chosen to stay back in Pakistan for all the rest of his life after the emergence of Bangaldesh in 1971.

He is known Ambassador-at-large and his contact information : Chakma House, 277, Gomal Rood E-7, Islamabad, Pakistan.

He was made the minister of Minorities Affairs (Being of Buddhist himself) in Bhutto's government. He also held the portfolio of tourism, and when Zia came into power, he was retained as an ambassador in a state of confusion at a length of time from the early stage of life and had to wend his way stirring up being the Buddhist minority himself in a principally Islamic country. He was a young romantic man when I met him on my board ship that barthed at Chittagong port with Pakistani consignment from Glasgow to Chittagong before India Pakistan war in 1964. He had many wits and converse brilliantly the won him respect from all the crews on board. All through his life he exercised superior knowledge and powers in bureaucracy.

WHATEVER HAPPENED TO...

Tridiv Roy, the Minority Monarch of East Pakistan

Until 1971, Tridiv Roy was the Raja (King) of the 200,000-strong Chakma tribe in the Chittagong Hill Tracts, a 13,000-sq.-km. tribal belt in the south-eastern corner of what is now Bangla-desh. A year before, he had won a seat in Pakistan's first democratically elected parliament; the Chakma leader was one of only two politicians who defeated candidates of Sheikh Mujibur Rahman's Awami League in East Pakistan. When Indian forces liberated Bangladesh in December 1971, Tridiv Roy was touring Southeast Asia. The Chakmas have not seen their Raja since: Tridiv Roy decided to give up his crown and kingdom for Pakistan, and flew straight to Islamabad.

Today, Raja Tridiv Roy, 47, is an adviser to the Pakistan government on minority affairs. But he is still at the centre of a tug-of-war involving the Bangladesh government and his tribal home. After Pakistan's defeat in the Bangladesh war, the government of Gen. Yahya Khan collapsed, and successor Zulfikar Ali Bhutto offered Tridiv a post in his new cabinet. Next day, Tridiv, a Buddhist, took the oath as Minister for Tourism and Minority Affairs. But after nearly two-and-a-half years, he faded out of the limelight and in 1974 he was made a governmental adviser.

Soon after Tridiv's appointment as a minister, Sheikh Mujibur had begun sending feelers to him. If he would return home, perhaps they could work out an arrangement. Tridiv declined; he was happy in Pakistan and he didn't want a relationship with Mujib's people. In September 1972, when Bangladesh was applying for membership of the United Nations, Bhutto sent the Raja as leader of Pakistan's delegation to the General Assembly. Mujib was delighted. If he could woo Tridiv to Bangladesh's side, it would be a diplomatic coup.

Mujib pulled every trick out of the hat to get the Raja to defect to Bangladesh. When his initial overtures were turned down, Mujib sent an ambassador to Tridiv's mother in Chittagong Hill Tracts. At the urging of Mujib's men, the Raja's mother flew to New York to see her son. But Tridiv was adamant. Unless the Bangladesh government gave the Chakmas more autonomy and pledged not to interfere in their internal affairs he could not even think of returning to the hill tracts. In Tridiv's place, the Bangladesh government installed his eldest son, Devasish Roy, as Raja of Chakma four years ago. "It was done with my knowledge and blessings," Tridiv told *Asiaweek* recently of the teenager's appointment. "But I think most Chakma still consider me as their Raja. Perhaps they think of me as the elder Raja and my son [now 22] as the younger Raja."

But while Tridiv Roy has been working in Islamabad, the Chakmas have been waging a war against the Bangladesh government. Some 3,000 armed Chakma tribesmen are involved in a guerilla battle against Bangladeshi soldiers and paramilitary troops. The dispute isn't new. The predominantly Buddhist Chakmas have traditionally been at loggerheads with Bengali Muslims who form the majority in Bangladesh. Before the 1971 civil war, Pakistan's federal administration was in the hands of West Pakistani Muslims who took a more neutral line between the Bengalis of Chittagong and Chakmas. Since Bangladesh's independence, however, the Chakmas have complained of atrocities and charged that Bengalis are encroaching on their rights.

Will Tridiv ever go back to the Chittagong Hill Tracts? "I'd sure like to go back. My sons, my mother, most of my family are there," he told Correspondent Assif Shameen. "But I won't go there as a Raja. I'd like to go there just to visit my family. I don't think I'd like to live there now." But that doesn't mean he would be unwilling to mediate in the ongoing dispute between the Chakmas and the Bangladesh government. "It's not for me to decide whether I have a role to play. It's up to the authorities in Dacca. If they think I have a role to play, I'll be glad to help." Until he gets an invitation from Dacca, however, Tridiv Roy has to be content with the routine of bureaucratic work in Islamabad. "I have very little work to do, intellectually," he says. "I only wish I could do more, perhaps serve the government in some other way."

484

Sir E. Jenkins (Punjab) to Rear-Admiral Viscount Mountbatten of Burma
Telegram, L/P & J/8/663 : f 24

Immediate *Lahore, 14 August 1947, 9.10 am*
Confidential *Received in India Office : 15 August, 1.05 am*

No. 234-G. Situation in Lahore City and Amritsar District still most unsatisfactory. Two trains reported attacked in Rawalpindi are a presumably by Moslems as reprisal for Sikh activities in Central Punjab. Re-arrangement of personnel as preliminary to partition completed. Situation will now be for new Governments to deal with.

Repeated to Secretary of State for India.

485

Rear-Admiral Viscount Mountbatten of Burma
of the Earl of Listowel
Telegram, L/P & J/10/117 : f 108

Immediate *New Delhi, 14 August 1947, 10.15 pm*
Received : 15 August, 2.30 am

No. 3408—S. A crisis has arisen over awards of the Boundary Commissions. I am reporting in full in my weekly report[15] the history of events which have led up to the present situation. In the meantime it is essential that H.M.G. should be in possession of outline of facts of the case, which are as follows.

2. I personally have scrupulously avoided all connection with Boundary Commissions, including interpretation of their terms of reference and putting before them the various points of view forwarded to me.

3. The leaders representing the two future Governments themselves.

(*a*) selected personnel of Commissions, including Radcliffe;[16]

(*b*) laid down terms of reference;[17]

(*c*) agreed inclusion of sub-clauses 3(4) and 4(3) of the Indian Independence Bill which made Chairman's decision binding;[18]

(*d*) issued a statement[19] from Partition Council pledging themselves to accept awards of Commissions whatever these might be: and, as soon as awards were announced, to enforce them impartially.

4. On 11th August Ismay received a verbal message from Liaquat to the effect that Gurdaspur, or a large portion of it, had been given to East Punjab by Boundary Commission; that it was reported that this was a political decision and not a judicial one; and that, if it was true, it was a grave injustice which would amount to a breach of faith on the part of the British.

5. In his answer[20] Ismay pointed out that award has not yet been sent in; and emphasized the points mentioned in paras. 2 and 3 of this telegram.

6. Radcliffe sent in the Bengal award on 12th August. This contained the allocation of Chittagong Hill Traces to Pakistan and I was warned that there would be serious reactions amongst Congress leaders at this.

7. On 13th I received a letter[21] from Patel, who had seen a deputation of Chittagong Hill Tribes and told them that the proposition that Chittagong Hill Tracts might be included in Pakistan was so monstrous that if it should happen they would be justified in resisting to utmost of their power and count on his maximum support in such relations [resistance]. He adds that any award against weight of local opinion and of terms of reference, or without any referendum to ascertain will of people concerned must, there fore, be considered a collusive or partisan awards and will have to be repudiated.

8. I have taken following action:

(*a*) I have decided not to publish awards myself;

(*b*) I have told Governors concerned that new Provinces must carry on notional partition boundaries on 15th and until awards are published and implemented,[22]

(*c*) I have arranged a meeting[23] of representatives of the two Governments on the (work) in order:

(*i*) to decide upon timing and method of publication and

(*ii*) to decide method of implementing undertaking of Partition Council to accept award and to enforce decision contained in it.

9. My next telegram[24] contains a summary of Boundary Commission's award.[25]

487

Minutes[26] of a Meeting between Rear-Admiral Viscount Mountbatten of Burma and representatives of India and Pakistan

L/P & J/10 117 : ff 19-22

CONFIDENTIAL

Those present at this Meeting held at Government House, New Delhi, on 16 August 1947 at 5.00 pm were: Rear-Admiral Viscount Mountbatten of Burma, Pandit Nehru, Mr Liaquat Ali Khan, Sardar Patel, Mr. Fazlur Rahman, Sardar Baldev Singh; Mr Mohammad Ali, Rao Bahadur, V.P. Menon, Lieutenant-Colonel Erskine Crum (Secretariat)

THE AWARDS OF THE BOUNDARY COMMISSIONS

1. The meeting considered the awards[27] of the Boundary Commissions, copies of which had been given to the Ministers after the Joint Defence Council meeting that morning.

Bengal

2. PANDIT NEHRU said that he had never considered that the allocation of the Chittagong Hill Tracts to East Bengal was possible under the terms of reference of the Boundary Commission. Eminent lawyers had confirmed this point of view. These Tracts were an excluded area, and were

not represented in the Bengal Council. He and his colleagues had given assurances to petty chiefs from the Chittagong Hill Tracts who had come to see them, that there was no question of the territory being included in Pakistan. The population of the Chittagong Hill Tracts, though small (approximately ½ million) was 97% Buddhist and Hindu. There was not the least doubt that the people themselves would prefer to form part of India. On religious and cultural grounds the Chittagong Hill Tracts should form part of India. Sir Cyril Radcliffe had no business to touch them.

3. THE GOVERNOR GENERAL explained the reasons why Sir Cyril Radcliffe has included the Chittagong Hill Tracts in East Bengal. He emphasized particularly the economic ties which bound Chittagong District and the Hill Tracts together. He stressed the importance to Chittagong Port of the proper supervision of the Karnaphuli River, which ran through the Hill Tracts.

4. MR. FAZLUR RAHMAN gave his opinion that the Chittagong Hill Tracts could not exist if separated from Chittagong District. In his view, the allocation of these Tracts to East Bengal was unquestionably permissible under the terms of reference. In fact the "contiguity" clause of the terms of reference would not have permitted their allocation to West Bengal.

5. THE GOVERNOR GENERAL said that it had been Sir Frederick Burrows' view that that whole economy of the Chittagong Hill Tracts would be upset if they were not left with East Bengal. However, he had confirmed that Sir Frederick had not expressed any view on this matter to Sir Cyril Radcliffe, so he could not be said to have influenced the decision.

6. THE GOVERNOR GENERAL suggested the possibility of a compromise whereby the upper waters of the Karnaphuli would be protected through the allocation of a

strip of territory on either side of the river to East Bengal, while the administration of the rest of the Hill Tracts would be undertaken by India.

7. This was not considered a satisfactory solution by either party. PANDIT NEHRU'S view was that India should undertake the administration of the whole territory; a strip on either side of the river allocated to Pakistan would cut the territory in two. If the Chittagong Hill Tracts were given to India, an agreement between the two Dominion government, whereby Pakistan would obtain all desired facilities, could well be made.

8. MR. LIAQUAT ALI KHAN said that he could not consider any suggestion of an adjustment in this territory alone. The awards of both Commissions must be looked at as a whole. If this was done, it would be found that Sir Cyril Radcliffe had completely ignored the fundamental basis of his terms of reference. Moreover, the Chittagong Hill Tracts were the only source of hydro-electric power in East Bengal.

9. THE GOVERNOR GENERAL then suggested that the two Governments might agree on an exchange of territory, whereby the Chittagong Hill Tracts would go to India and some predominantly Muslim area which had been allotted by the commission to India would go to Pakistan.

10. MR. LIAQUAT ALI KHAN emphasized that the awards of the Commission, taken as a whole, had been so unfavourable to Pakistan, that he could not consider any minor modification only, such as had been suggested. Finally, Indian leaders exchanged CHT for Ferozpur junction between villages Rattoke, Sahjra and Mabbuke. The line will then run north-east between the villages Rattoke and Mabbuke to the junction of villages Rattoke, Mabbuke, and Gajjal. From that point the line will run along the boundary

between villages Mabbuke and Gajjal, and then turn south along the eastern boundary of village Mabbuke to its junction with village Nagar Aimanpur. It will then turn along the north-eastern boundary of village Nagar Aimanpur, and run along its eastern boundary to its junction with village Masteke. From there it will run along the eastern boundary of village Masteke to where it meets the boundary between the tahsils of Kasur and Ferozepore.

For the purpose of identifying the villages referred to in this paragraph, I attach a map[28] of the Kasur tahsil authorized by the then Settlement Officer, Lahore District, which was supplied to the Commission by the Provincial government.

The line will then run in a south-westerly direction down the Sutlej River on the boundary between the Districts of Lahore and Ferozepre to the point where the districts of Ferozepore, Lahore and Montgomery meet. It will continue along the boundary between the districts of Ferozepore and Montgomery to the point where this boundary meet the border of Bahawalpur State. The district boundaries, and not the actual course of the Sutlej River, shall in each case constitute the boundary between the East and West Punjab.

It is my intention that this boundary line should ensure that the canal head works at Sulemanke will fall within the territorial jurisdiction of the West Punjab. If the existing delimitation of the boundaries of Montgomery District does not ensure this, I award to the West Punjab so much of the territory concerned as covers the head works, and the boundary shall be adjusted accordingly.

So much of the Punjab Province as lies to the west of the line demarcated in the preceding paragraphs shall be the territory of the West Punjab. So much of the territory of the Punjab Province as lies to the east of that line shall be the territory of the East Punjab.

Appendix II to No. 488

L/P & J/10/117 : ff 40-47

New Delhi, 12 August 1947

REPORT

To :

His Excellency the Governor-General.

1. I have the honour to present the decision and award of the Bengal Boundary Commission, which by virtue of section 3 of the Indian Independence Act, 1947, is represented by my decision as Chairman of that Commission. This award relates to the division of the Province of Bengal, and the Commission's award in respect of the District of Sylhet and areas adjoining thereto will be recorded in a separate report.

2. The Bengal Boundary Commission was constituted by the announcement of the Governor-General dated the 30th of June, 1947, Reference No, D50/7/47R. The members of the Commission thereby appointed were

Mr. Justice Bijan Kuman Mukherjee,

Mr. Justice C.C. Biswas,

Mr. Justice Abu Saleh Mohamed Akram, and

Mr. Justice S. A. Rahman.

I was subsequently appointed Chairman of this Commission.

3. The terms of reference of the Commission, as set out in the announcement, were as follows:—

> "The Boundary Commission is instructed to demarcate the boundaries of the two parts of Bengal on the basis of ascertaining the contiguous [majority] areas of Muslims and non-Muslims. In doing so, it will also take into account other factors,"

We were desired to arrive at a decision as soon as possible before the 15th of August.

4. After preliminary meetings, the Commission invited the submission of memoranda and representation by interested parties. A very large number of memoranda and representations was received.

5. The public sittings of the commission took place at Calcutta, and extended from Wednesday the 16th of July 1947, to Thursday the 24th of July 1947, inclusive, with the exception of Sunday, the 20th of July. Arguments were presented to the Commission by numerous parties on both sides, but the main cases were presented by counsel on behalf of the Indian National Congress, the Bengal Provincial Hindu Mahasabha and the New Bengal Association on the one hand, and on behalf of the Muslim League on the other. In view of the fact that I was acting also as Chairman of the Punjab Boundary Commission, whose proceedings were taking place simultaneously with the proceedings of the Bengal Boundary Commission, I did not attend the public sittings in person, but made arrangements to study daily the record of the proceedings and all material submitted for our consideration.

6. After the close of the public sittings, the remainder of the time of the Commission was devoted to clarification and discussion of the issues involved. Our discussions took place at Calcutta.

7. The question of drawing a satisfactory boundary line under our terms of reference between East and West Bengal was one to which the parties concerned propounded the most diverse solutions. The province offers few, if any, satisfactory natural boundaries, and its development has been on lines that do not well accord with a division by contiguous majority areas of Muslim and non-Muslim majorities.

8. In my view, the demarcation of a boundary line between East and West Bengal depended on the answers to be given to certain basic questions which may be stated as follows:—

(1) To which State was the City of Calcutta to be assigned, or was it possible to adopt any method of dividing the City between the two States?

(2) If the City of Calcutta must be assigned as a whole to one or other of the States, what were its indispensable claims to the control of territory, such as all or part of the Nadia River system or the Kulti rivers, upon which the life of Calcutta as a city and port depended?

(3) Could the attractions of the Ganges–Padma–Madhumati river line displace the strong claims of the heavy concentration of Muslim majorities in the districts of Jessore and Nadia without doing too great a violence to the principle of our terms of reference?

(4) Could the district of Khulna usefully be held by a State different from that which held the district of Jessore?

(5) Was it right to assign to Eastern Bengal the considerable block of non-Muslim majorities in the districts of Malda and Dinajpur?

(6) Which State's claim ought to prevail in respect of the Districts of Darjeeling and Jalpaiguri, in which the Muslim population amounted to 2.42 per cent of the whole in the case of Darjeeling, and to 23.8 per cent of the whole in the case of Jalpaiguri, but which constituted an area not in any natural sense contiguous to another non-Muslim area of Bengal?

(7) To which State should the Chittagong Hill Tracts be assigned, an area in which the Muslim population was only 3 per cent of the whole, but which it was difficult to assign to a State different from that which controlled the district of Chittagong itself?

9. After much discussion, my colleagues found that they were unable to arrive at an agreed view on any of these major issues.[29] There were of course considerable areas of the Province in the south-west and north-east and east, which provoked no controversy on either side: but, in the absence of any reconciliation on all main question affecting the drawing of the boundary itself, my colleagues assented to the view at the close of our discussions that I had no alternative but to proceed to give my own decision.

10. This I now proceed to do: but I should like at the same time to express my gratitude to my colleagues for their indispensable assistance in clarifying and discussing the difficult questions involved. The demarcation of the boundary line is described in detail in the schedule which forms Annexure A to this award, and in the map attached thereto, Annexure B. The map is annexed for purposes of illustration, and if there should be any divergence between the boundary as described in Annexure A and as delineated on the map in Annexure B,[30] the description in Annexure A is to prevail.

11. I have done what I can in drawing the line to eliminate any avoidable cutting of railway communications and of river systems, which are of importance to the life of the province: but it is quite impossible to draw a boundary under our terms of reference without causing some interruption of this sort, and I can only express the hope that arrangements can be made and maintained between the two States that will minimize the consequences of this interruptions as far as possible.

CYRIL RADCLIFFE

Annexure A to Appendix II

A line shall be drawn along the boundary between the Thana of Phansidewa in the District of Darjeeling and the Thana Tetulia in the District of Jalpaiguri from the point where that boundary meets the Province of Bihar and then along the boundary between the Thanas of Tetulia and Rajganj; the Thanas of Pachagar and Rajganj, and the Thanas of Pachagar and Jalpaiguri, and shall then continue along the northern corner of the Thana Debiganj to the boundary of the State of Cooch-Behar. The District of Darjeeling and so north of the District of Jalpaiguri as lies north of this line shall belong to West Bengal, but the Thana of Patgram and any other portion of Jalpaiguri District which lies to the east or south shall belong to East Bengal.

A line shall then be drawn from the point where the boundary between the Thanas of Haripur and Raiganj in the District of Dinajpur meets the border of the Province of Bihar to the point where the boundary between the Districts of 24 Parganas and Khulna meets the Bay of Bengal. This line shall follow the course indicted in the following paragraphs. So much of the Province of Bengal as lies to the west of it shall belong to West Bengal. Subject to what has been provided in paragraph I above with regard to the Districts of Darjeeling and Jalpaiguri, the remainder of the Province of Bengal shall belong to East Bengal.

1. In my view, the question is limited to the districts of Sylhet and Cachar, since of the other districts of Assam that can be said to adjoin Sylhet neither the Garo Hills nor the Khasi and Jaintia Hills nor the Lushai Hills have anything approaching a Muslim majority of population in respect of which a claim could be made.

2. Out of 35 thanas in Sylhet, 8 have non-Muslim majorities; but of these eight, two—Sulla and Ajmiriganj (which is in any event divided almost evenly between Muslims and non-Muslims), are entirely surrounded by preponderatingly Muslim areas and must therefore go with them to East Bengal. The other six thanas comprising a population of over 530,000 people stretch in a continuous line along part of the southern border of Sylhet District. They

are divided between two sub-divisions, of which one, South Sylhet, comprising a population of over 515,000 people, has in fact a non-Muslim majority of some 40,000; while the other, Karimganj, with a population of over 568,000 people, has a Muslim majority that is a little larger.

3. With regard to the District of Cachar, one thana, Hailakandi, has a Muslim majority and is contiguous to the Muslim thanas of Badarpur and Karimganj in the District of Sylhet. This thana forms, with the thana of Katlichara immediately to its south, the sub-division of Hailakandi, and in the Sub-division as a whole Muslims enjoy a very small majority being 51% of the total population. I think that the dependence of Katlichara on Hailakandi for normal communications makes it important that the area should be under one jurisdiction, and that the Muslims would have at any rate a strong presumptive claim for the transfer of the Sub-division of Hailakandi, comprising a population of 166,536, from the Province of Assam to the Province of East Bengal.

4. But a study of the map shows, in my judgment, that a division on these lines would present problems of administration that might gravely affect the future welfare and happiness of the whole District. Not only would the six non-Muslim thanas of Sylhet be completely divorced from the rest of Assam if the Muslim claim to Hailakandi were recognized, but they form a strip running east and west whereas the natural division of the land is north and south and they effect an awkward severance of the railway line through Sylhet, so that, for instance, the junction for the town of Sylhet itself, the capital of the district, would lie in Assam, not in East Bengal.

5. In those circumstances I think that some exchange of territories must be effected if a workable division is to result. Some of the non-Muslim thanas must go to East Bengal and some Muslim territory and Hailakandi must be

retained by Assam. Accordingly I decide and award as follows:—

A line shall be drawn from the point where the boundary between the Thanas of Patharkandi and Kulaura meets the frontier of Tripura State and shall run north along the boundary between those Thanas, then along the boundary between the Thanas of Patharkandi and Barlekha, then along the boundary between the Thanas of Karimganj and Barlekha, and then along the boundary between the Thanas of Karimganj and Beani Bazar to the point where that boundary meets the River Kusiyara. The line shall then turn to the east taking the River Kusiyara as the boundary and run to the point where that river meets the boundary between the Districts of Sylhet and Cachar. The centre line of the main stream or channel shall constitute the boundary. So much of the District of Sylhet as lies to the west and north of this line shall be detached from the Province of Assam and transferred to the Province of East Bengal. No other part of the Province of Assam shall be transferred.

6. For purposes of illustration a map marked A[31] is attached on which the line is delineated. In the event of any divergence between the line as delineated on the map and as described in paragraph 13, the written description is to prevail.

CYRIL RADCLIFFE

489

Viceroy's Personal Report No. 17
L/PO/6/123: ff 245-63

TOP SECRET

AND PERSONAL

16 August 1947

This last week of British rule in India has been the most hectic of any. We have been working longer hours and under more trying conditions, and with crises of differing magnitudes arising every day, and sometimes two or three times a day. The problem of the States continued to occupy most of my time, particularly of those Rulers who have kept changing their mind up to the last moment, whether to accede to India, to Pakistan, or to neither. I paid my farewell visit to Karachi, and took part in unbelievable scenes on the day of the transfer of power in Delhi. The issue which has created the greatest and most serious crisis to date has been the awards of the Boundary Commissions, a summary of which is given in Appendix I.[32]

2. I had always anticipated that the awards could not possibly be popular with either party, and that both would probably accuse the Chairman of the Boundary Commissions of being biased against them. I have therefore taken the greatest pains not to get mixed up in the deliberations of the Commissions in any way. In fact, though I have repeatedly been asked both to interpret the Boundary Commissions' terms of reference and to put forward to them certain points of view (for example on behalf of the Sikh Princes), I have resolutely refused to do this.[33] I have firmly kept out of the whole business but I am afraid that there is still a large section of public opinion in this country which is firmly convinced that I will settle the matter finally.[34] For this reason I made my position as regards the Boundary awards absolutely clear in my address to the Indian Constituent Assembly (Appendix II).[35]

3. I feel it necessary to put on record a brief review of the history of the Boundary Commissions, for the crisis that has been caused is in my opinion the most serious we have ever had to meet, and might have undone all the work of the past four months—so bitter have been the feelings.

4. On 10th June, Nehru wrote agreeing to the proposal that each Commission should consist of an independent chairman and four other persons of whom two would be nominated by the Congress and two by the Muslim League.[36] This proposal was agreed to by Jinnah.[37]

5. On 12th June, Nehru sent in the proposed terms of reference for the Boundary Commissions[38] which were accepted by Jinnah on 23rd June.[39] These were the exact terms which were subsequently issued, namely:—

For the Punjab

The Boundary Commission is instructed to demarcate the boundaries of the two parts of the Punjab on the basis of ascertaining the contiguous majority areas of Muslims and non-Muslims. In doing so it will also take into account other factors.

For Bengal

The Boundary Commission is instructed to demarcate the boundaries of the two parts of Bengal on the basis of ascertaining the contiguous majority areas of Muslims and non-Muslims. In doing so it will also take into account other factors.

For Sylhet

In the event of the referendum in Sylhet Diştrict of Assam resulting in favour of amalgamation with Eastern Bengal, the Boundary Commission for Bengal will also demarcate the Muslim majority areas of Sylhet District and contiguous Muslim Majority areas of adjoining districts.

6. At a Partition Council Meeting on 27th June[40] the leaders of both parties agreed that Sir Cyril Radcliffe, whose name had been put forward as a candidate for the Arbitral Tribunal, should be asked to be Chairman of both Boundary Commissions. At a Partition Council Meeting on 10th July,[41] it was agreed that no direction in addition to the terms of reference should be given to the Boundary Commissions; and that it should be left to their own discretion to interpret their terms of reference.

7. At this same Partition Council Meeting it was agreed that the Secretary of State should be asked to add the following sub–clause to the Indian Independence Bill[42]. It

was added as sub–clause (4) and sub–clause (3) to Section 3 and 4 respectively:—

"In this section, the expression 'award' means, in relation to a boundary commission, the decisions of the chairman of that commission contained in his report to the Governor–General at the conclusion of the Commission's proceedings."[43]

8. At a Meeting on 22nd July,[44] the Partition Council issued a statement in which they pledged themselves to accept the awards of the Boundary Commissions whatever these might be; and, as soon as the awards were announced, to enforce them impartially.

9. The first indication that the reception which the awards were likely to have was going to be even worse than anticipated was contained in a message given to Ismay on behalf of Liaquat Ali Khan by the Pakistan Cabinet Secretary (Mohamed Ali) during a vist to Delhi from Karachi. This was a verbal message, but very strongly worded, to the effect that if indeed it proved true that the Gurdaspur district in the north Punjab area or even a large part of it had been given to East Punjab by the Boundary Commission, this would be regarded as a most serious fact by Jinnah and the Pakistan Government. If it turned out that this was a political and not a judicial decision, then this would amount to so grave a breach of faith as to imperil future friendly relations between Pakistan and the British.

10. In answering Liaquat, on 11th August,[45] Ismay (while pointing out that even I had not received the award) reminded him that I had had nothing to do with the Boundary Commissions; that I was determined to keep clear of the whole business; and that the Indian leaders themselves had selected the personnel of the Boundary Commissions, drafted their terms of reference, and undertaken to implement their awards.

11. It was on Tuesday, 12th August, that I was finally informed by Radcliffe that his awards would be ready by noon the following day, just too late for me to see before leaving for Karachi. For some time past, I and my staff had been considering the question of when and how these awards should be published.[46] From the purely administrative point of view, there were considerable advantages in immediate publication so that the new boundaries could take effect from 15th August, and the officials of the right Dominion could be in their places to look after the districts which had been allotted to their side before that date. However, it had been obvious all along that, the later we postponed publication, the less would the inevitable odium react upon the British.

12. The matter came to a head at the Meeting which I held with members of my staff on the evening of the 12th.[47] The Bengal award had by then been sent in but I had deliberately refrained from reading it. I was told however that it allotted the Chittagong Hill Tracts to Pakistan. My Reforms Commissioner, V.P. Menon, was present at the meeting and was able to warn me of the disastrous effects that this was likely to have on the Congress leaders. He went so far as to say that Nehru and Patel were both certain to blow up, since they had only recently assured a delegation from the Chittagong Hill Tracts that there was no question of their being allotted to Pakistan, (V.P. Menon admitted that they had no possible authority for making such a statement).

13. V.P. Menon went on to say that if the details of the award were given to them before the 15th he thought they might well refuse to attend the meeting of the Constituent Assembly which I was to address. If given to them later in the day he thought they would refuse to come to the State banquet and the evening party. In any case he said that unless the situation were handled with the utmost care, Congress would blow up. I have never known V.P. Menon

to mislead me, and I decided that somehow we must prevent the leaders from knowing the details of the award until after the 15th August; all our work and the hope of good Indo–British relations on the day of the transfer of power would risk being destroyed if we could not do this.

14. On 13th August[148] I therefore wrote to Jinnah and Nehru telling them that I had not received all the awards by the time I left for Karachi, though I expected them that afternoon; and suggesting that there should be a meeting at Government House on the 16th August to decide upon the timing and method of publication, and also the method of implementing the undertaking of the Partition Council to accept the award and to enforce the decisions contained in it.

15. Just as I was signing the letter to Nehru a letter arrived from Patel which is so incredible that I attach a copy of the complete letter as Appendix III.[49] From this it will be seen that the one man I had regarded as a real statesman with both feet firmly on the ground, and a man of honour whose word was his bond, had turned out to be as hysterical as the rest. Here he was suggesting that if indeed the Chittagong Hill Tracts were put into East Bengal the people would be justified in resisting this award by force and that the Central Government would be bound to support them! So much for his undertaking on behalf of India to accept and implement the awards what ever they might be.

16. The crazy part about all this is that Burrows had explained to me that the whole economic life of the people of the Hill Tracts depends upon East Bengal, that there are only one or two indifferent tracks through the jungle into Assam, and that it would be disastrous for the people themselves to be cut off from East Bengal. The population consists of less than a quarter of a million, nearly all tribesmen who, if they have any religion at all, are Buddhists (and so are technically non-Muslims, under the

terms of the Boundary Commission). In a sense Chittagong, the only port of East Bengal, also depends upon the Hill Tracts; for if the jungles of the latter were subjected to unrestricted felling, I am told that Chittagong port would silt up. Candidly I was amazed that such a terrific crisis should have blown up over so small a matter. However, I have been long enough in India to realize that major crises are by no means confined to big matters.

17. Once more I had cause to thank the invaluable V.P. Menon for deliverance from the disaster which would have followed on my publishing the awards in good faith without prior reference to the leaders. Having deciced not to announce the awards before the 15th August I had no alternative but to send instructions to the Governors[50] that the Governments of the two halves of the split Provinces would have to take charge up to the *national*[51] boundary on 15th August, pending publication and implementation of the awards or of mutually agreed boundaries.

18. When I was at Karachi, although Liaquat saw the absolute need for him to come to Delhi on the 16th both to discuss the terrible situation in the completed by the end of February 1948. We do not however consider it necessary to modify our above conclusions in the light of this fresh information.

TEDDER.

R.R. MCGRIGOR, V.C.N.S.

F.E.W. SIMPSON, V.C.I.G.S.

No. 335

363

Sir F. Burrows (Bengal) to Rear-Admiral Viscount Mountbatten of Burma Telegram, R/31/153: f 231

IMPORTANT

SECRET

26 June 1947, 7.40 pm

Received: 27 June, 9 am

174–S. My telegram 161-S dated 18th June,[52] Indian Dominion Bill. I have following supplementary comment. Under clause 3(3)(b) of the Bill[53] Chittagong Hill Tracts will, until otherwise determined, fall within the new Province of West Bengal. For reasons indicated in my immediately succeeding telegram I regard this as entirely impracticable proposition since all of the Hill Tracts' links are with Chittagong District. Pending negotiations between the two Dominions, I would strongly press for amendment of the Bill to allow Hill Tracts to be treated at all events temporarily as part of territories of East Bengal.

364

Sir F. Burrows (Bengal) to Rear–Admiral Viscount Mountbatten of Burma Telegram, R/3/1/153: ff 232–3

IMPORTANT

CONFIDENTIAL

26 June 1947, 7.40 pm

Received: 27 June, 9 am

No. 175–C. My immediate preceding telegram. Chittagong Hill Tract. Constitutional position of the Hill Tracts was fully discussed in memorandum about their future administration forwarded with para. 4 of my General Letter F.J.B.–24 dated May 7th.[54] It was recommended that Hill Tracts should continue to remain attached to the Province of Bengal and that their future administration should rest with the Provincial Government. Their only easy means of communication with outside world is through Chittagong District and all their commerce and administrative ties are with that District. It would be wholly impracticable for them to be administered as part of West Bengal Province.

Population figures in 1941 Census are:

Tribals	—	233,392
Muslims	—	7,270
Hindus	—	4,881
Others	—	1,510
Total	—	247,053

When I saw the three Chiefs of the Tracts on May 3rd they strongly deprecated being placed under the Muslim Province of East Bengal and indicated preference for federation with Tripura and Assam States; (group corrupt) admitted that all their links were with Bengal. Great weight need not be attached to opinion of the Chiefs who are more concerned with personal aggrandisement than the welfare of the population.

3. Neither major political party has yet evinced any strong interest in tracts which as an excluded area have been outside the main stream of political life of the province. But League are likely to press for inclusion in East Bengal, if only because hydro–electrical project for electrification of Chittagong Area depends on the dam at Barkal on Karnaphuli River in the interior of tracts. Congress will naturally try to keep any non-Muslim Area out of Muslim hands.

4. Though reference to "Other factors" in terms of reference of the Boundary Commission gives Commission considerable scope, *I assume that the fate of Hill Tracts would be a matter for negotiation between the two Dominion Govts. or their Constituent Assemblies and not for decision of Boundary Commission.*

5. Your Joint Secretary *Christie* was Deputy Commissioner Hill Tracts for two years and will be able to give you much local colour.

365

Rear-Admiral Viscount Mountbatten of Burma to the Earl of Listowel Telegram, R/3/1/153: ff 227–8

MOST IMMEDIATE

SECRET

NEW DELHI, *26 June 1947, 10 pm*

Received: 26 June, 7.20 pm

No. 1598–S. Indian Independence Bill. Your telegrams 8155, 8156, 8162, 8163, 8176, 8184, 8185 and 8194 of 25th June.[55] All textual amendments communication.

430

Minutes by Lieutenant–Colonel Erskine Crum, Sir G. Abell and Rear–Admiral Viscount Mountbatten of Burma R/3/1/153: f 290

30 June 1947

1. Since the Staff Meeting, Sundaram and I have been in communication with V.P. Menon about the proposal to raise, at the meeting tomorrow, the question of the Chittagong Hill Tracts.[56] Menon is very strongly of the view that to arise this question tomorrow would lead to extreme trouble. He even offered to dress immediately and come over and personally convince H.E. on this point. He says that the Governor of Bengal[57] is looking at the matter from a purely provincial point of view. To depart from the "Muslim-majority" principle at this stage would be exceedingly dangerous and lead to endless complications.

2. I have also looked up an extract from a letter of 16th May from Pandit Nehru, which reads:—

> "There is no mention in the document of the Chittagong Hill areas which are predominantly Hindu and Buddhist. These are Excluded areas lying to the east of East Bengal. They have nothing in common with Chittagong District or with East Bengal. They will

naturally line up with some of the Hindu States to the north of them and possibly with Assam."

3. I have prepared the papers about the Chittagong Hill Tracts, but recommend that these should not be produced unless the Muslim League representatives raise the matter tomorrow. Sundaram agrees.

V.F. ERSKINE CRUM

I am going to see V.P. Menon tonight, but I put this up for immediate information. I think the Chittagong Hill states must at least be mentioned though the feasible alternative are limited to:

(1) leaving things as they are for future discussion, and

(2) insisting that some arrangement be made before the appointed day to ascertain the will of the inhabitants.

G.E.B. ABELL

No action is to be taken to raise this issue with any of the leaders unless the League raise it. I hope to discuss it with VP about 10.15.

4. As regards the Portuguese, Sir G. Bajpai said that the Government of India would probably ask us to take some action with the Portuguese government. (As I would know, their relations were far from good, as India had opposed Portugal's admission to U.N.O.). I said that, speaking personally, I thought it might be very difficult for H.M. Government to do this on behalf of India; what action did he contemplate asking us to take? He replied "soundings". I suggested that before pursuing the matter of the Portuguese possessions, it might be advisable for the government of India to see whether some accommodation could be reached with the French. But I rather expect that Nationalist exuberance after August 15th will incline them to push ahead.

452

Sardar Patel to Rear-Admiral Viscount Mountbatten of Burma

L/PO/6/123: ff 273–5

MOST IMMEDIATE

AND PERSONAL

NEW DELHI, *13 August 1947*

A deputation of the Chittagong Hill Tribes saw me this morning and expressed to me their grave apprehension that their area was going to be included in East Bengal under the Boundary Commission award. I am unaware of the source of their information, but they seemed to be well-convinced that this was going to happen. I have told them that the proposition was so monstrous that if it should happen they would be justified in resisting to the utmost to their power and count on our maximum support in such resistance.

2. Personally, I feel it is inconceivable that such a blatant and patent breach of terms of reference should be perpetrated by the Chairman of the boundary commission. We have all along felt that the future of this area was not at all in doubt. No fair reading of the terms of reference or appreciation of the factual position could make a ninety-seven per cent non-Muslim area a part of the award relating to the boundary of East Bengal. Such a decision would also jeopardise the position of the adjoining Tripura State which is a Hindu State with predominantly Hindu population, and which has acceded to the Indian Dominion and has joined the Union Constituent Assembly.

3. I, therefore, fell bound to draw you attention to the serious consequences which would follow such a manifestly unjust award. There is no doubt from the report of the Tribal Areas Committee who collected impeachable evidence on the spot and whose views I represented to the Chairman of the

Commission in a letter (copy enclosed) which I sent to him as Chairman of the Advisory Committee of the Constituent Assembly, that the entire population of this area is in favour of remaining in the Indian Union.

4. Any award against the weight of local opinion and of the terms of reference, or without any referendum to ascertain the will of the people concerned must, therefore, be construed a collusive or partisan award and will have, therefore, to be repudiated by us. I make this statement with a full sense of responsibility as one who was party to the setting up of the Commission. But you cannot clearly expect us to submit to a proceeding which would be in violation of the basic conception underlying the commission's terms of reference.

5. I must also point out that public reaction would wholly and overwhelmingly support us in such repudiation. Already there is considerable doubt whether they would get an impartial award under the novel and strange procedure adopted by the Chairman of not even hearing the arguments. Many persons have come and complained to me that he has rendered himself liable, by this means, to being influenced by circles in your Secretariat whose antipathies to India and sympathies with the League are well known. The selection, as Secretary of the Commission, of one of the European officers of the Punjab, who are generally associated in public mind with pro-League sympathies, had not mended matters. I have generally adopted an indifferent attitude to these complaints, but if the award confirms the worst fears entertained by the public, it is impossible for me to predict the volume of bitterness and rancour which would be let loose and I am certain that this will create a situation which both you and I may have to regret.

Yours sincerely,

VALLABHBHAI PATEL

Enclosure to No. 452

Copy of letter No. CA/38/COM/47, dated the 25th July, 1947, from the Chairman, Advisory Committee on Minorities, Fundamental Rights, Tribal and Excluded Areas, Constituent Assembly of India, Council House, New Delhi, to The Chairman, The Bengal Boundary Commission, Calcutta.

Subject:—Chittagong Hill Tracts

I have the honour to address you on behalf of the Advisory Committee set up in pursuance of paragraph 20 of the Statement of the 16th May 1946[58] by the Constituent Assembly of India. A Sub-Committee was set up by the Advisory Committee to report on a scheme of administration for the Excluded Areas. This Sub-Committee visited the Chittagong Hill Tracts, which is an Excluded Area, in April 1947 and took the evidence of local official, non-officials and associations who were interested in the future administration of the area. The Sub-Committee have recently considered the future administration of the Chittagong Hill Tracts and although they are not in a position to send their complete report yet, they have pointed out that the people of the Chittagong Hill Tracts were unanimously against the Tracts forming a part of Bengal (as it then was) and that in view of the predominantly non-Muslim character of its population the area should in no circumstances be included in East Bengal. They have also pointed out that the Tracts adjoin and form part of the Lushai Hills of Assam and that communications exist between them.

I have the honour to bring the views of the Sub-Committee on behalf of the Advisory Committee to your notice and to say that I am fully in agreement with them. A copy of the evidence recorded by the Sub-committee is enclosed herewith.[59]

453

Rear-Admiral Viscount Mountbatten of Burma to Sir F. Burrows (Bengal) and Sir E. Jenkins (Punjab). Repeated to Mr. Christie,

New Delhi

Telegram, R/3/1/157: f 281

MOST IMMEDIATE

BY TELEPHONE

CAMP KARACHI, *13 August 1947, 9.00 pm*

No. 2907–S. No objection to your announcing that since the award of the Boundary Commission is unlikely to be READY FOR PUBLICATION BEFORE 16TH AUGUST the Government of East and West Bengal/Punjab will take charge up to the *national* repeat *national* boundary pending publication and implementation of the Award.

(For J.P.S.V. only: Please make similar announcement in Delhi after securing concurrence of Pandit Nehru. Pakistan Government have agreed).

454

Rear-Admiral Viscount Mountbatten of Burma to Pandit Nehru

R/3/1/157: f 277

NO. 1446/17

Dear Mr Nehru,

14 August 1947

I am advised that Sir Cyril Radcliffe is sending me the Award of the Boundary.

References

1. Mililarization and CHT by Chndra Ray.
2. Neither Here Nor there by Rosenmary Zoramchans.

3. When Chakmas people were happy by Adam Curle.
4. The Tribes of Brahmaputra Valley by L.A. Waddel.
5. The Shrine on the Hill by Raja Tridir Roy.
6. Peace Accord CHT (1997).
7. Survival Statement in the CHT for the European Human Rights Conference in June 17, 2005.
8. The Daily Pratom Alo by Saiful Alam and A.K. Rana on 14.8.2004.
9. The Boundary Commission's report on the creation of East and West Bengal.
10. No. 489, paras. 2–18.
11. See Vol. XI, Nos. 128, 175, Iten 2, 207, 317 and 369 para. II
12. See *Ibid.*, Nos. 158 and 311, para. 2.
13. See No. 52, Case No. P.C. 26/4/47 and No. 164.
14. No. 224.
15. No. 428.
16. No. 224.
17. No. 452.
18. See No. 446; also No. 453.
19. See No. 454 and its note 2, and No. 472.
20. Not printed. The awards of the Boundary Commissions are printed as Appendices to No. 488.
21. In tel. 579 of 16 August Sir A. Carter asked Sir T. Shone to convey to Lord Ismay a message which referred to the above telegram from Lord Mountbatten (and the telegraphic summary of the award which succeeded it) and continued: 'In view of great importance of this matter could you arrange to Shone know privately of any significant developments in this matter up to the time of publication of the awards, whenever that may be, so that Shone can keep Secretary of State for Commonwealth Relations secretly informed of the position.' L/P&J/10/117: ff 104–5.
22. In his letter of 19 August to Sir T. Shone, Commander Nicholls explained that he had been asked by Lord

Mountbatten to forward a copy of these minutes and referred to the message from the Commonwealth Relations Office (see No. 385, note II). Shone then forwarded the minutes to Sir A. Carter on 22 August and explained: 'I am grateful to His Excellency for sending me this paper, but I am sure you will agree that its contents and the fact that it has been communicated to me and by me to you, should be treated with the utmost secrecy.' L/P&J/10/117: ff 18 and 17.

23. See Appendices to No. 488.
24. A Photostat of this map may be found in an envelope at the back of L/P&J/10/117. Sir C. Radcliffe signed the map in the following manner: 'Attached to my Report d. 12 August 1947 for reference Cyril Radcliffe. Chairman, Punjab Boundary commission.'
25. The Reports by the Members of the Bengal Boundary Commission may be consulted at the I.O.L.R. on a microfilm of Partition Proceedings supplied by the National Documentation Centre, Pakistan. IOR Pos. 3658.
26. The Reports by the Members of the Bengal Boundary Commission relating to Sylhet District and the adjoining districts of Assam may be consulted at the I.O.L.R. on a microfilm of Partition Proceedings supplied by the national Documentation Centre, Pakistan. IOR Pos. 3658.
27. See above, note 20.
28. Not printed. For the awards of the Boundary Commission, see Appendices to No. 488.
29. See Nos. 367, 378, 405, 427 and 441.
30. cf. No. 326.
31. Reproduced here as appendix I.
32. Vol. XI, No. 128.
33. See *Ibid.*, No. 175, item 2.
34. *Ibid.*, No. 158.
35. *Ibid.*, No. 311, para. 2.
36. *Ibid.*, No. 369, para. 11 and its note 10.
37. No. 52, Case No. P.C. 30/4/47.

38. *Ibid.*, Case No. 26/4/47.
39. See No. 164
40. See No. 224.
41. No. 428.
42. See No. 389, Item I and its note 3.
43. See No. 436 and its note 2.
44. See No. 454 and its note 2.
45. Not printed; see No. 452.
46. See Nos. 446 and 453.
47. Emphasis in original.
48. No. 335.
49. See No. 271, note 10.
50. See No. 191.
51. Not printed.
52. The Minutes of the Viceroy's Fiftieth Staff Meeting record that: 'There was discussion on the Chittagong Hill Tracts, and His Excellency indicated the outline of a note which he wished to be preprared on this subject' ; and that the Viceroy 'directed Con. Sec. to draft a note on the Chittagong Hill Tracts, for discussion, if necessary, with the Indian Leaders the following day'. Mountbatten Papers.
53. Nos. 363 and 364.
54. Vol. X, No. 464, para. 8.
55. No. 450.
56. Vol. VII, No. 303.
57. Not printed.
58. Emphasis throughout in original.
59. Mr. Christie noted on 14 August : 'Pandit Nehru Agrees' R/3/1/157 : f282.

3

Buddhism Religious Faith of Daily Life

(A Variety of Sheer Richness of Buddhism)

Hirodotus father of Historians writes:

The Scythian (nomadic race), were one of the earliest tribes in the Central Asia, those who moved in the west are known to be fairer Aryans, and those who moved in the far oriented became known as the great yellow race – the semantic of the word Sakyan. The Aryans are seen as a separate cultural group, but not as a distinct race. The earliest human beings were rather ignorant, imaginary and justifying everything by fate, act of God (God's will), treating animals and abstract things as God. The Hindus are anthropomorphic race. The Hindu philosophy is mainly dealing with the identity of Brahman (the highest caste, social group of Hindus, who traditionally become priest in the Hindu religion), and Atma (Soul), which is the central thought of linking them with God (Supreme soul) an imagery idea. This religious conviction is based on 'theism,' the belief that there is only one God, who is completely separate from those things (the earth, people etc.), he has created rather than being part of them. As the principle of all religions, except Jainism and Buddhism, has the God as the creator, preserve and destroyer. Aphoristically, religion in two ways: God indicated dignity (elevation of mind) and the other rationalism (endowed with reason, logic) against prejudice. The theory that only the self exists or proven to exist is termed Solipsism (Philos), univocal in Buddhism. Dukkha (Suffering). Trishna (craving), Nirodh (fend off) and Restrain (8 fold path).

Sila : Right view, Right thinking, Right speech, Right activity, Right livelihood, Right diligence.

Samadhi : Right mindfulness
Right meditation

Wisdom : Perfect knowledge of truth.

Buddha's enlightenment steered as under :

1st period 6 – 10 p.m. = recalling past lives

2nd period 10 – 2 a.m. = Analysis of Karma

3rd period 2 – 6 a.m. = Dharma four noble truth, (Dependent Originations)

Now, what is Dukkha (vedana); it rises by eye contact, ear contect nose contect, tongue contact body contact, mind contact respectively. Similarly, Trishna has links of dependent origination.

Samskara, Vijnana, namarupa, sparsha, vedana, trishna, upadana, Bhava, jati, jaramarana, Aridya. A pictorial provider of all as below :

Skandha Circle (How we see the world : objective outer experience only subjective inner experience).

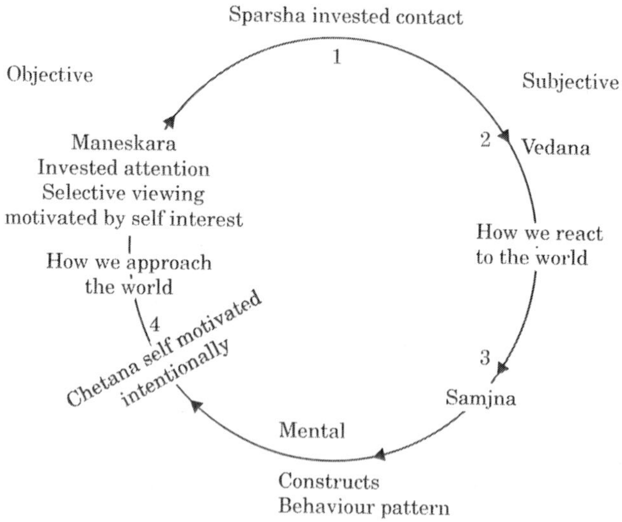

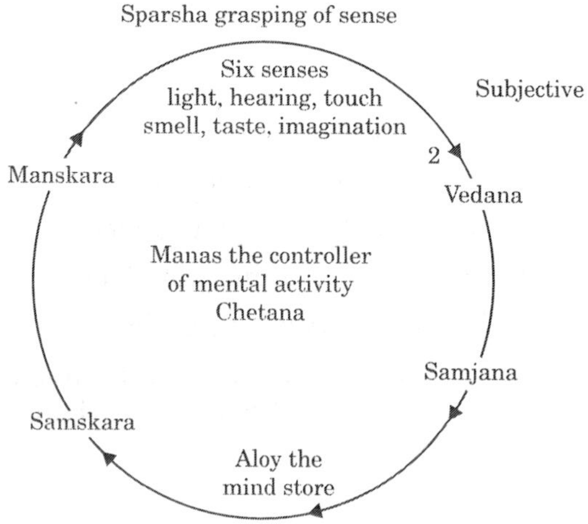

No : The five omnipresent factors related to Skandha process.

There are 12 links of dependent origination:

1. Avidya pratyaya, sanskara
2. Sanskara pratyaya, Vijnana
3. Vijnama pratyya, namarupa
4. Nama rupa pratyaya, Shadayatana
5. Sadayatana pratyaya, Sparsha
6. Sparsha pratyaya, Vedana
7. Vedana pratyaya, trishna
8. Trishna pratyaya, upadana
9. Upadana pratyaya, Bhava
10. Bhava pratyaya, jati
11. Jati pratyaya, jaramarana
12. Jaramarana pratyaya, Avidya

According to some study in Buddhism basically besides four noble truths there has been dependent origination impermanance etc. in the courses of Buddha Gautama. It was retrieved by Nagarjuna (C1CE) from the Nagas (mythical serpent like being who had been entrusted to preserve the most profound of Buddha's teaching until the prophelization of Nagarjuna. The next was the great master Asanga (300-390 CE) which advocated the mind only—Yogachara. There has been many denominations in the present worldlike the veins of a leaf. The belief that only one's experience and existence can be known with absolute certainty. This is basically the doctrine of Hinayana (Therovada) Buddhism. In some respect, the Mahayana form of Buddhism arose in contrast to it, and this is specially clear in its concept of the insight which gives rise to liberation in times and space in the cosmos. Meditation is basically solipsism leading to personal development (Nirvana); *Ni-Ban ie Ni or Nil+tie* (no attachment or desire). This is the fundamental concept of Paticca Samuppada of Therovada Buddhism. While in Mahayana Buddhism it is of Dependent Arising and Sunyata. Because the original nature (E) in the phenomena of Dependent Arising is emptiness, therefore (E) can arise in different phenomenal forms depending on different causes or conditions. The ideal Buddhist way of acquisition of knowledge of holism and deriving knowledge as co-reclusion from something already known with the act of deductive reasoning, inductive knowledge: A typical form is "All A is C; All B is A; therefore All B is C". Thus, is the dissimilarities with the conventional religion. They cling to "Act of God, God's will! Law of God! Buddha's word of freedom of thought : do not believe anything because it is believed by parents, teachers learned men of high rank or by the public or because it is thought to be given by divine inspiration or by on aracle, or because it is handed down by tradition, or because it is found in book or because some one proclaims it to be true, but believe anything if it agrees with reasons, investigation and experienced knowledge. But, Gautama Buddha propagated the Law of Nature and one can make way up by the acquisition of knowledge. The meaning of Buddha means awakened. In Buddhism the power of knowledge (ability, capacity, potentiality) called 'iddhi' six kind of spiritual powers : 1. Determination, 2. Transformation, 3. Spritual Creation, 4. Penetrating knowledge, 5. Power of penetrating concentration, 6. Noble power (Ariya iddhi) iddhi to be cultivated on discursiveness. To be going on Buddhist way of life, one should maintain purity and is supposed to live on surfeit (no excess or over fullness) open and clear. Buddhism is enshrined in the cultural paradigm of Chakmas. Bhikkhus on the whole maintain asceticism and their sanctity for sanctimonious utterances enshrined in their traditional culture. It gives joy to the family as they accept it with alacrity and religiosity. Chakmas Buddhist persuasion has remained in unperfidiousness albeit Gagon the dream they use to refer Gautama Buddha supreme truth. Mahavagga Pitaka how the Buddha attained supreme enlightenment, how be discovered the famous law of Dependent origination how he gave his first sermon on the noble truths (Dhammacakkappa vandama sulta) and later the discourse on non-self (Anatta Lokahana-Satta). Observing the rains retreat (varsa) and Kathina Chibar Dana Ceremony were annual making and offering of robes takes place. It is implicitly clear that the Chakma Buddhist religion is one of those traditional systems from the very ancient times (Buddhist life). Like the Kathina Chibara Dana, according to Vinaya Sutta how the Buddha attained supreme enlightenment the famous law of dependent origination, how he gave his first sermon on four noble truth (dhamma cakkappa vandona sutta) and later the discourse on non-self (Anatta Lokhana Sutta). Observing the rain retreans (Vassa) Kathina ceremony were annual making and offering of robes take place in Therovada Buddhism. There life is undergoing a great evolution through the ages – as Spencer, a great thinkers says: "Life is an evolution, it is continuous adjustment of interrelations to external relations." The present perennial value of Buddhism is in world Buddhism which advocated Buddhist activities more unitedly through the ideology get more clarified in a credible way through wisdom and knowledge. The mind (cause), the matter (effect) and the unity of both, that reflects in Buddhism. Gautama Buddha spoke in this verse :

> *"Wealth and destiny come from one's destiny.*
> *From causes planted in lives in the past.*
> *People who hold to this simple principle*
> *will reap good fortune in lives in the future.*
> *Kind men and women, listen to the causes*
> *Hear and remember this Sutra's reminder*
> *of the causes and effects of karmic deeds*
> *In the past, in the future, and in the present.*
> *Cause and effects is no small case,*
> *True are my (Buddha's) words; don't take them lightly,*
> *Why are some people officials at present?"*

Buddhist religion is the manifestation of the following :

1. They are the producer of highest number of Bhikkhus (Monks);
2. They are not confined to Therovada Buddhism alone, and many have ardent faith in Mahayanaism and pursuing practices there.

There are images of Buddha in every household. The most customary worshipping place for them is on a *machan* (raised from the ground) in front of their dwelling house. It is a solitary place. They are aiming to achieve individual attainment *Araht i.e.* no suffering in this life itself: Therovada Buddhism, while Mahayanist the aim of life is for benefiting all living creatures. At one time the Chakmas were adhering to Tara originated in India it became very popular in 7th Century *Tara* which means goddess saviour. In China Tibet it is the manifestation of the wisdom, compassion, love and in particular the skillful activity of all enlightened beings. *Tara* means Shakti (perfect knowledge, heart Sutta in Mahayana, *Prajna Paramita*). According to Tibetian doctrine Kalachakra Tantra King Suchandra of the north eastern India kingdom Shamhala requested teaching from the Buddha that would allow him to practice the Dhamma without renouncing his wordly enjoyment and responsibilities. In response to his request the Buddha taught the first Kalachakra root Tantra in Dhanyakataka present day Amaravai in Andhra Pradesh South India. The Mahayana Buddhism which branched off at the time of Asoka (C 250 BC) had long remained popular in Mayanmar before the rise of Pagan (mid 9th century). The renowned Buddhist monk scholar, Dipankara Srijana Atisa (920–1054 AD) who is supposed to have spent twelve years in "Suvarnabhumi" (South of Myanmar) before going to Tibet to reform the Tantric tradition there. The 'Ari'-ism (corrupted form of Buddhsim, medley of Tantric and Therovada) ended in Myanmar and became fully influenced by Therovada in the middle of 18th century and swamed over Chittagong Hill Tracts. Hence, the ideal of an altruistic enlightened man who caringly resolves. May the fruits austerities and meditations alleviate sufferings of all sentient creatures, even moment of giving birth. The universe is holistic and secular, *Sabbe Satta Sukhito hontu*.

Owing to the differences on the death of Sakyamuni among the monks in the Ist council itself, they were divided. In the 2nd Council at Vaisali (about 300 B.C.) they split into two camps. Therovadin and Mahasanghikas (Mahayana). They together are called Sarvas tirading (dialectical materialism mind and matter are independent mind is evolution process and matter is a form of energy. There are many denominations of Buddhism like the vein of a leaf In the moden world many people practice varying degrees of Buddhism and liturgy exists in wider variety of subjective manner at the back, but the prime objective of personal improvement of enlightenment as shown by Gautam

Buddha. Coming next Buddha gave five precepts for one week to his followers which is the origin of Therovadins, while in the second phase it is represented by the Avatamsaka Sutra first which Buddha delivered for 21 days to convert all those with Bodhis all (future Buddha) potential. So that the eyes of Mahayana Bodhisattvas as would open to the view and awareness of Buddhas. Buddha continued the Avatamsaka for twenty one days to convert all those with Bodhisatta potential. There monks can not eat together with lay persons, but not in Mahayana.

Therovadin Vinaya there are 227 rules for the Bhikkhus and 311 for the Vhikhhunis. For Bhikkhus in China, the few Bhikkhus and Bhikkhunis in japan and those in Korea and Vietnam follow Dharmaguptaka Vinaya, which has 250 rules for the Bhikkhus and 348 for the Bhikkhunis. Buddhist in Tibet and Mongolia follow Mulasarvastivada Vinaya which has 253 rules for Bhikkhus and 364 rules for Bhikkhunis. There are many supplimentary rules. They believe in 'Tantric' enlightenment through one's own body (Tantra-means a sexuality between male and female monks like brother and siter in the priory sacred union of opposite energies—Mandala, achieved between men and God in Moksha or Nirvana. In true sense, after achieving Moksha one would still remain in the terristerial world or might return, but in Nirvan there is no return.

Satipattana Buddhism Theology of Chakmas

The Chakmas adhere to Satipattana Buddhist theology (Deep Philosophy) and the ardent believer of the 10 (ten) fetters (tie) in the doctrine of Buddhism which are as follows: Satipattana wisdom has six stages. 1. Anapana breathing, 2. standing (walking meditation), 3. remain watchful and aware, 4. knowledge of holy and unholy sanctity, 5. realisation of five elements (four natural Air, Heat, Water and Earth+Body), 6. Grandeur way of analysing of dead body.

The 10 fetters:

1. The delusions (ignorance) of Selfhood.
2. Doubt (Don't belief and accept till you agree with analysis and evidence).
3. Belief in the efficiency (effectiveness) of ritual observation for deliverance.
4. Sensual craving/Sentience feeling.
5. Ill will (mental power, intention's).
6. Craving for from existence.
7. Craving formless existence.
8. Conceit (pride)
9. Restlessness
10. Ignorance.

The five elements of human body, eye, ear, nose, tongue and touch which operate with mind (intellectual power/ science) graded at different levels, which is subject of development/purification. The self-purification on these, cannot be reborn lower than human in the wheel of life. Their aim is to destroy these fetters. Their religious faith is beholden to their community and Nirvana means supreme tranquility and does not mean destruction of existence. The Chakma social entities (Stratum) is purely on religious ritual and practices which has undergone variant, changes in the ages in different Buddhist practices.

Robe Offering Ceremony

One of their oldest religious practices is known to be Kathina Chibra Dan (Robe offering Ceremony, according to Vinaya Sutta in Therovada Buddhism. It is the solemn invocation of divine blessings of Buddha and it invokes his divine memory traditionally Buddha's garments consist of four parts :

1. Antarvasa (A transparent piece of cloth below the wrist).
2. Uttarasanga (A yellow brown robe).

3. Sanghati (Scapular covering shoulders)
4. Kathinabhandi (belt).

It is celebrated one month after the rain, which lasts for three months to offer robe to those monks, who had observed Varsha vash (at a fixed place) not in wandering and preaching, but in meditation and giving instruction to his disciples. The Buddhist monks accordingly follow his examples and live in a monastery giving religious instruction to the people. Incantation is the monk's pre-occupation which is believed to have magical effect. It is called kathina Chibara Dan as it is hard to complete entire processing of spinning of the raw cotton, making and dying of the fibres, weaving of cloth on handlooms and completing the Chibar (Robe) in 24 hours which is still alive in Chakma religion festivals. That is why there is a difference between ordinary Chibar offering and the Kathina Chibar offering. It is interesting to know that it becomes the main concern of women to partake in its preparation. In the Buddha's time, out of loyalty and faithfulness the Sakyan issued a decree that each family should provide one son to the centre of Buddhas Sangha. It is being followed upon in Sakyan which is most shining saving characteristics of Chakmas. It continues among all his followers since then – as a proof of their intangible faith in Buddhism.

Shiv Saran Chakma

It is the last dot of Buddhism that survived in the erstwhile eastern Bengal over thousand years ago, whose written record in Buddhist texture was dominantly found in the Chakma society composed by Shivsaran Chakma a poet composer whose biodata is as under: Father's name-Dhongi Birth Place – Village – Batoli on the Bank of River Karnaphuli near Kaptai. His classic contributions writings are called Gogen Lama, Genghuli Yog Alam and Fakira Alam that relates to Tantric Buddhism. Lakshi in Mahayana is transformation in human life (Seat of consciousness, where as in Hinduism, Laxmi is the goddess of prosperity). There is some mystic element in it. In the midst of life wherever unhappiness arises it was the customery to the Chakmas to make Lakshi pala which is performed by pious spirituality who will invite holi spirit by Gengkhuli—descending autometically from mouth all through the night. He made Buddhism more profounder with more devotional recitative songs in the culture life of Chakma. This is most precious works of a cleric that crystallises with a vision. Their preconceived notion ideas that they are the torchbearers of Buddhism. Lakshi in Mahayana is transformation in human life (seat of consciousness, where as in Hinduism, Laxmi is the goddess of prosperity). There is some mystic element in it. In the midst of life whenever unhappneess and sex it was the customery to the chakmas to make Lakshi pala which is performed by pious spirituality who will invite holi spirit by Gengkhuli—descending automatically from mouth all through the night. In the present era, most primate Bana Vante, the forest monk in the Chittagong Hill Tracts, Bangladesh (dwell on prive retreat) when people believe to have attained pretarnatural powers. There is a general acceptance of his pieties providence. It is so obviously seen on him. The psychological sping off the phenomenon is tremendous – the entire Chakma Community in many countries feels elevated. As a monk he believes (trust) in divine providence that he would receive any offering, if it is offered to him even if it is from far distance, because of his psychic "Iddhi" power. An edification after meeting him, because of his attainment of Arahathood highest stage of holiness in Therovada before Nirvana, whose physical sensation (Consciousness ceses and mind remains concentrated on subject moditating). He has been in the puritan streak line as Sramana receiving premptory instructions of his senior as a naïve monk since the full-moon day (Bengal month Phalgun, March 1949) in the monastry Nandan Kanan, Chittagong under Mahastavir Dipankar. After being ordained to full Bhikkuhood he became known by the name Sadhana Nanda Mahastavir since 1970 in Dighinala monastry in CHT. From 1976 he has been living in the Raj bana Vihar at Rangamati in Bangladesh and great edification has been taking place in his prediency, as he is the product of great religious ecstacy in this region. He has become the religious icon for the community, as they have had spiritual and deeper communion on religious belief by his teaching.

Chakma Buddhist Organizations

Besides this there are many notable Chakma Buddhist organizations to speed up their progress to being with their life over again when lifes tenor is going on other ways, namely :

1. Monoghar in CHT, Contact information P.O. & Dt. Rangamati, Bangladesh.
2. Sishu Karuna Sangha Motri Nagar in Kolkata, Contact information P.O. Rajarhat Hatiara West Bengal.
3. Chakma Buddhist foundation in Bodh Gaya, Contact information Buddhagaya Bihar, India.
4. Sneha in Arunachal Pradesh, Contact information P.O. Diyun Dt. Changlang.
5. The Ashok Buddha Vihar, New Delhi, Contact information Rajghat, New Delhi.
6. Peace Campaign Group in New Delhi, Contact information RZ-1-71/211 West Sagarpur.
7. Mahabodhi Society Bangalore contact information 14 Kalidasa Road, Gandhi Nagar.
8. Parbatya Buddha Mission contact information PO & Dist. Khagarachari, CHT, Bangladesh.
9. Rangamati Parbatya Buddha Moitree Sangha P.O. Rangamoti (behind Food Godown), CHT, Bangladesh.

Many other similar organizations are present in different

states in India and abroad. The success of these organizations was greater than one could have hoped. Many luminaries of them are now already wide spread around the globe. It is amazing how they progressed with their own endeavour. It is revealing something of sheer richness of Buddhism.

It is heralding of a new era of Buddhism. According to Buddhist cosmology, there are three worlds viz the Kamaloka (the world of Sensuous experience); The Rupalaka (the world of subtle form), and the Arupaloka the world without subtle form. These realms correspond to the level of consciousness that can be attained in meditation.

Epigram:

"Science without religion is lame,
Religion without science is Blind."

–Albert Einstein

References

1. Hiouen—Tsang's report.
2. Avtamsaka Sutta, p. 148.
3. The smaller Sukhavati—Vyuha Sutta, p. 161.
4. The ways of enlightenment, p. 172.
5. History of Buddhist Chronology, p. 180.
6. Buddha canonical literature.

IMPORTANT RACIAL AND LINGUISTIC REFERENCES

Imperial Gazetteer of India—WW Hunter (1885)

Chapter: Burma British (page – 183, 449)

"It is probable that the lower part of the valley of the Ganges was formerly occupied by people speaking languages of the class sometimes called Mramma before the advents of the Aryans, but as regards the Burmese, it seems more natural to believe, as Sir Arthur Phayre writes, that they passed from the tableland of Central Asia round the eastern Himalayas. A kingdom was formed at Tagaung; and thence, it is said, a portion of the people went westwards into Arakan, while the remainder moving southwards, founded fresh kingdoms in Prome and Tounggu, where the Burmese language is still supposed to be spoken in greater purity than elsewhere in Burma.

The hill tribes of Arakan who live near the Kuladan river and its tributaries, namely the Sak, Chaw, Kwaymi, Kuo, Mro and Sandhu belong by Burmese, and their language belongs to what is sometimes called Tibets Burman family.

Linguistic References

Kadu of south Central Yunnan (now known in the Chinese literature as Kaduo) is now classified as one of the severities of Hani. What is the history of Kadu people, from where they had derived? Do they have any progenitory history? Can it be possible to identify them distinctly? Which are the places of their concentration in Yunnan? What is their racial history?

Characteristics of Mon (Burma) and Pollard Seripts

Some Anthropologists patch them with the Chakmas as lost tribe. Their language resembles to that of the Saks or Thets.

History of Chakma Buddhist

THE UNSWERVING ETHNIC TRIBAL BUDDHISTS. (This was written for Living Buddhism the Amida Trust Journal of April, 2000) By Sakya Talukdar

Introduction

There are few loyalists of Buddhism in the main land of India. Uptill 1947, the Chittagong Hill Tracts was a part of greater Bengal in India. "On 15 August 1947, the Indian tricolour went up a flag post in Rangamati, the main town in the Chittagong Hill Tracts. The Chakma leaders had believed during the tortuous negotiations leading up to partition that, given the religious composition of the largely Buddhist CHT, their district would be parcelled out to India."

The CHT with 2,75,000 people out of which 98 per cent ethnic Buddhists was awarded to (east) Pakistan arbitrarily against the partition axiom of India by the Radcliff Commission. The Buddhist religion was given away – to satisfy the Hindus and Muslims. The long and the short of it, they all plotted treason and from thenceforth the days of travail had begun for Tribal Buddhists.

Historical Background

The ethnic tribal Buddhists are the earliest settlers of CHT which geographically is at the tail end of Arakan Yoma (in Myanmar) an extensive stretch of mountainous country arising from the Himalayan Mountain ranges at the foot hills of which Kapilavastu (Sakya Kingdom) had once come up into great prominence at the time of Buddha. According to conceivable history the Sakyas came to racial encountering and massacre which resulted uprooting of Sakyas from Kapilavastu. When the Chinese pilgrim Fa Hien visited Kapilavastu in 435 AD the country around looked deserted and there were heaps of ruins. This was the break on the wheel of Sakya prominence.

Sakyas were diverged into many groups, sub-groups, branches etc. with the passing of the ages, years. Many of them must have lost their tracks or co-mingled with others in the long run. But yet many preserved Buddhism and Buddhist culture. CHT was considered as the Buddhist preserve by the distinctive group of Tribal people, who refer their ancestry from Sakya clan and their chiefs consider themselves from the Sakya rulers. The majority of the tribal people are known by the term Chakmas (in English) and the word is spolt as Tsakma (in Burmese). There are many offshoots of this terminology of ethnic people who are in river and mountain valleys of Irrawadi (in Mayanmar) Brahmaputra (India).

To be going on with Buddhism was most difficult in India as it opposed the Brahman ceremonial and caste pretensions (which is still alive) and preached non-sectarianism and racialism. After Buddha's death Buddhism and its psyche got broken down. People began to disavow Buddhism. But there were some pertinacious Buddhists in the smaller places and tribal republics in India. The final crusade came by the Mohammedan invasion which began in the year 1001 AD that destroyed and massacred all Buddhist precinct, learning centres, monks and finally Buddhist tenets. Buddhist people had undergone a change and not a single Buddhist was left over in the mainland of India. In this background, CHT remained the Buddhist preserve, where the earnest pertinacious Buddhist found it to be their safe sanctuary. "Buddhism is a living religion in Chittagong proper, in the Hill Tracts, and in Tripura. It was introducted in these district about the ninth century AD direct from Magadha." The Mahayana Buddhist Tradition which about that time prevailed in Magadha became completely extinct and forgotten in the mainland India, but it was blooming in CHT and got resonance for the ethnic tribal Buddhists upto to-day. There are Buddhist tenets as 'Agartara' (personification of Nirvana) among them which is similar as 'Arya Tara' who identified with Sakti or the female principle. In Tibet she is called Yum-Chenmo, the great mother, in Nepal she is personified as Prajna Paramita or transcendental Wisdom.

Cut under British Rule

There is not much of allusion of CHT before 1763 (the British took over the control of Chittagong from Mughals in 1760). It was for the first time the Chakma Chief's area (the head of Buddhist ethnic tribe) was drawn out as "All the hills from Pheni river to the Sangoo and from Nizampur road in Chittagong to the hills of the Kuki Raja", who were in the distant hills (unsurveyed areas) at the animism stage. They began murderous attacks on the British subjects in Assam, Tripura and CHT. It became most vital to the British Government to protect its subjects from the great Kuki invasions in 1847, 1848, 1859 and 1860. The British Government had a real gloom when a six years British girl of a tea planter was taken captive (from Alexanderpore in Cachar, Assam) by the savage tribes. The British Government had to take up with administration, to penetrate till the last outpost in British rule. An act on CHT was framed in 1860 and the Chakma chief was asked to shift his headquarters to Rangamati inside CHT. In 1866, Capt. T.H. Lewin was posted as the superintendent of the District and in 1867 the official designation was changed from 'Superintendent of the Hill Tracts' to the 'Deputy Commissioner of the tracts'. The ethnic tribal Buddhists were in great peace and fulfilling happiness. They could get on with their simple life and local forest conservation could meet all their demands. They had a most natural life, enough of everything. They practiced a great deal Buddhism in their social life, they are quoted "I had often heard of the vicious excess and drunken debauchery of the savage races for ought I know this may be the case of the coast of Africa or New Guineas; but here in the Hill Tracts, through out the three days' Carnival, I have not seen any one drunken man nor witnessed any discourtesy to a woman. They seemed an honest kindly people, happy in their homes and in their simple Buddhist faith and I doubt much if they had anything to gain from the introduction of European ideas. The Lushais and Sindhus were made of different stuff and need very different dealing with"[3].

The British administration understood that the CHT Act of 1860, was needed to be amended as it had not given adequate safeguard to the ethnic tribal from powerful races. Finally in 1900 a new regulation on CHT was introduced under which migration in the CHT was prohibited and the tribals were entrusted with limited Self Government through their Chiefs.

CHT Under Pakistan

"As a part of Pakistan, the CHT lost its special status and autonomy under an amendment to the Pakistan constitution in 1963. Pressure for land to cultivate had in the past led to the migration of large number of non-tribal people from other parts of Bangladesh into the CHT. This process was actively encouraged by Governments since the 1960's"[4]. Lest CHT should go to India, the Pakistan Government was bent to change to demographic position by immigrating Bengali Muslims and also made an outrageous scheme by setting up of a hydroelectric project on the river Karnaphuli to uproot and displace the ethnic tribals.

"The origin of the problem in the CHT is believed to be the completion of a dam at Kaptai near Rangamati between 1957 and 1963 when the area was administered by Pakistan. At least 54,000 acres of settled cultivable land, mostly farmed by the Chakma Tribes were lost in 1957 when the Government began the Construction of the Karnaphuli hydroelectric project. Over 400 square miles of land were submerged with far-reaching effects on the economic life style of the tribal people there. Some 100,000 people lost their homes and prime agricultural lands. Compensation for lost land was inadequate and over 40,000 Chakma tribal crossed the border into India where the majority have sought Indian citizenship' [5]. They are still stateless. At least 20,000 more left for the Arakan hills in Myanmar where they are now settled.

CHT Under Bangladesh

The political expediency of Pakistan gave birth of Bangladesh in 1971. The pressure of Bengali Muslim immigration had undoubtedly fueled xenophobia among the ethnic tribals. They decided to remain in peace and neutral during the bad days of the Bangladesh liberation movement. Therefore, the sore point of the Bengali Muslims became more hardened against the Tribal Buddhist after the liberation of Bangladesh as Bengalis looked upon the tribals as pro-Pakistanis. A large blood let was perpetrated in CHT by the Muslim Bengalis in the name of liberation. The ethnic Buddhist had no place to keep them on their guards as the Bangladesh Government (at that time) was against them. The Buddhist leaders then demanded for the constitutional safe-guards, but it was rejected outright (it is said that the President of Bangladesh angrily threatened to drown the ethnic people in a flood of people from plains). Since then the ethnic Buddhist leader felt parting with their ways of peaceful dialogue with the Bangladesh Government an formed and underground armed wing 'Shanti Bahini' (peace force) in January 1973. The dispute with Government began smoldering, but the violent army operation in the CHT began in March 1980 onwards. More than 8500 rank and files of 'Shanti Bahini' were killed.

Prior to the creation of Bangladesh in 1971, the population in CHT were almost entirely of indigenous tribes (13 different groups). The phenomenal population increase in CHT as recorded in the census (1981) is Tribal population (4,39,458) while Bengali total population (2,68,998), but in the next census (1991) the Tribal total population remained (4,98,595) while Bengali population increased to (4,68,825); the ratio of Tribal and non-tribal being 51:49. The home land of ethnic Buddhist Tribals becamc the living space of the Bengali Muslim. In fact they have already been out-numbered by new settlers (Muslim immigrants) in many areas. The Government was bringing economic growth and large benefits to them while tribals were systematically burdened and finally uprooted. During the years 1981-1994 the blood lust situation in CHT became a great concern to many humane Government of the world. Because of their insistence finally on 2 December 1997, an agreement generally known as 'Peace Accord' was signed between National Committee on CHT and the Parbatta Chattagram Jana Sanghati Samiti (the political wing of Shanti Bahini) in the presence of the Prime Minister of Bangladesh. The insurgency violence had continued for almost 20 years. This resulted fleeing of many ethnic tribals (60,000) to Tripura. After the peace treaty the refugees had returned to CHT, but many of them had not yet been able to get back their ancestral lands. Also the implementation of peace accord is yet to get a start. The long and short of it, there has not been any change as yet. The mind sets of tribals Buddhist and Bengali Muslims are different.

The heading and the writing are two different. The heading relates to p. 143 in Mizoram.

The writing to be transparred after the first para of page 142 (before A petal of Buddhism).

Rai Sarat Chandra. Its Bahadur, C.I.I., a brother of Babu Nabin Chandr Das has given the following account of the history of Buddhism in Chittagong:—"Buddhism is a living religion in Chittagong proper, in the Hill Tracts, and in Tippera. It was introduced in these districts about the ninth century A.D. direct from Magadha, when the eastern provinces of Bengal extending from Rangpur down to Ramu (Romya Bhumu in Chittagong, were under the sway of a Rajput prince named Gopipala. The Mahayana Buddhism, which about that time prevailed in Magadha and Tibet, was preached in Chittagong by Bengali Buddhists. In the 10th century A.D. Chittagong, in a manner, became the centre of the Buddhism of Bengal". The chief feature of Mahayana Buddhism is that the has taken in the entire Hindu pantheon and added innumerable fancied deities to it. In this enlarged pantheon the ruling deity is Arya Tara (a personification of Nirrdna), who is dentified with Sakti or the female principle. In Tibet she is called *Yum-chenna*, the great mother; in Nepal the Eastern Bengal District Gazetteers (1908) by L.S.S. O'Malley, Chittagong, p. 66. The word Tara is commonly use in Barma and Assam indicating consort of Buddha.

A Petal of Buddhism in Eastern Mountain Region in India

In Assam : The geographical limit of CHT was bounded with Kuki land (now Mizoram state, previously a part of Assam); Pheni river which borders with Tripura State of India and Sangoo river which borders with Arakan of Myanmar. Till the British period people from all the neighbouring areas gravitated into CHT as it was ideally peaceful for living. The distance rebellious animist tribes were overwhelmed by the British troops with the faithful assistance of the Chakmas; whose area was originally a far as Tuichong river, now forming a part in India, so they are ipso facto, Indian origin. More than 32 per cent of the total Chakmas of the world are living in India. It is mentioned that 'Tsakma' Chittagong Hill Tracts are the ethnic people of Brahmaputra valley. They do not have as much right to the assets and opportunities strown around them as they have not achieved any success in life. Their social ladder is still on the ground.

In Arunachal Pradesh : Ground down by years (from 1963) of stateless condition, Chakma Buddhist Tribals (80,000 population) are in grim face and reproving look in Arunachal Pradesh. They are starved of their basic human necessities like education, health care and right to public assets whenever they highlight the demand of their citizenship right, the powerful political groups start creating troubles to them. Since their uprooting from their ancestral land they are in sorry/dreadful plight.

In Mizoram : A portion of Mizoram state is the original home land of the ethnic Buddhist tribal Chakmas. Ex-chief

Labamoni Chakma of Lokisurj received compensation of the government Assam. They find it hard to understand in the present day why they have been out-played by the animist (of a century back). In the last 100 years there was not much to do here except impregnation of Christianity to the animist. The number of Christian people (from zero at the beginning of 20th century) phenomenally increased to 92 per cent today and the remaining 8 per cent are pertinacious ethnic Chakma Buddhists.

In Tripura: The settlement of Tripuris in CHT and Chakmas in Tripura vice-versa displayed a sign of fraternal relationship between the two rulers from very ancient time. The two were the adjacent states separated by the river boundary Pheni. Therefore, Chakmas are the origins of Tripura. Later political compulsions to escape the brunt of torture resulted migration from CHT to Tripura. The refugees who recently came had been sent back to CHT. The ethnic Tribal Buddhists in Tripura are in a position to take a decisive role in making the people aware of Buddhism.

So in the present day the ethnic tribal Buddhists are wide spread swimming in different non Buddhist society. The effect could be seen in their grinding poverty. Their centre piece of life is Buddhism. It always dwells in their thought. This has to be kept alive.

Assam is the heart of North East region of India comprising of seven states *i.e.* Assam, Arunachal Pradesh, Nagaland, Manipur, Mizoram and Tripura – Seven Sisters. This region is forged with multi races who were originally Buddhists or Animist. Majority of them are now either Hindu or Christian. The Buddhists are in marginal numbers in the cities. The capital city Guwahati of Assam is a cosmopolitan city and posed to be on the super international highway – India's main surface link route to the South- east Asian countries within a decade. The ethnic Buddhist have envisaged to build up a Buddhist precinct with a monastery, an accommodation for pilgrims and a community centre on the city Guwahati in Assam, India.

Buddhism Discouraged

During the ninth century, the Pal dynasty rose to power in the country formerly known as Anga and gradually extended their sway over the whole of Bihar and north Bengal. Traces of their rule are very common in the south of Dinajpur, where the memory of Mahipal, in particular, is preserved both in the traditions of the people and in numerous names of places. Like the kings of Pundra, they were Buddhists, but they were tolerant towards Hinduism. They were driven from Bengal proper, about the middle of eleventh century, by a king named Vijaya Sen of the Sen family, but they continued to rule for some time longer in Bihar. The Sen rose to power in east and deltaic Bengal towards the end of the tenth century, and eventually included within their dominions the whole of Bengal proper from the Mahananda and the Bhagirathi and the west to the Karatoya and the old Brahmaputra on the east. The Sens were Hindus, and during their rule Buddhism was actively discouraged.

(Imperial Gazetteer of India Vol. VII, p. 210)

Vikramsila Monastery (University) was on the Ganges. It was revealed post excavation work carried out at Antichak just off to north Kahalgaon (Bhagalpur) now in Bihar. It was an ancient university founded by Dharmapala, the Pala king during the 8th century AD. It had been set up to complement the dipping standard of Nalanda University. Supposedly the place was marked in the 13th century through its remnnts which offer a vibrant poop into the by gone world of history. It had international fame. Some Buddhist Luminaries of there monasteries including Dipankara Srijana Atisa (980-1053 AD) head of Vikramsila establishment went to Tibet and preached Dharma which has been translated into a thousand ways – religious merit, righteousness, truth, nature etc.

Dhamma

Dhamma also refers to the natural and moral behaviour appropriate to an individual or group of individuals to a society as a whole. And Dharma to individual differs according to their own nature physical cum morality – own conscience. For a conscious being, to exist is to change to change is to with the nature, to nature is to go on creating self endlessly – Dhamma (Duty in conscieneeness).

It is well known that these are two editions of the council books of Sakya Muni's religion – one in Sanskrit, discoursed by Hodgson in Nepalese monasteries; and the other in Pali or Magadhi, in the possession of the Sinhalese priests. These two collections, although written in somewhat different language since Pali is the popular and Sanskrit the cultivated and even sacred dialect. Thoroughly agrees as to the substance.

Hiouen-Thsang

He knew of three councils—one that was held immediately after the death of Sakya-muni; a second one under Asoka and a third under Kaniskha, king of Kashmir, on the first one he dwells at great length. According to tradition, which he repeats, it was not far from Rajagriha, two miles from the bamboo grove at Kalanta, in a large house situated in the midst of another wood, that the Arahats of the first Council assembled, Kasyapa, who had chosen them—they numbered nine hundred and ninety-nine—directed all the labours from which sprung the *Tripitaka,* and he presided over the learned assembly. Hiouen-Thasang shows him as exercising a kind of supervision, admitting some, excluding others as unworthy, and only receiving Ananda himself on the condition of his performing a long penance. They had been in retreat for fifteen days, when

Kasyapa made Ananda take the chair, inviting him to read the *Sutra-Pitaka*, or commentary on the Sutras. The assembly, who respected the profound knowledge of Ananda, which had been recognized by the Tathagata himself, received the Sutras from his lips, and wrote them down under his dictation. Then Kasyapa ordered Upali to read the *Vinaya-Pitaka*, or Commentary on the Discipline; after which he himself read the *Abhidharma-Pitaka*, or Commentary on Metaphysics. At the end of three months the work of the Council was finished. The writings of the three Commentaries were collected; Kasyapa had them transcribed on palm-leaves, and sent them out all over India. As he had presided over the monks, his school was called the School of the President (*Sthavira-Nikaya*).

Those, however, who had been excluded from the Council by Kasyapa's severity, assembled at a places near there. They numbered several thousands, laymen as well as monks, and, basing themselves on the principle of equality that had always been inculcated by the Tathagata among his disciples, they deemed themselves in a fit state to make their own Collection of Sacred Writings. This they composed of Five Commentaries, first the three first, then a collection of miscellanies, and a collection of Magic Formulas. This second school was called the School of the Great Council (*Maha-Samgha-Nikaya*), and its partisans became celebrated under the name of Mahasamghikas.

In Hiouen-Tsang's memories it was written there were eighty-eight thousand stupas from east to west from the kingdom Tamralipta to the border of Sindh.

1st Buddhist Council immediately death of Sakyamuni, 2nd council under king Asoka, 3rd Council under Kanishka king of Kashmir.

The Buddha and his religion —J. Barthelmy Saint Hirairee London 1914.

Buddha Canonical Literature

Historically, Mahayana school developed from its Indian Buddhist root, but the basic source of writing material were from Kashmir and Gandhara, Central Asia, Tibet and China. Much of the Buddhist scholarly works has only appeared in Mahayana producing sub-schools, as seen in the canonical literature of Mahayana. Mahakasyapa presided over first Buddhist council at Rajgraha soon after there month of Sakyamuni's Parinirvana. The very first recitation of Mahakashyapa of the Buddha's teaching were not accepted by the Arahat Purana. He preferred to hold to what he had himself from the lips of Sakyamuni. The second council was held at Vaishali where there was dispute among Arahats of accepting donations of money from laity. In the third council there were two distinct bodies of opinion on the subjects of Arahat's behavior. The fourth council was held at Gandhara (Kabul) during the reign of king Kushan where developed sub-sect of Buddhism Zen (Dhyan) of Mahayan School. In fact, leading to the dispute since very early time a large body of Arahat (Sthavirs) made a disaffected withdrawal to Kashmir and beyond and thereafter called themselves Sarvastivadin (selfless) in the school of Mahayana. Kashmir was a strong centre of Buddhist learning in the ancient time. From here it passed to central Asia and China. The earliest account of Buddhist activity could be traced in the 1st century AD proceeding to china. This is the background of Buddhist canonical literature. It is note- worthy the contribution of leading Indian scholarly monks like Dipankara Srijana Atisa (AD 980-1053), who was the head of Vikramshila monastery to Tibet. The two main division of Tibetan are Kanjur and Tanjur. The first one included works esteemed as canonical including Tantras which originated in Bihar. India and Jogini Tantra in Assam in 5th AD. The second is composed of exposition of scriptures and also of many treaties on subjects as medicine, astronomy and grammer (Tantric Buddhist Literature Lamaism Vijrayana). The Mahayanist scholars were most notable for their creativity, such as those of Asvaghosa, Nagarjuna, Atisa, Padmasambabha, Asanga, Vasubandhu, Santideva and many others.

AVATAMSAKA SUTRA

(The Flower Garland Sutra)

{Practices and Vows of the Bodhisattva Samantabhadra}

Take a look at the commentary, Precious Garland

[The first part of this document is an excerpt from one of the great Buddhist sutras (Book One Begins below) Buddha Shakyamuni preached it in heaven shortly after his attainment of Buddhahood. The sutra reveals different causes and ways of cultivation of many great Bodhisattvas, such as Ten Grades of Faith, Ten Stages of Wisdom, Ten Activities, Ten Transference of Merits, Ten Stages of Bodhisattvas, Absolute Universal Enlightenment, Wonderful Enlightenment, etc. It also reveals how to enter Avatamsaka World (Buddha's world) from the Saha World. "The Flower Adornment Sutra" – whose full title is the "Great Means Expansive Buddha Flower Adornment Sutra"—is the longest Sutra in Mahayana Buddhism. Referred to by Buddhist scholars as "the King of Kings of Buddhist scripture" and the "epitome of Buddhist Thought, Buddhist sentiment, and Buddhist experience," the Flower Adornmen. Sutra is 81 rolls (bamboo scrolls) long and contains more than 700,000 Chinese characters.] At one time Samantabhadra addressed the assembled, having praised the exalted merits and virtues of Buddha Vairocana, the Bodhisattva Bodhisattvas, along with Sudhana, as follows :

"Good men, even if all the Buddha's of all the ten directions were to speak continuously, for as many eons as there are fine motes of dust in a incalculable number of Buddha lands (worlds), the merits and virtues of the Buddha could never be fully described.

"Those wishing to achieve these merits and virtues should cultivate ten vast and great practices and vows. What are these ten?

First, Pay homage and respect to all Buddha's.

Second, Praise all the Buddha's.

Third, make abundant offerings.

Fourth, Repent misdeeds and evil karma's (actions).

Fifth, Rejoice in others' merits and virtues.

Sixth, Request the Buddha's to teach.

Seventh, Request the Buddha's to remain in the world.

Eighth, Follow the teachings of the Buddha's at all times.

Ninth, Accommodate and benefit all living beings.

Tenth, Transfer all merits and virtues universally."

After explaining the significance of the first eight vows, the Bodhisattva Samantabhadra continues :

Ninth Vow,

"Sudhana, to accommodate and benefit all living beings is explained like this: throughout the oceans of worlds in the ten directions exhausting the Dharma realm (cosmos) and the realms of empty space there are many different kinds of living beings. That is to say, there are those born from eggs, the womb-born, the transformational born, as well as those who live and rely on earth, water, fire and air for their existence. There are beings dwelling in space, and those who are born in and live in plants and trees. This includes all the many species and races with their diverse bodies, shapes, appearances, life spans, families, names, and natures. This includes their many varieties of knowledge and views, their various desires and pleasures, their thoughts and deeds, and their many different behaviors, clothing and diets.

"It includes beings who dwell in different villages, towns, cities and places, as well as gods, dragons, and others of the eight divisions, humans and non-humans alike. There are also footless beings, beings with two feet, four feet, and many feet, with form and without form, with thought and not entirely with thought and not entirely without thought.

"I will accord with and take care of all these many kinds of beings, providing all manner of services and offerings for them. I will treat them with the same respect I show my own parents, teachers, elders, Arhats, and even the Buddha's. I will serve them all equally without difference.

"I will be a good Physician for the sick and suffering. I will lead those who have lost their way to the right road. I will be a bright light for those in the dark night, and cause the poor and destitute to uncover hidden treasures.

"The Boddhisattva impartially benefits all living beings in this manner.

"Why is this? If a Bodhisattva accords with living beings, then he accords with and makes offerings to all Buddha's. If he can honor and serve living beings then he honors and serves the Buddha's. If he makes living beings happy, he is making all Buddha's happy. Why is this? It is because all Buddha's take the mind of great compassion as their substance. Because of living beings, they develop great compassion. From great compassion the bodhi mind is born; and because of the bodhi mind, they accomplish supreme, perfect enlightenment (Buddhahood).

"It is like a great regal tree growing in the rocks and sand of a barren wilderness. When the roots get water, the branches, leaves, flowers, and fruits will all flourish. The regal Bodhi-tree growing in the wilderness of birth and death is the same. All living beings are its roots; all Buddha's and Bodhisattvas are its flowers and fruits. By benefiting all beings with the water of great compassion, one can realize the flowers and fruits of the Buddha's and Bodhisattvas wisdom. Why is this? It is because by benefiting living beings with the water of great compassion, the Bodhisattvas can achieve supreme perfect enlightenment; therefore, Bodhi belongs to living beings. Without living beings, no Bodhisattva could achieve supreme, perfect enlightenment.

"Good man, you should understand these principals in this way : When the mind is impartial towards all living beings, one can accomplish full and perfect great compassion. By jsing the mind of great compassion to accord with living beings, one perfects the offering of the Dharma to the Buddha's. In this way the Bodhisattva constantly accords with living beings.

"Even when the realms of empty space are exhausted, the realms of living beings are exhausted, the karma's of living beings are exhausted, I will still accord endlessly, continuously, in thought after thought, without cease. My body, speech and mind never weary of these deeds.

Tenth Vow

"Moreover, good man, to transfer all merits and virtues universally is explained like this: all merits and virtues, from the first vow, to pay homage and respect up to and including the vow to accommodate and benefit all living beings throughout the Dharma realm (cosmos) and to the limits of empty space. I vow all living beings will be constantly happy without sickness or suffering. I vow that no one will succeed in doing any evil, but that all will quickly perfect their cultivation of good karma. I vow to shut the door to evil destinies and open the right paths of humans, gods and that of Nirvana. I will stand in for living beings and receive all the extremely severe fruits of suffering which they bring around with their evil karma. I will liberate all these beings and ultimately bring them to accomplish unsurpassed Bodhi (Buddhahood). The Bodhisattva cultivated transference's in this way.

"Even when the realms of empty space are exhausted, the realms of living beings are exhausted, the karma's of living beings are exhausted, and the afflictions of living beings are exhausted, I will transfer all merits and virtues endlessly, continuously, in thought after thought without cease. My body, speech and mind never weary of these deeds.

"Good man, these are the ten great vows of the great Bodhisattvas in their entirety. If all Bodhisattvas can follow and abide by these great vows, then they will succeed in bringing all living beings to maturity. They will be able to accord with the path of the supreme, perfect enlightenment and complete Samantabhadra's sea of conduct and vows. Therefore, good man, you should know the meaning of this...

"Further, when a person who recites these vows is on the verge of death, at the last instant of life, when all his faculties scatter and he departs from his relatives, when all power and status are lost and nothing survives, when his "Prime Minister, great officials, his inner court and outer cities, his elephants, horses, carts, and treasures of precious jewels" can no longer accompany him these great vows alone will stay with him. At all times they will guide him forward, and in a single instant he will be reborn in the land of ultimate bliss arriving there, he will see Amitabha Buddha, The Bodhisattvas Manjushri, Samantabhadra, Avalokiteshvara, Maitreya, and others. The appearance of these Bodhisattvas will be magnificent and their virtues and merits complete. Together they will surround him.

"This person will see himself born from a lotus flower and will receive a prediction of Buddhahood. Therefore, he will pass through a incalculable number of eons and, with his power of wisdom, he will accord with the minds of living beings in order to benefit them everywhere, throughout the countless worlds of the ten directions.

"Before long he will sit in front of the Bodhi-mandala (place of enlightenment), subdue the demonic armies, accomplish supreme, perfect enlightenment, and turn the wonderful Dharma Wheel (Preach Buddhism). He will cause living beings in worlds as numerous as the fine motes of dust in Buddha lands to develop the Bodhi mind (Mind of Enlightenment).

"According with their inclinations and basic natures, he will teach, transform, and bring them to maturity.

"To the exhaustion of the oceans of future eons, he will greatly benefit living beings... "

At that time the great Bodhisattva Samantabhadra, wishing to restate his meaning, contemplated everywhere in the directions and spoke in verse.

1. Before the Buddha's "Lions Among Men,"
   Through out the worlds of the ten directions,
   in the past, in the present, and also in the future,
   With Body, Speech and Mind entirely pure,
   I bow down before them all, omitting none.
   With the awesome power of Samantabhadra's Vows,
   I appear at the same time before every Buddha,
   And in transformed bodies as numerous as motes of dust in all lands.
   Bow to the Buddha's as numerous as motes of dust in all lands.
2. With oceans of sound I every where let fall
   Words and phrases, wonderful and endless,
   Which now and though all the eons of the future,
   Praise the wide, deep sea of the Buddha's Merits and Virtues.
3. Flower garlands, supreme and wonderful,
   Music, perfume, parasols, and canopies,

And other decorations rich and rare,
I offer to every Buddha.
Fine clothing, superior incense,
Powdered and burning incense, lamps and candles,
Each one heaped up as high as mount Sumeru,
I offer completely to all Buddha's
With a vast, great, supremely liberated mind,
I believe in all Buddha's of the three periods of time,
With the strength of Samantrabhadras conduct and vows
I make offerings to all Buddha's everywhere.

4. For all the evil deeds I have done in the past,
Created by my body, speech, and mind,
From beginning-less greed, anger, and delusion,
I now know shame and repent them all.
5. I rejoice in the merits and virtues,
of all beings in the ten directions,
from the most humble to the Arhats,
Pratyekabuddhas, Bodhisattvas and Buddha's.
6. Before the "Lights of the Worlds" of the ten directions,
Who have just accomplished supreme Bodhi,
I now request and beseech them all,
To turn the foremost, wondrous Dharma Wheel.
7. If there are Buddha's who wish for Nirvana,
I request with deep sincerity,
That they dwell in the world for a long time,
To bring benefits and bliss to every being.
The good roots gained,
from following and rejoicing in merit and virtue
and from repentance and reform,
I transfer to living beings and the Buddha way.

8. I study with the Buddha's and practice
   the perfect conduct of Samantabhadra;
   I make offerings to all the Buddha's of the past
   and to all present Buddha's throughout the ten directions
   All future "Teachers of Gods and Men"
   Whose aspirations and vows have been completed,
   I will follow in study throughout the three periods of time
   And quickly attain the great Bodhi...
   I vow that every being in all directions
   Will be peaceful, happy, and without worry.
   May they obtain the proper Dharmas profound aid,
   And may their afflictions be wiped away,
   Without exception.
   In my practice striving for Buddhahood,
   I will gain the knowledge of my past lives
   In all destinies.
   I will always leave the home-life and cultivate pure precepts,
   Without default, never broken, and without stain.
   Be they Gods, Dragons, Yakshas, or Kumbhandas,
   Humans, Non-humans, and the rest,
   In the many languages of all such living beings,
   With every sound I will speak the Dharma.
   I will cultivate the pure paramitas with vigor,
   and never abandon the Bodhi Mind.
   I will banish all Obstructions and defilement's,
   And fulfill all wondrous practices.
   From all delusions, karma's, and demon states,

amid all worldly paths, I will be freed,
As the lotus does not touch the water,
As Sun and Moon do not stop in Space.

9. Ending the sufferings of the paths of evil,
And to everyone equally bringing joy,
May I for eons like the motes of dust
in all the lands
ever benefit all in the ten directions
Always in accord with living beings,
Cultivating through all future eons
The vast conduct of Samantrabhardra,
The unsurpassed Bodhi will I perfect.
I vow always to meet Buddha's face-to-face
And the hosts of disciples who gather around them;
I will raise offerings, which are vast and great,
Untiring to the end of future eons.
I will hold high the subtly wondrous Dharma
And illuminate all the practices of Bodhi;
I will be ultimately pure in Samantabhadra's way,
Practicing until the end of time.
Inexhaustible blessings and wisdom,
I cultivate throughout all worlds;
By concentration, wisdom, skillful means, and samadhis,
I will gain an endless store of merits and virtues.
In one mote of dust are lands as numerous as motes of dust;
In each land are incalculable numbers of Buddha's.
In every place where Buddha's dwell I see the host assembled

Endlessly proclaiming all the practices of Bodhi.

In ten directions everywhere, throughout the sea of lands,

Every hair-tip encompasses oceans of past, present and future.

So, too, there is a sea of Buddha's, a sea of Buddha lands;

Pervading them all I cultivate for seas of endless time.

The speech of all Buddha's is pure;

Each word contains an ocean of sounds.

According with what beings like to hear,

The Buddha's' seas of eloquent flows forth...

I can penetrate the future

And exhausting all eons in a single thought.

In a single thought I compress

All eons of the three periods of time.

In one thought I see all "Lions of Men"

Of the past, present, and future;

I constantly fathom the Buddha's' states,

Their magical samadhis and their awesome strength.

On the tip of an extremely fine hair,

Appears jeweled lands of past, present and future;

Lands on hair-tips as numerous as dust motes in all lands of the ten directions,

I deeply enter, adorn, and purify...

The seas of lands I everywhere adorn and purify,

And I liberate all living beings, without exceptions.

With skill I make selections from among the seas of Dharmas

And enter deeply into the wisdom sea...
Each Buddha has an elder disciple
Named Samantabhadra, Honored One.
I now transfer all good roots, and I vow
To perform deeds of wisdom identical to his.
I vow that my body, speech and mind will be forever pure,
And that all practices and lands will be also.
I now in every way to be identical
To the wisdom of Samantabhadra.
I will wholly purify Samantabhadra's conduct,
And the great vows of Manjushri as well.
All their deeds I will fulfill, leaving nothing undone.
Till the end of time I will never tire.
Infinite and measureless is my cultivation;
Boundless merit and virtue I obtain.
Amid limitless practices I will dwell in peace,
And penetrate the strength of spiritual powers.

10. Manjushri has wisdom, courage and bravery;
Samantabhadra's conduct and wisdom are the same.
I now transfer all good roots
In order to follow them in practice and in study...
In the three periods of time, all Buddha's praise
such vows as these, lofty and great.
I now transfer all good roots, wishing to perfect
The supreme practices of Samantabhadra
I now that when my life approaches its end,
all obstructions will be swept away;
I will see Amitabha Buddha,

And be born in his land of Ultimate Bliss and Peace.
When reborn in the western land,
I will perfect and completely fulfill,
without exception, these great vows,
To delight and benefit all beings.
The assembly of Amitabha Buddha is completely pure;
When from a matchless lotus I am reborn,
I will behold the Buddha's Measureless light as he appears before me
To bestow a prediction of Buddhahood.
Receiving a prediction from the Buddha,
I will take countless appearances and forms,
and with wisdom power vast and great, pervade ten directions to benefit all the realms of living beings.
Realms of worlds in empty space might reach an end,
And living beings, Karma's and afflictions be extinguished;
But they will never be exhausted,
and neither will my vows.
With myriad jewels in boundless lands in all directions,
I make decorations and offerings to the Buddha's,
For eons as numerous as the motes of dust in all lands,
I bring the foremost peace to gods and humans.
Yet, if anyone believes in these great vows,
as they pass by the ears a single time,
And in search of Bodhi thirstily craves these vows,
The merits and virtues gained will surpass these

offerings

With bad advisers forever left behind,

From paths of evil he departs for eternity,

Soon to see the Buddha of limitless light

And perfect Samantabhadras supreme vows.

Easily obtaining the blessings of long life,

Assured of a noble rebirth in the human realm, before long he will perfect and complete

the practices of Samantabhadra.

In the past, owing to a lack of wisdom power,

The five offenses of extreme evil he has committed;

In one thought they can be wiped away by reciting

The great vows of Samantabhadra.

His clan, Race, features and characteristics with his wisdom are all perfected and complete;

Demons and externalists will have no way to harm him, and he will be a field of merits in the triple realm.

To the regal Bodhi tree he will quickly go, and seated there subdue hordes of demons,

Supremely and perfectly enlightened, he will turn the Dharma Wheel,

To benefit all sentient beings.

If anyone can read, recite, receive, and hold high

Samantabhadras vows and proclaim them,

His reward only the Buddha's will know,

and he will achieve Supreme Enlightenment.

If anyone recites Samantabhadras vows,

I will speak of a portion of his good roots:

in one single thought he can fulfill
the pure vows of sentient beings.
The supreme and endless blessings from
Samantrabhadras conduct
I now universally transfer;
May every living being, drowning and adrift,
Soon return to the pure land, the land of
Limitless light!

When the great Bodhisattva Samantabhadra finished speaking these pure verses on the great Vows of Samantabhadra before the Buddha, the youth Sudhana was overwhelmed with boundless joy. All the Bodhisattvas were extremely happy as well, and the Buddha applauded saying "Good indeed, Good Indeed..."

The Smaller Sukhavati-Vyuha Sutra

Translated from Chinese by Hisao Inagaki

[1] Thus have I heard. At one time the Bhagavat was staying in Jeta Grove monastery in Anathapindada's Garden at Shravasti, together with a large company of twelve hundred and fifty monks, who were all venerable shravakas and well-known great arhats. They were headed by eminent shravakas, such as the Venerable Shariputra, Mahamaudgalyayana, Mahakashyapa and Aniruddha. He was also accompanied by innumerable bodhisattvas, mahasattvas, who were all dwelling in the Stage of Non-retrogression and were adorned with immeasurable merits and virtues, headed by great bodhisattvas, such as Bodhisattva, Bodhisattva Ajita, Bodhisattva Nityodyukta and Bodhisattva Anikshipta-dhura. Also in the assembly were a hundred thousand kotis of nayutas [of devas] headed by Shakra along with the King of Mahabrahma Heaven,

the Lord of Saha world, as well as the Four Guardian Kings and others. Many demi-gods, innumerable heavenly and human beings, asuras and others assembled and took their seats to.

[2] The Bhagavat said to Shariputra: "Do you know that if you travel westwards from here, passing a hundred thousand kotis of nayutas of Buddha-lands, you come to the land called Utmost Bliss,' where there is a Bhagavat named 'Amitayus' or 'Amitabha' with ten titles, including Tathagata, Arhat and Samyaksambuddha. He is living there at this very moment, teaching the profound and wonderful Dharma to sentient beings to give them supreme benefit and bliss.

[3] "Why, Shariputra, is that land called 'Utmost Bliss'? Shariputra, beings in that land suffer no afflictions and pain but experience only pure immeasurable joy and happiness. For this reason, that land is called 'Utmost Bliss.'

"Again, Shariputra, in the pure Buddha-land of Utmost Bliss there are seven rows of jewelled balustrades, seven rows of jeweled tala-trees, and sevenfold jewelled nets, which surround everywhere and are completely decorated with four jewels, namely, gold, silver, beryl and crystal. Shariputra, that Buddha-land is full of such glorious adornments of supreme qualities, which are most pleasing to the mind. For this reason, that land is called 'Utmost Bliss.'

"Again, Shariputra, in the pure Buddha-land of Utmost Bliss here and there are many seven-jewelled ponds filled with water of eight excellent qualities, namely, (1) pure, (2) cool, (3) sweet-tasting, (4) soft, (5) moistening, (6) comforting, (7) quenching thirst, hunger and many other needs, and (8) nourishing the senses, increasing the activities of the four elements and producing superior goodness. Sentient beings with a large stock of merits always enjoy using such water. The bottom of these ponds is lined with gold sand,...

"In the ponds, at all times, lotuses of various colours as large as chariot-wheels are in bloom. Blue flowers radiate blue light, brilliance and splendor; yellow ones radiate yellow light, brilliance and splendor; red ones radiate red light, brilliance and splendour; white ones radiate white light, brilliance and splendor; four-coloured ones radiate four-coloured light, brilliance and splendor. Shariputra, that Buddha-land is full of such glorious adornments of supreme qualities, which are most pleasing to the mind. For this reasons, that land is called 'Utmost Bliss.'

"Again, Shariputra, in that pure Buddha-land of Utmost Bliss limitless exquisite music is spontaneously played at all times. The sound is harmonious and most pleasant to hear. When sentient beings hear its excellent sound, their evil passions are completely removed, numerous good acts multiply, and they soon attain the highest perfect Enlightenment. Shariputra, that Buddha-land is full of such glorious adornments of supreme qualities, which are most pleasing to the mind. For this reason, that land is called 'Utmost Bliss.'

"Again, Shariputra, the ground throughout that pure Buddha-land of Utmost Bliss is of true gold. It is soft to the touch and refreshing, shining boundlessly and adorned with rare jewels. Shariputra, that Buddha-land is full of such glorious adornments of supreme qualities, which are most pleasing to the mind. For this reason, that land is called 'Utmost Bliss.'

"Again, Shariputra, in that pure Buddha-land of Utmost Bliss, six times during the day and night, various heavenly blossoms of rare beauty continuously rain down from the sky. They are brilliant and refreshing, soft and variegated, pleasing to the mind and the senses. They do not rouse greedy attachment, but increase countless inconceivable merits in sentient beings. Six times during the day and night, the beings in that land offer those blossoms to Amitayus in homage. Every morning they take those heavenly blossoms and, in such a short time it takes for a meal, fly to innumerable other lands to pay homage to a hundred, thousand kotis of Buddhas. They offer to each Buddha a hundred thousand kotis of such blossoms and return home to the Pure Land, as if to enjoy leisure in a heavenly abode. Shariputra, that Buddha-land is full of such glorious adornments of supreme qualities, which are most pleasing to the mind. For this reason, that land is called 'Utmost Bliss.'

"Again, Shariputra, in that pure Buddha-land of Utmost Bliss there are always many rare species of beautiful birds of various colours, such as swams, geese, herons, storks, cranes, peacocks, parrots, kalavinkas and jivamjivakas. Six times during the day and night, those birds form a flock and sing with melodious and delicate tones, producing diverse sounds to proclaim numerous wonderful teachings, such as the [four] mindful acts, the [four] ways of stopping evils, the [four] miraculous powers, the [five] roots of goodness, the [five] powers, the [seven] factors of wisdom, and the [Eightfold] Noble Path. Having heard their singing, the sentient beings in that land gain innumerable merits through mindfulness of the Buddha, Dharma and Sangha, and their bodies long retain the perfume of virtue. Shariputra, do you think that the birds in that land belong to the evil realm of animals? Do not hold such a view! The reason is that none of the three evil realms, not even their names, exist...

"Again, Shariputra, in that pure Buddha-land of Utmost Bliss soft breezes always blow. When they waft through the jewelled trees and jewelled nets, wonderful sounds are produced. As if a hundred thousand kotis of celestial musical instruments were playing together to produce exquisite sounds, when soft breezes which constantly arise in that land waft through the jewelled trees and jewelled nets, they produce various excellent sounds, which proclaim many teachings of the Dharma. Having heard those sounds, sentient beings in that land give rise to numerous meritorious acts, such as mindfulness of the Buddha, Dharma and Sangha. Shariputra, that Buddha-land is full of such glorious adornments of supreme qualities, which are most pleasing to the mind. For this reason, that land is called 'Utmost Bliss.'

"Shariputra, in that pure Buddha-land of Utmost Bliss there are wonderful manifestations such as those, which are innumerable and inconceivable. Even if a hundred thousand kotis of nayutas of innumerable tongues should praise their excellent qualities for a hundred thousand kotis of nayutas of kalpas, each tongue producing immeasurable voices, they would not be able to praise them to the full. For this reason, [that land] is called the Land of Utmost Bliss.

[4] "Again, Shariputra, why is the Buddha of the pure Buddha-land of Utmost Bliss called 'Amitaytus'? Because, Shariputra, the life-span of that Tathagata and all beings living there last for immeasurable and innumerable great kalpas, the Tathagata of that land is called 'Amitayus.' Shariputra, why is the Buddha also called 'Amitabha'? Shariputra, the Tathagata always emits boundless and innumerable rays of glorious light, illuminating all the Buddha-lands of the ten directions without hindrance, so as to display Buddhist ac...

"Again, Shariputra, the Buddha Amitayus of that pure Buddha-land of Utmost Bliss always has shravaka disciples, all of them arhats, who are possessed of various excellent merits and whose number is unlimited and incalculable. Shariputra, the Pure Land of that Buddha is full of such glorious adornments, which are most pleasing to the mind. For this reason, that land is called 'Utmost Bliss.'

"Again, Shariputra, the Buddha Amitayus of that pure Buddha-land of Utmost Bliss always has innumerable bodhisattva disciples, all of them in the Stage of Becoming a Buddha after One More Life. They are possessed of various excellent merits, and their number is unlimited and incalculable. Even if one praised their merits for innumerable kalpas, one would not be able to praise them fully. Shariputra, that Buddha-land is filled with such glorious adornments, which are most pleasing to the mind. For this reason, that land is called 'Utmost Bliss.'

[5] "Again, Shariputra, sentient beings born in that land all dwell in the Stage of Non-retrogression, and will not fall again into an evil realm, be born in a border-land or in the state of debased people or mlecchas. They always enjoy visiting pure lands of other Buddhas. With their excellent vows and practice advancing and developing every moment, they will unfailingly realize the highest, perfect Enlightenment. Shariputra, that Buddha-land is full of such glorious merits, which are most pleasing to the mind. For this reason, that land is called 'Utmost Bliss.'

"Again, Shariputra, if sentient beings hear of the glorious manifestations of countless merits in that pure Buddha-land of Amitayus, they should all awaken aspiration to be born there. The reasons are: first, those born there will meet those Great Beings adorned with such countless merits as mentioned above; second, they will enjoy the pleasure of the Mahayana Dharma intrinsic to this pure Buddha-land adorned with such innumerable merits; and third, with their own immeasurable vows and practice advancing and developing every moment, they will quickly realize the highest perfect Enlightenment. Shariputra, those who are to be born in that Buddha-land do not have few but already countless and unlimited merits, *so* such sentient beings can attain birth in the pure Buddha-land of Utmost Bliss of the Buddha Amitayus.

"Again, Shariputra, if good men or women of pure faith, having heard Amitayus Buddha's name of innumerable, boundless and inconceivable merits and also heard of the glor...

"Shariputra, as I perceive that such blissful benefits are matters of great importance, I pronounce these words of truth: Good men and good women of pure faith who hear Amitayus Buddha's name of inconceivable merits and also learn of the pure Buddha-land of Utmost Bliss should all receive [the teaching] in faith, arouse aspiration, practise the method as prescribed, and attain birth in that Buddha-land.

[6] "Shariputra, just as I praise the innumerable, unlimited and inconceivable merits of the Buddha-land of Amitayus, so do the Buddhas of the eastern direction as numerous as the sands of the Ganges, such as Aksobhya Tathagata, Meru-dhvaja Tathagata, Mahameru Tathagata, Meru-prabhasa Tathagata, and Manju-dhvaja Tathagata. While dwelling in their own pure lands of the east, they extend their long, broad tongues and, encompassing with them the universe of a thousand million worlds, pronounce these words of truth: Sentient beings should all receive in faith this gate of the Dharma concerning praise of the inconceivable merits of the Buddha-land and protection by all Buddhas.

[7] "Again, Shariputra, there are in the southern direction Buddhas as numerous as the sands of the Ganges, such as Candra-surya-pradipa Tathagata, Yashah-prabha Tathagata, Maharci-skandha Tathagata, Meru-pradipa Tathagata and Ananta-virya Tathagata. While dwelling in their own pure lands of the south, they extend their long, broad tongues and, encompassing with them the universe of a thousand million worlds, pronounce these words of truth: Sentient beings should all receive in faith this gate of the Dharma concerning praise of the inconceivable merits of the Buddha-land and protection by all Buddhas.

[8] "Again, Shariputra, there are in the western direction Buddhas as numerous as the sands of the Ganges, such as Amitayus Tathagata, Amita-skandha Tathagata, Amita-prabha Tathagata, Amita-dhvaja Tathagata, Maheshvara Tathagata, Mahaprabha Tathagata, Jvalana Tathagata, Maharatna-ketu Tathagata and Sphuta-rashmi Tathagata. While dwelling in their own pure lands of the west, they extend their long, broad tongues and, encompassing with them the universe of a thousand million worlds, pronounce these words of truth: Sentient beings should all receive in faith this gate of the Dharma concerning praise of the inconceivable merits of the Buddha-land and protection by all Buddhas.

[9] "Again, Shariputra, there are in the northern direction Buddhas as numerous as the sands of the Ganges, such as Amita-prabha-vyuha-abhijna- buddhi Tathagata, Mahaskandha Tathagata, Amrita-divya-dundubhi-vaishvanara- nirghosa Tathagata, Jaleni-prabha Tathagata and Salendra-raja Tathagata. While dwelling in their own pure lands of the north, they extend their long, broad tongues and, encompassing with them the universe of a thousand million worlds, pronounce these words of truth: Sentient beings should all receive in faith this gate of the Dharma concerning praise of the inconceivable merits of the Buddha-land and protection by all Buddhas.

[10] "Again, Shariputra, there are in the nadir Buddhas as numerous as the sands of the Ganges, such as Sarva-saddharma-darshana-yukti-sada-jvalana-rajottama-shri-prabha Tathagata, Simha Tathagata, Yashas Tathagata, Yashah-prabhasa Tathagata, Dharma Tathagata, Saddharma Tathagata, Dharma-dhvaja Tathagata, Guna-mitra Tathagata and Guna-nama Tathagata. While dwelling in their own pure lands of the nadir, they extend their long, broad tongues and, encompassing with them the universe of a thousand million worlds, pronounce these words of truth: Sentient beings should all receive in faith this

Dharma-gate expounding praise of the inconceivable merits of the Buddha-land and protection by all Buddhas.

[11] "Again, Shariputra, there are in the zenith Buddhas as numerous as the sands of the Ganges, such as Brahma-ghosa Tathagata, Naksatra-raja Tathagata, Gandha-prabhasa Tathagata, Utpala-shri-kalpa Tathagata and Sarvartha-darsha Tathagata. While dwelling in their own pure lands of the zenith, they extend their long, broad tongues and, encompassing with them the universe of a thousand million worlds, pronounce these words of truth: Sentient beings should all receive in faith this gate of the Dharma concerning praise of the inconceivable merits of the Buddha-land and protection by all Buddhas.

[12] "Again, Shariputra, there are in the south-eastern direction Buddhas as numerous as the sands of the Ganges, such as Uttama-vipula-megha-ghosa-raja Tathagata. While dwelling in their own pure lands of the south-east, they extend their long, broad tongues and, encompassing with them the universe of a thousand million worlds, pronounce these words of truth: Sentient beings should all receive in faith this gate of the Dharma concerning praise of the inconceivable merits of the Buddha-land and protection by all Buddhas.

[13] "Again, Shariputra, there are in the south-western direction Buddhas as numerous as the sands of the Ganges, such as Uttama-surya-prabha-yasho-guna Tathagata. While dwelling in their own pure lands of the south-west, they extend their long, broad tongues and, encompassing with them the universe of a thousand million worlds, pronounce these words of truth: Sentient beings should all receive in faith this gate of the Dharma concerning praise of the inconceivable merits of the Buddha-land and protection by all Buddhas.

[14] "Again, Shariputra, there are in the north-western direction Buddhas as numerous as the sands of the Ganges,

such as Amita-guna-jvalanadhipati- prabhasa Tathagata. While dwelling in their own pure lands of the north-west, they extend their long, broad tongues and, encompassing with them the universe of a thousand million worlds, pronounce these words of truth: Sentient beings should all receive in faith this gate of the Dharma concerning praise of the inconceivable merits of the Buddha-land and protection by all Buddhas.

[15] "Again, Shariputra, there are in the north-eastern direction Buddhas as numerous as the sands of the Ganges, such as Asamkhya-shata-sahasra-koti- nayuta-vipula-buddhi Tathagata. While dwelling in their own pure lands of the north-east, they extend their long, broad tongues and, encompassing with them the universe of a thousand million worlds, pronounce these words of truth: Sentient beings should all receive in faith this gate of the Dharma concerning praise of the inconceivable merits of the Buddha-land and protection by all Buddhas.

[16] "Shariputra, why is this sutra named the Dharma-gate expounding praise of the inconceivable merits of the Buddha-land and protection by all Buddhas? Shariputra, it is revealed in this sutra that the inconceivable merits of Amitayus Buddha's Land of Utmost Bliss are praised and glorified and that all Buddhas, Bhagavats, of the ten directions, while dwelling in their own lands, display glorious and wonderful manifestations and pronounce...

"Shariputra, if good men or women, who have heard this sutra, now hear or will hear it, have already awakened or will awaken deep faith, they are embraced by those Buddhas, Bhagavats, dwelling in the ten directions, as numerous as ten times the number of the sands of the Ganges. All who practise as prescribed will not regress but will definitely attain the highest perfect Enlightenment and be born in the Pure Land of Utmost Bliss of Amitayus. For this reason, Shariputra, all sentient beings should receive in faith and understand well my words and the words of the Buddhas, Bhagavats, of the ten directions, and should make great efforts and diligently practise as prescribed. Do not allow any doubt to arise.

"Again, Shariputra, if good men or women have already aspired or will aspire or now aspire to the glorious adornments in the Pure Land of Utmost Bliss of Amitayus, they will be definitely embraced by those Buddhas, Bhagavats, dwelling in the ten directions, as numerous as the sands of the Ganges, even ten times that number. All who practise as prescribed will not regress but will definitely attain the highest perfect Enlightenment and be born in the Pure Land of Utmost Bliss of Amitayus. For this reason, Shariputra, good men and women of pure faith should all believe deeply in Amitayus Buddha's Pure Land of Utmost Bliss and aspire to be born there. Do not be indolent.

[17] "Shariputra, just as I now praise and glorify the inconceivable merits of Amitayus Buddha's Land of Utmost Bliss, all other Buddhas, Bhagavats, of the ten directions likewise praise my boundless inconceivable merits, saying: 'How marvellous it is that Shakyamuni, Shakya Dharma-King, Tathagata, Arthat, Samyaksambuddha, Possessed of Wisdom and Practice, Sugata, Knower of the World, the Unsurpassed, Tamer of Men, Teacher of Gods and Humans, Buddha and Bhagavat, has appeared in this Saha world during the period of the five corruptions: namely, those of time, sentient beings, passions, views and life-span, and that, having attained the highest perfect Enlightenment, delivered this teaching, most difficult for the world to accept, in order to guide and benefit sentient beings and give them peace and bliss.'

"Thus, Shariputra, you should know that I have appeared in this Saha world of various defilements during the period of the five corruptions and, having attained the highest...

[18] When the Bhavagat had delivered this sutra, all the great shravakas, such as the Venerable Shariputra, and bodhisattvas, mahasattvas, together with all beings, including innumerable devas, humans and asuras, greatly rejoiced at the Buddha's exposition and received it in faith.

By Bhikkhu Sasena Kiffi alias Rev. Hye Dahl, South Korea.

The Ways of Enlightenment

Verse 1. Suffering Follows The Evil-Doer

> ***Manopubbangama dhamma***
> ***manosettha manomaya***
> ***manasa ce padutthena***
> ***bhasati va karoti va***
> ***tato nam dukkhamanveti***
> ***cakkamva vahato padam.***

Verse 1: All mental phenomena have mind as their forerunner; they have mind as their chief; they are mind-made. If one speaks or acts with an evil mind, 'dukkha' (suffering) follows him just as the wheel follows the hoofprint of the ox that draws the cart.

Verse 2. Happiness Follows The Doer of Good

> ***Manopubbangama dhamma***
> ***manosettha manomaya***
> ***manasa ce pasannena***
> ***bhasati va karoti va***
> ***tato nam sukha[1] manveti***
> ***chayava anapayini.***

Verse 2: All mental phenomena have mind as their forerunner; they have mind as their chief; they are mind-made. If one speaks or acts with a pure mind, sukha (happiness) follows him like a shadow that never leaves him.

The above two verses are taken from the Dhammapada, the famous Buddhist book which contain 423 verses of the Buddha. In the above verses, mind, which is the main focus of the Buddhist practice, has been given foremost importance by the Buddha. Mind, the origin of all kinds of thoughts, forms the very basis of all of our future suffering and happiness. The origin of thoughts in our mind and the resulting speech and action determines our future states. So the practice or cultivation of mind is to keep the mind fully free from all kinds of defilement because the pure mind without any defilement means the blissful state or happiness.

Mind is considered as originally pure and without any defilement. It is contaminated only when it is stained by passions and delusions. The purity of the mind is often compared with the cloudless sky or with the mirror that does not have even the tiniest particle of dusts or with the unpolluted water of the pond where everything in the bottom can be clearly visible. Sentient beings live in the world of torment and delusion but the Buddha is one who has completely transcended such a world. The delusion-free state of the mind is also called the state of supreme enlightenment. Sometimes it is called No Mind. And the aim of the practice is to achieve this state of supreme enlightenment through the elimination of all delusions. Based on the sutras, there are 84,000 delusions that are classified into two major groups as conscious and unconscious. The thoughts or the delusions at the conscious level can be cognizable but there are tiny unconscious delusions stored in the Alayavinnana or the "storehouse" consciousness which are extremely difficult to cognize. Even a Bodhisattva at the 8th level of sainthood or an Arahant are not aware of delusions at this level. This can be known fully only by those who have achieved Supreme Enlightenment, by the Buddha.

Giving the utmost priority of these ideal teachings of the Buddha, practitioners (meditators) who seek ultimate liberation from the sufferings of the world, engaged themselves in the practice of mental cultivation or purification of the mind. All the negative forces of the mind such as greed, aversion, delusion etc. form the hindrances to the practice of mental purification. These defilements of the mind are regarded as the enemy or foe (pali-ari). Totally uprooting them (ari-foe, enemy; hant-destroy, conquer) by the practitioner makes the realization of the spiritual culmination called Arahant in the Theravada tradition. Thus an Arahant has conquered or destroyed all kinds of defilements of the mind. Thus one who has attained arahantship has "laid down the burden" and realized the goal of Nibbana, the culmination of spiritual life.

In the Pali Canon, the Buddha has described the Arahant as the Worthy One or the highest grade of a noble person, "Ariya Puggala." The word Arahant was also used as an epithet of the Buddha himself as well as his disciples. However, arahantship could not be directly realized or attained. Based on the purification level of the mind, there are four stages of spiritual attainment. Arahant is the highest one, having fully purified the mind, and the other three are sotapanna, sokadagami and anagami. Attainment of all these stages of spirituality is classified on the basis of purification level of the mental defilements, by the practitioners. The mental defilements which are mainly the three poisons such as greed, aversion and delusion can also be explained on the basis of Ten Fetters. The Ten Fetters, also known as the Ten Chief Hindrances and the children of Mara, which are claimed by the Buddha specifically and Buddhism generally as standing in the way of enlightenment.

The Ten fetters are as follows :

1. *Personality belief (sakkaya-ditti)*
2. *Skeptical doubt (Vicikiccha)*
3. *Addherence to wrongful rites, rituals and ceremonies (Silabbataparamasa)*
4. *Sensual desire (Kama-raga)*

5. *Ill will or hatred (Pathiga)*
6. *Craving for fine material-existence (rupa-raga)*
7. *Craving for non-material existence (arupa-raga)*
8. *Conceit or arrogance (Mana)*
9. *Restlessness (Udhacca)*
10. *Ignorance (Avijja).*

The first five Fetters are known as Lower Fetters (orambhagiya-samyojana) because they bind us to the sensuous world. The second five Fetters are known as Higher Fetters (uddhambhagiya-samyojana) because they bind us to the rupa and arupa worlds.

The removal of the first three fetters makes one a stream enterer or sotapatti, one who's final awakening is assured within seven further rebirths.

The removal of the first three fetters and the dilution of the next two makes one a "once returner" or sakadagami in other words there will be only one more rebirth as a human being before enlightenment.

The complete abandonment of the first five fetters makes one a "non-returner" or anagami and therefore leads to rebirth in one of the Buddhist pure abodes where final awakening is assured.

An Arahant is one in whom all ten fetters have been destroyed and no more further rebirth takes place. After fully uprooting or destroying the mental defilements, an Arahant, after biological death, is not reborn into any samsaric realm because all causes of future becoming have been removed.

The Arahant creates no new Karma; he has gone beyond both good and evil, but he must still live with the Karmic effects of his previous actions.

In the Ratana Sutta, it says: "Their past is dead, the new no more arises, Mind to future becoming is unattached, and the germ has died. They have no more desire for growth.

Those wise (and steadfast ones) go out just as this lamp has gone out." (Sutta Nipata, 14)

Many great disciples of the Buddha have attained parinibbana. To name a few: Sariputta, Moggalana, Mahakassapa, Ananda, Upali, Assaji, etc.

Every practitioner in the Theravada tradition aspires to become an Arahant and attain the spiritual stage which is free from all kinds of samsaric suffering.

But with the growth of Mahayana tradition, the ultimate aim of attainment of arahantship as the final spiritual stage has been shifted to the ideal of becoming a Bodhisattva.

Unlike an Arahant that does not reborn again, the bodhisattva postpones his/her liberation (final enlightenment) and is reborn again and again to help other sentient beings in the world to attain spiritual progress. Indeed, the bodhisattva vows to save all sentient beings before going to full nirvana. Thus, the bodhisattva out of compassion for the living beings in the world chooses to be reborn again and again in samsara voluntarily in order to aid all living beings to become enlightened.

Although those on the path of Arahant also help others, often extensively, that helps ends with the entering of Nibbana because the Arahant is not reborn again. So sometimes, it is branded as narrow as it limits liberation only to an individual.

The reference of the bodhisattva ideal can be found in the original text of the Theravada tradition. In the Jataka stories, there are numerous references of the Buddha's former life as a Bodhisattva. It is mentioned in the Jataka Stories that the bodhisattva has undergone numerous rebirths in different forms of life in different realms of existence as a Bodhisattva (aspirant of enlightenment). The Bodhisattva has to fully develop the six paramis (ten in Theravada) to become a fully enlightened one. In the course of perfecting the paramis, the Bodhisattva undertakes various activities out of compassion, helping and guiding the sentient beings through the path of liberation. We find in the Jataka stories that the Bodhisattva on many occasions has even sacrificed himself for the cause of saving other living beings.

But Bodhisattva carries a different meaning in Mahayana Buddhism to Theravada Buddhism. In the Pali scriptures the Tathagata when relating his own experiences of self-development uses a stock phrase 'when I was an unenlightened Bodhisattva'. Bodhisattva thus connotes here the absence of enlightenment (Bodhi) of a person working towards that goal. In Mahayana Buddhism, on the other hand a Bodhisattva is an "enlightened being" who has reached ultimate understanding, and delays the final enlightenment to help others make spiritual progress. Thus the Bodhisattva seeks to put the welfare of others before their own, forfeiting their own final enlightenment until all beings are saved.

To quote His Holiness the Dalai Lama: "Nirvana may be the final object of attainment, but at the moment it is difficult to reach. Thus the practical and realistic aim is compassion, a warm heart, serving other people, helping others, respecting others, being less selfish. By practicing these, you can gain benefit and happiness that remain longer. If you investigate the purpose of life and, with the motivation that results from this inquiry, develop a good heart - compassion and love. Using your whole life this way, each day will become useful and meaningful."

To save all sentient beings, the bodhisattva undertakes what is called the bodhisattva vows. Following are the four great vows of the Bodhisattva :-

1. *However innumerable sentient beings are, I vow to save them.*
2. *However inexhaustible the defilements are, I vow to extinguish them.*

3. *However immeasurable the dharmas are, I vow to master them.*
4. *However incomparable enlightenment is, I vow to attain it.*

There is in the Mahayana metaphysics a whole cosmology full of heavenly Bodhisattvas. Many celestial bodhisattvas are worshipped along with the Gautama Buddha and the buddhas of other worlds. The most important celestial bodhisattvas are Avalokitesvara, the bodhisattva of compassion; Manjusri, the bodhisattva of wisdom; and Maitreya, who presently abides in Tushita heaven awaiting to be reborn as the next Buddha.

The term is also used for human beings who have taken the Bodhisattva Vow to heart to such an extent that they will keep it through all their future lives.

However, to practice the Bodhisattva ideal one must first generate "bodhicitta". Bodhicitta is translated as an enlightened (Bodhi) mind (citta). It is the mind that is based on compassion and love upon which the bodhisattva vows to attain enlightenment in order to be of the greatest benefit to all sentient beings. A popular Mahayana saying is that the Buddhas are born from bodhisattvas and bodhisattvas from the bodhicitta.

The rise of Mahayana Buddhism has brought many fascinating and new developments in Buddhism. The most important factor is the renewed emphasis on compassion and the significance of Bodhisattva (a Buddha to be), postponing his or her own liberation to bring all sentient beings to the state of Nibbana by becoming a fully enlightened Buddha. As each of us has an inherent Buddha nature, everybody can and will become a Buddha at some point in time. The Theravadins still hold the view that though attaining Buddhahood is the highest ideal, it is too difficult and beyond most people's capabilities. Indeed they hold the view that only one Supreme enlightened Buddha (Samma

Sambuddha) can exist in each global time period. Similarly, we can also see in the Mahayana countries the practice of offering prayers and devotion to the divine Bodhisattvas while requesting help and protection. The feeling is that people in this age cannot reach enlightenment. What they can do is ask a Bodhisattva for help, and these Bodhisattvas will, in return for devotion, ensure that you reincarnate into a heavenly world (the pure land), after which enlightenment is a simple step.

Many Buddhists, especially the westerners, tend to see both the Theravada and the Mahayana approaches as not being contradictory or in opposition but rather as contemporary to each other. The Mahayana is often seen as an expansion of or commentary on Theravada teachings.

To conclude, there can be of no points of difference for any practitioner seeking spiritual attainment, since mind forms the beginning as well as the end of our practice. Indeed we don't need to seek some place outside ourselves to: Buddha nature or Tathagathagabbha (seed of Buddha) is inherent in our mind. "Its brightness is not something that we have to produce; rather it is the intrinsic nature of mind, the citta." (Ajahn Amaro in Silent Rain) The most important step in spiritual growth is the first: we must begin by making a decision to avoid unwholesome and cultivate wholesome states within our stream of being. On the basis of this fundamental discipline every spiritual quality becomes possible, even the eventual perfection of Buddhahood.

1. *Dhammapada (Sacred book of the East)*

   Translated by Daw Mya Tin, M.A.

   Edited by Editorial Committee, Burma Tipitaka Association Rangoon, Burma, 1986.

   The sun is bright by day

The moon shines bright by night
The warrior is bright in his armour
The Brahmana is bright in his meditation
But Buddha, the awakened
Is bright with splendor day and night.

2. *"Generating the bodhimind" by His Holiness Kybje Ling Rimpoche, senior tutor of His Holiness The Dalai Lama.*
3. *"Echoes from Mt. Kaya" selections on Korean Buddhism by Ven. Song chol, Patriarch of the Korean Chogye Order.*
4. *"Silent Rain" Ajahn Amaro.*
5. *The Ten Fetters of Buddhism presented by.*
6. *The rise of Mahayana by Graeme Lyall.*

History of Buddhism - Chronology

563-483 B.C.

Life of Siddharta Gautama, otherwise known as Buddha, the founder of Buddhism, [short description of his life]. Buddha's foremost disciple was Shariputra. Buddha's closest companion was Ananda.

History writes after the king Prasenjit who was a great admirer of Buddha he was succeeded by his son Vidudhava who massacred the Sakya clan in Kapilvastu (50,000) in one day), sparing neither men or women and children. That was virtually the end of Sakya clan there in Buddha's life time. many moved out from there and established kingdom and returned to Sakya clan outside Kapilavastu in Burma (myanmar). They hatted at many places on the route.

486 B.C./483 B.C.

- First Buddhist Council at Rajagriha, under the patronage of King Ajatasattu. Oral tradition established for the first time.

383/386/350 B.C.

- Second Buddhist Council at Vesali about 100 year after the Parinirvana.
- First schism of the Sangha occurs in which the Mahasanghika school parts ways with the Sthaviras or Theras (elders), regarded as the founders of Therevada Buddhism.

269/272 -233/231 B.C.

- Reign of *Indian Emperor Asoka* who converts and establishes the Buddha's Dharma on a national level for the first time. He also sends out Buddhist missionaries all around the then known world. Traceble are the emergence of Buddhism all over India and in Indonesia.

250 B.C.

- Third Buddhist Council at Pataliputra under the patronage of Emperor Asoka about 200 years after the Parinirvana. This council is not recognised among Mahayana Buddhists.

240 7' 247 B.C.

- Asoka's son and missionary Mahinda established Buddhism in Sri Lanka.

50 B.C.

- Modern scholars believe that Buddhism was in fact being introduced into China by at least this date by traveling merchants, if not by missionaries.

30 - 100 B.C. or 35-32 B.C.

- Entire scriptural canon of Theravada School was committed to writing on palm leaves in Pali at the Aloka Cave, near Matale, Sri Lanka.

2 BCE

Ashvaghosa wrote an inspired biogaphy of Buddha and gave rise to Buddhism.

[0 A.D.]

- The alleged birth of Christ, the beginning of the Christian Era on which all the date, here mentioned are based.
- During the first century A.D. Buddhism reached China from India. Buddhism was one of the few foreign influences that had a deep impact on chinese life. It spread along caravan trade routes (Silk routes) that linked India to China and western world.

c. 150-250

- Indian Buddhist philosopher Nargarjuna founds the school of Madhyamika ('the Middle Way'), one of the major schools within Mahayana Buddhism.

c. 320-400

- Asanga and his brother Vasubandhu develop the new school of Yogacara Buddhism. They were very reknowned Buddhist Teacher and founder of Both Hinayana and Mahayana and greatly developed Buddhist Psychology.

375

- King Sosurium, the 17th ruler of the Koguryo Kingdom of Korea, establishes Buddhism as the spiritual foundation of the state and Confucius's teachings as its legal base. This marks the start of Buddhist influence all over Korea, though in some portions of the land Buddhists are persecuted in this era.

4th Century – 5th century

- Translation of Buddhist texts into Chinese by Kumarajiva (344-413) and Hui-yuan (334-416).

5th Century

- Amitabha (Amida) Pure Land sect emerges in China, founded by Hui Yuan, a convert from Daoism.

- Buddhaghosa composes the Visuddhimagga and major commentaries in Sri Lanka. He thereby systematizes Therevada Buddhism's doctrines.

c. 500-528

- Buddhists are persecuted by Hindus in India, leading to a Buddhist migration east into southeastern Asia.

c. 500-535

562-645 Pure Land Buddhism under the influence of Tan Luan's

- Chan Buddhism (in Japanese Zen) is introduced to China through Bodhidharma, probably from India.

1133-1212

- Founder of the Jodo Shu Saigo the first independent pure land Buddhist school in Japan.

1173-1262

- Disciple of Honen Shinran and founder of the Jodoshi Shu School. He advocated reliance in faith upon Amida.

1197 A.D.

- Muhammed-i-Bakhtyar Khilji conquered Bihar and Nalanda Buddhist university and massacred the Buddhists. Two years later he advanced to Bengal and took possession of Gaur, the Scythions Kingdom.

1239-1289

- Ippen founder of the Jishu, a school of pure land Buddhism.
- History continues mentioning chinese scholar Hiuen Tsiang visited north Bihar that was divided into Vreji to the north and vaisali to the south, both the countries stretching eastwards to the Mahananda south of Ganges the present manghyr and south Bhagalpur (Champa kingdom), the santal paraganas

and Bhirbhum. Muhammad Khilji destroyed the capital Odantopuri and massacred the Buddhist monks assembled there. The glorified history of that time has not been excuvated by the archeologists till the present day.

1357-1419

- Tsong-kha-pa becomes a major Tibetan Buddhist reformer and founder of Dge-lugs-pa (or Gelugpa, or 'Yellow Hat') order. He abolishes marriage for the lama's in his order.

15th Century

- Beginning of Dalai Lama lineage in Tibetan Buddhism. The current is the 14 (fourteenth) Dalai Lamas of Gelungpa, practicing Kalachakra. The present Dalai Lama has given thirty Kala Chakra initiations all over the world.

1616-1651

- Ngawang Namgyal (1594-1651), a Tibetan monk, arrives in Bhutan, in flight from the Dalai Lama. After defeating rival religious leaders, he becomes the spiritual head of the country. As Bhutan's first national figure he is regarded as the father of this nation.

19th Century

- First Western translation of the Dhammapada. (German-1862).
- German translation of Lotus Sutra, 1852 and pioneer Buddhist scholars: - Neumann and Odlenburg, first German monk, Nyanatiloka.
- The history of Buddhism is dominated by Western Colonialism. Colonialism is seen as both a suppressing agent for Buddhism, in the form of Christian Missionaries, for instance, as well as a

reinvigorating agent as old libraries are newly studied.

- Buddhism will grow to be intertwined with nationalistic and independence movements in various Asian nations.

1875

- A public debate takes place in Sri Lanka between a Buddhist monk and several Christian missionaries. It is the intent of the Christians to convince the people of the presumed superiority of Christianity, but in fact the lone monk makes a strong case for Buddhism. Published reports of the debate will have considerable influence in convincing various Westerners of the value of Buddhism.

1880

- Colonel Olcott, president of the Theosophical Society [see *Theosophical Chronology]* and H.P. Blavatsky come to Sri Lanka where they embrace Buddhism by *taking Pansil.* Colonel Olcott will be instrumental in founding various Buddhist schools, often lead by theosophists, creating the first Buddhist Catechism and in creating the Buddhist flag. All this was part of his effort to reinvigorate Buddhism and other eastern religions. In the end his work was criticised for being too much a mixture of various traditions, with the result that none felt he was being true to theirs.
- Anagarika Dharmapala met Olcott and Blavatsky and became a member of the Theosophical Society. He is encouraged by H.P. Blavatsky not to work for theosophy, but for Buddhism.

1891

- The Maha Bodhi Society was founded by Anagarika Dharmapala, member of the Theosophical Society, in 1891.

Bana Bhante (Forest Monk) Mahastavir Sadhana Nanda

1893

- World Parliament of the Religions, Chicago. Anagarika Dharmapala is there represent Theravada Buddhism and becomes very popular.

1907

- Buddhist Society of Great Britain was founded.

1924

- The Buddhist Society was founded, by the late Christmas Humphreys, member of the Theosophical Society, building on the pioneer work of the Buddhist Society of Great Britain and Ireland (1907 to 1925-6) and it is one of the oldest Buddhist societies in Europe. From its inception it has not been attached to any one school of Buddhism, remaining non-sectarian in character and open in principle to the teachings of all schools.

1952

- Founding of World Fellowship of Buddhists.

1959

- Dalai Lama flees Tibet to India.

1989

- H.H. Dalai Lama receives Nobel Peace Prize.

Sources

- The Wilson Chronology of the World's Religions, edited by David Levinson, New York, 2000.
- http://www.buddhanet.net/e-learning/history/b_chron-txt.htm (checked October 20th 2004)
- The White Buddhist, The Asian Odyssey of Henry Steel Olcott.
- http://www.thebuddhistsociety.org/ (checked October 20th 2004)
- http://www.bbc.co.uk/cchecked October 20th 2004).

2004-2005

References

1. Hiuen Tsang's report
2. by Bhikkhu Sarana Kitti alias Rev. Hye Dahl, South Korea-Vyuha Sutra
3. The ways of enlightenment
4. History of Buddhism – Chronology
5. Buddha Canonical Literature
6. Chittagong Hill Tracts (Refugees within, Refugees without) by Sanjay Hazarika.
7. Eastern Bengal District Gazetteer, Chittagong by L.S.S. O' Malley, 1908.
8. A fly on the wheel by Capt. T.H. Lewin.
9. Amnesty International – Report – ASA13/01/00 February 2000.
10. Amnesty International – Report – ASA 13/01/00 February 2000.
11. The Tribes of the Brahamaputra Valley by L.A. Waddel.
12. The Tribes of the Brahamaputra Valley by L.A. Waddel.

4

Chakma Language and Script

Origin

Comparative evidences shows Chakma alphabetical scripts[1] have shared characteristics in curvic style and tonal affinities with Tai scriptures[2]. Historically during king Ashokas period (BC 232) Tai scriptures spread through Buddhist religious texts in many South-Asian countries[3]. Their curvic form is almost identical with Tamil Dravidian character of Southern India. There is another view – the Chakma language written in an alphabets (originally) which, has its curvic form and is almost identical with the Khmeer character, which was formally in use in Cambodia, Laos, Annan, Siam (now Thailand) and at least the Southern of Burman Mon Type (Burma, Myanmar). These Khmeer alphabets are in turn, the same as that which was in South India in the 6th and 7th centuries. There is another legacy activating our knowledge to know the root of Chakma Scriptures and language. The local communication language of Gautam Buddha's time was Prakrit in 6th B.C. In Buddha's time their Brahma Desha comprised of Kasi. Kosal, Videha and Magadhi. Chakmas have many distinguishing words in their language. The origin of Brahmi script is not known. But has Greek influence as the Indians of the Gangetic valley were in close contact with Greek people. In 1907 the reknowned scholar.

Hara Parshad Shastri discovered in the repository of king Nepal some ancient writing bearing no title on it. Later he named it *Charya pad* and it was published by Bengal literary society in 1916, in the name *Buddhist in Bengal* 1000 years ago. In 1916, Dr. Sunity Kumar Chatterjee, national professor of India came with judgment that Charya Pad is in the Original Bengali form which is discreetly in the form of Buddhist text in poetry songs like "ode" poems addressed to a person or things or celebrating an event which was like Gangkhuli songs or old Chakmas writings in poetry forms like prominent writing of Pranhari Talukdar and Shivcharan Chakma. He Dr. S.K. Chatterjee is of the opinion among the various forms of Bengali, the Chakma language of CHT is one of them, but very little has been done for its study, and there has been no serious work in the language on scientific mission. The language compared with any other form of vocabulary there are words from Arakan (Barma), and a number of unexplained words which makes its study very tantalizing[4] Chakma language has intricacy with Magadhi and Arakanese one of the offshoot of Tai language. As Chakmas were in Bengal province, the Bengali language was their literary language and their original language became their home dialect, and it has changed life. They have great linguistic similarity with language in the eastern India (Assamese, Orissa, Bihar, Bengal of Magadhi language. In Tibetain it is called the wonderful songs.

The central facts is that the study of Chakma language, we have the reflection of pre- and post- Buddhist era of closer relation among nations. Buddhism survived in India till 1000 BC; and so the Buddhist patronage. I quote from James Merill:

> *'lost, is it buried? One more missing piece?*
> *But nothing's lost, or else: all is translation*
> *And every bit of lost in it.*
> *(or found-I wonder through the ruins of S*
> *Now and then, wondering of peacefulness.'*

Literary Works

Chakma's oldest literary works are Shristi Pattam, Agar Tara, Gengkhuli, Gogenlama, Radha Mohan Dhan Pudi and many others. The original writing is not traceable. Heinz Bechart German Anthropologist make a reference of *Agar Tara* (20 sets of books) in his book *Buddhism in East Bengal*. There is also a reference of Arya Tara (a personification of Nirvana) in the *Imperial Gazetter*[5] Categorizing people in India on linguistic basis, which has been admitted as a home rule, where people are united on language (linguistic state). So the language of the majority are surviving and ethnic languages are on threat of extinction. Their identity of being somebody is lost. It says :

Lose your language and you lose your culture.

Lose your culture and you lose your identity.

Lose your language and you will lose mutual understandings.

Lose mutual understandings and you lose harmony, mutual support and peace.

Lose your peace and you lose your brotherhood.

Lose your brotherhood and you will lose your destiny.

Queen Kalindi Rani of Chakma used Bengali as court language during her reign. Bengali was also court language of the British Colonial rulers. So Bengali became the School language for Chakma students. Since 1870, and their native language has fallen into disuse ever since. As a result, over the space of time there have been some pre-eminent writers in Bengali, one such celebrated writer is Pranendra Mohan Regei (head of Regei clan). Pran Hari Talukdar, who brought into light Chakma History, Rhyme, Folk Songs, Poetry and many others. The central idea of some of the poems has been translated into English by R. Excelicia Curville which are adjoined[6-12] (original writing in Bengali).

Among the various forms of Bengali, the Chakma dialect of Chittagong and Chittagong Hill Tracts, which has also spread into Burma, is of very great linguistic importance. It would appear to be a form of South-Eastern Bengali as spoken in Chittagong, but there has been a very widespread phonetic decay or development, and at times along new lines. Then the morphological system also shows some new inflections. Further, the syntax has some special characteristics of its own. The language, compared with any other form of Bengali, appears to be very much abbreviated and attenuated. In its vocabulary there are words from Arakan (Burma), and a number of unexplained words which make its study very tantalising.

Unfortunately very little has been done in the study of

Chakma. Excepting one or two small monographs or notes there has been; no serious work in the language. It has become just a village patois and has no real literature to boast of. There are some songs and poems of a popular nature, partly religious and partly narrative, and excepting for two books which were collected and published by Sri Tripur Chandra Sen, no printed literature is available using the Bengali script. Through the influence of the Bhikkhus from among the Chakma people, who used to have their training in Buddhism and Pali in Burma, the Burmese script along with Pali manuscript was introduced among the Chakmas some generations ago. They were cut of from the main trend of Bengali literature, and in their isolation some of them employed a kind of simplified Burmese script to write their Bengali dialect. Some literature in this Burmese-Chakma Bengali is found in manuscript writing, and already with a view to bring out books in Burmese-Chakma an enterprising Publisher had a fount of these special Burmese-Chakma script cast for the language. But as this is very recondite, and as it is not at all popular, it is fast going out of use, and excepting for a few old people nobody can write it. The best proposition for the Chakma dialect would be to write it in Bengali characters as it has been done successfully.

As students of Bengali and Indo-Aryan linguistics,we are very much interested in the development of Chakma studies.One or more Chakma young man or woman with a knowledge of the language as it is spoken, combined with a good knowledge of Bengali as well as English, should immediately take up the task of preserving this language for posterity by both study and publication of texts in it. There is no lack of highly edudated and cultured peoples among the Chakma speakers including some members of the landed aristocracy as well as men in the professions. Just to perpetuate a knowledge of their home dialect, they should form themselves into an association for the preservation and development of Chakma (Chakma, Bhasha-Prabardhini Samiti).

I would suggest that some of the young men and women studying for higher degrees in Calcutta should form themselves into a Study-Group and start collecting materials in Chakma, both such specimens of folk-poetry and folk-literature as can be gleaned from among the older generations and also by creating a literature of translations from standard Bengali or other languages into Chakma. But the more important thing would be to preserve the language by its study and by gathering the floating material which is on the way to passing into oblivion.

I trust that the leaders of the Chakma community in Bengal and elsewhere will pay serious attention to this matter and find out ways and means to keep up a study of their language which is unique among the dialects of Bengali for some of its intrinsic characters and qualities.

(Suniti Kumar Chatterji)?

Emeritus Professor of Comparative Philology, University of Calcutta? Ex-Chairman, West Bengal Legislative Council and National Professor of India in Humanities.

How beautiful our homeland Hill Chatal

Wondrous wonder: beautiful Hill Chatal
Enwrapped by surrounding hills
Over and beyond;
Shaped by river Karnaphuli:
Its turns and bends meandering
From valley to valley.

Valleys, peopled by those who till the land
Watered by those perennial mountain falls
Painting the hillsides green
Capturing the heart.

Hill Chatal: blessed with fruitful forest
And moving river, gliding in and out
Like a snake, yielding transport to
Earth-given products.

The surrounding hills are but
Demons bowing down to that
Sublime Peak: Chatal
Standing like a temple
Beckoning all to see its glory.

Sounds in the forest, sounds of the wild-Tiger,
elephant, deer, bird : the
ferocious and the benign, yet peace reigns they live in harmony.

Ever grateful to Kapti hydroelectric
Purposed on the vast river to
Accelerate development.
Here the engine boats move and
Fish dwell; giving rise to fish culture,
And varied trades move in
Intermingling in renewed lives
Enhancing modes of living.

Colonial rule broken, now comes progress
Speeding its way for men and women
Barriers pulled down, schools planted
Calling people to education
And technical perfection:
Doctors, engineers spring up
Taking their stand in this world.

(translated by R. Excelicia Cunville)

XXXXXXXXXXXXXXXXXXXXXXXXXXXXXXXXX

AURA of Power

Power - forceful power:
Wherein lies its reason?
This force called POWER
Attacking the weak
Crumbling the little
Yet with no defined shape
Unforeseen in its ways:

But, so willingly worshipped
In all its man-made forms:
Wealth, Authority,
Knowledge, Physique
And alas : Ferocity;
How they bow to it
With fear.

Look forth to the Jataka stories
Behold Buddha's life:

High moral principles
Kindness, compassion
Melt gruesome POWER
Love takes control
That is True Power.

xxxxxxxxxxxxxxxx

Somewhere, in eternity
The world was born
Etched as a playground
For its living beings:
Men, women, children
All playing their parts
Phases linked by intermezzos
A festival of varied people
Who simply go by.

Were there no attacks on life
No illness, no fightings within
The WORLD renamed PE
Life, people would still go by
Simply, calmly, eternally.

xxxxxxxxxxxxxxxxx

A world peace poem

Humans, proud: the highest of all creation
Attaining wisdom and knowledge untold
Nothing to stop them, barriers all broken
Conquering all, their pride unfolds.

Humans: ruling this world, taking their reign
Over all: animals, birds, illness, nature
Even darkness of night under their domain
Only death uncontrolled, they cannot shake its structure.

Human knowledge surpassing physics that destroys:
Cyclone, earthquake, tsunami, starvation,
Desiccated and removed, ignorance now is coy

While wisdom moves on, bringing more adoration.

New states they create, these wise people
Yet at some point they with each other battle
And along comes UNO playing its deified role
Pacifying, harmonising, uniting mankind from pole to pole.

(translated by R. Excelicia Cunville)

What is wisdom and its shape?

House of wisdom - human mind
Wealth of knowledge untold:
Where does it come from?
Who created the seed?
Wonder yet to be behold.

It lies asleep, but not for long
Awakening, it touches the senses
Sprightly waking some to light
But others still slumber
Under a cloud; they cannot shine.

Wisdom began with the world
Circling with time and space
Yet can widen its horizon —
through practice; Light gives Light -
no end; not so, Ignorance.

Ignorance, destroyer
Bringer of unreasonable fear
Blinding eyes from the Light:
No enlightenment, only destruction - the end of everything.

Nations fight
Can't see the Light
Behold the birth of United Nations
But still - no Peace, 'coz deep within
Ignorance, the destroyer still rules:

Leading to craving unsatisfied
Turning to unresolved struggling:

Husbands, wives, fathers, children
Cannot see eye to eye.
There is no freedom when bound to struggle

(translated by R. Excelicia Cunville)

3 RHYME

Behold the wedding celebration of Khuki Rani
Instruments fill the air with lilting melody
While Khoka adorns himself, ready to go and see
The scene around, and in her splendour - his bride Khu Ki Rani.

Like a doll sequenced with jewels glittering
Diamonds and pearls her neck, ears, wrists bedecking
Face lit up, and on her head a crown
Such beauty C'en in a princess ne'er was found.

Khoka will Khuki Rani in her new attire see
From head to foot so resplendent with beauty, she
Astounding beauty - that will hearts on fire set
Beauty so perfect - only matched by the flower bed.

As fireworks light up the sky
She lets out a satisfied sigh
As music fills the air around
Wordless she stands, her heart with joys abound

Art of Writing and Literaus

A language boundary comprising of Phonology (sound): Morphology (structure and form), Syntax (grammatical arrangement of words), orthography (the accepted way of spelling and spelling of words), Lexicography (the activities of writing standard was of words), Syntactic (arrangement of words) etc, Chakma language lacks in this field of work (Chriteria). A few only, have the knowledge of art of writing, which is considered a most powerful way to sharpen the mental saw on deep level of thoughts, feeling and ideas to understand effectively. So the society can not be called literate (when the art of writing becomes a matter of social possession, a society may be called literate). Looking briefly the society may have been literate one time but it is now facing a break (halt). Some institutions in the present world are most concerned with the indigenous languages and it has become the subject matter of study. Like Osaka University, Japan. Chakma language has been included in their study since 1964, and already published papers on it edited by Prof. Toshitaka Amano[13]. Clifford Geertz written in his book *The Interpretation of Cultures*: The most important, the linguistic study (and along with it, information theory and class logic) also defines its basic units, its constituent elements, not in terms of their common properties but their differences that is, by constructing them in pairs. Binary opposition - that dialectical chasm between plus and minus which computer technology has rendered the Lingua franca of modern sciences - forms the basis of savage thought as it does of language. And indeed it is this which makes them essentially a variant form of the some thing – Communication System. There is a bright ray of hope for Chakma language, as it has already been introduced in the schools upto class VII under the programme (SARVA SIKSHA) education for all in the Chakma District Council, (CADC) in Mizoram. Considering the enormous difficulties and disadvantages faced by the Chakmas in the southern part of Mizoram particularly during the uprising of Mizo insurgency in 1966, Government of India accorded self autonomy to a section of Chakmas independency in internal affairs of the community. In the earlier time they were in a very critical stage with no opportinity of education/ schooling that was a marval of contrivace with the rest Mizoram. Now, they are happy just as they were with no big ideas. Their greatest achievement of success to acquire a sustainable life with a job. It is swinging a balance of communal unity of a limited geographical area whose headquarter is at Kamalangar, in 1971 and since then many have made upward mobility. It has attracted the impulse of the Chakmas and they are now being uplifted in all fronts of progress compared to their counterparts who are also in Mizoram but outside the territorial area of the Autonomous

Chakma District (ACDC) under the general supervision of the State Government of Mizoram. There has been an impulse force of wind to keep Chakma indigenous language alive in literary works and on this line various institutions are engaged in bringing out magazines periodicals, etc. in Roman, Bengali and Chakma scripts in all Chakma concentrated area in India and Bangladesh.

Chakma, Tsakma, Tasak, Thek (Burm)

Sub-tribes	*Septs*
There are numerous septs among chakmas : 1. Chakma 2. Doingnak 3. Tungjainya Septs of the Chakma sub-tribe	Amu. Bamu, named after rivers Barbora Baruwa Batalya, a chisel Boga Borsege Bung Bungza Darjea Dawin Dhaona, he of the mended cloth Dhurjya, the wearer of *bhimraj* feathers Durjea Ichapocha, the eater of rotten shrimps Kala, a plantain tree Kengragati,[1] the giver of the big crab Khambe Khiongje Kura, named after rivers Kurjya, the idle one Kutua Larma Leba Loskra Molima, named after rivers.

Septs of the Chakma sub-tribe-*concluded*	Molima-Sege Phaksa Phe-dang-sirri Phedungsa Phema Pirabhanga, the fat man who broke the stool Poa Poma Rangyacelunya, the lover of shells or mother-of-pearl Ranyin Sadonga Sege Sekowa Shoalyia, the jester Theya
Septs of the Tungjainya sub-tribe	Toinya Uksarri Warggu, name of a river Aruyai, the man as thin as a skeleton Badal, a chisel Bangal, descended from a Bengali father Bhumar, he of high back ribs Bola, he whose family was as numerous as the wasps Dunya Fariansa, he who excelled in wickedness Gochalya, the strong man Icha, he who was too fond of shrimps Kachui, they who built their houses in a row Karua Lambacha Lulang,[1] the devil Millong Mongla Mo-u Ongyo Puma.

Chakma Alphabets

No.	Letter	Name	Sound
1.		Ka - Ji	Ka
2.		Chhuchangya - Ka	
3.		Kha - Khai	Kha
4.		Gujangya - Kha	
5.		Ga - nge	Ga
6.		Chandya - Ga	
7.		Gaha - ji	Gha
8.		Tindalya - Gha	
9.		Nga (free tongue This free tongue can't be expressed in Roman or Bengali Script	Nga // ua
10.		Chilan Nga	
11.		Ca - Lwon	Ca
12.		Didalya ca	
13.		Chha - Lin	Chha
14.		Mojara - Chha	
15.		Ja - gweri	Ja
16.		Dipadala - ja	
17.		Jha - Mainswi	Jha
18.		Ura - Uri - Jha	
19.		Nya (touching tongue up)	Na
20.		Silachya Nya	
21.		Ta - than - lung - chit	Ta
22.		Diya - dyat - ta	
23.		Tha - wan - be	Tha
24		Funda - diyal - tha	
25.		D/r-yan-kouk (did)	Da
26.		Adu - vanga - D/r	

No.	Letter	Name	Sound
27.		Dh/rh- ri - mook (aspiratd)	Dha
28.		Lej-Vharat - Dh/rh	
29.		Na - jii	Na
30.		Petuwa - Na	
31.		Ta - wam - pu	Ta
32.		Gha - nga - dat - ta	
33.		Tha - sun - thoo	Tha
34.		Ga - ga- dat - tha	
35.		Da - Daw - e	Da
36.		Do-lo-nit-da	
37.		Dha - oo - chit	Dha
38.		Tal - muwat - dha	
39.		Na - ng - ye	Na
40.		Fur - Banya - Na	
41.		Pa - Chuk	Pa
42.		Palya - pa	
43.		Fa - wo - thwok	Fa
44.		Ubar - fundya - fa	
45.		Ba - la - chit	Ba
46.		Ubar - muya - ba	
47.		Va - Kwon	Va
48.		Cherdalya - va	
49.		Ma	Ma
50.		Bugat Padala - Ma	
51.		Ya	Za/ya
52.		Jilya ya	
53.		Rakawk	Ra
54.		Didajya Ra	

No.	Letter	Name	Group
55.		La	La
56.		Talmuya La	
57.		Wa	Wa/sa
58.		Bhajunya wa	
		TS (Tongue pressed by both tooth) Namo Tsya	Sa
		Bhudi Bukya TS	
		Ha	Ha
		Ubar Muya - ha	
		Laggi	Special words sounds
		(Pet phada hla)	
		Ah	
		Dimajya Ah' 	
		(Bi-i-i)	
		(Dhumka Sound)	

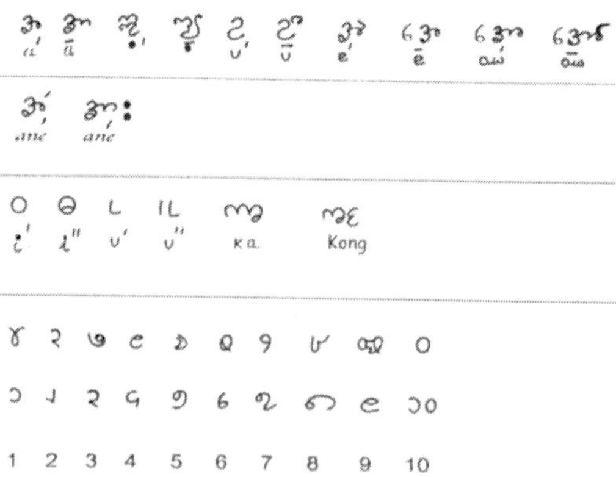

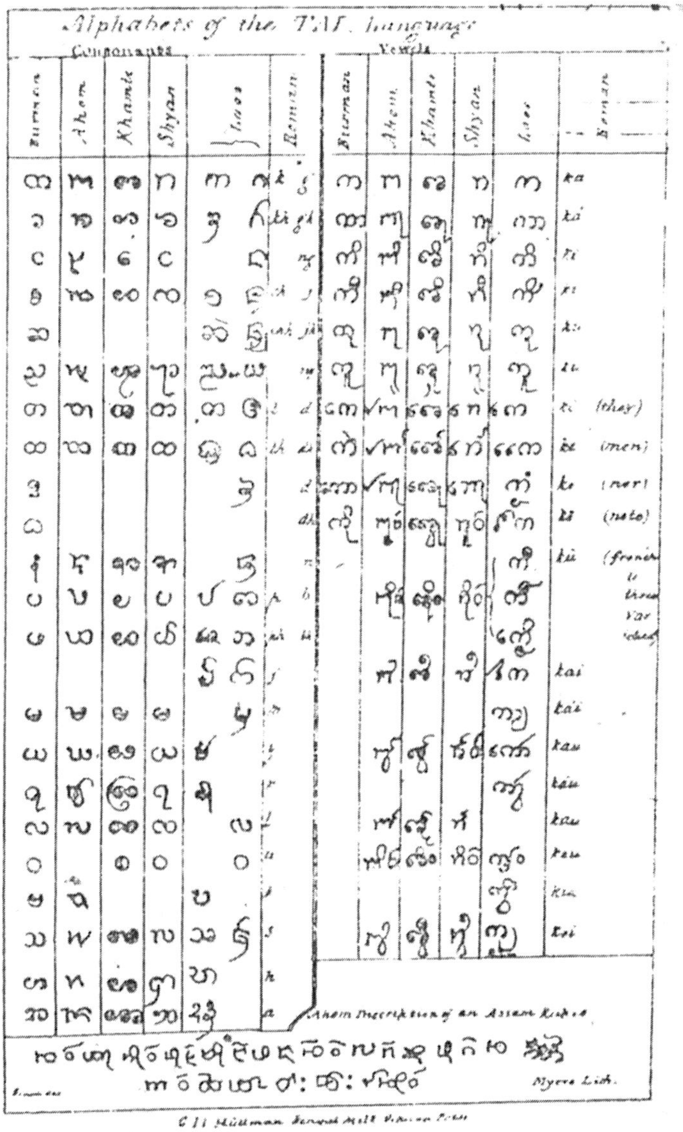
Alphabets of the TAI language
Consonants
Vowels
Burman
Ahom
Khamti
Shyan
Laos
Roman
(they)
(men)
Myers Lith.

CHAKMA RAJ

Religious Places

Karatoya : Old river of eastern Bengal and Assam, which rises in the Baikuntpur jungle in the estreme north-west of Jalpaiguri district in 26°51′N and 88°28′E and meanders through Rangpur until after a course of 214 miles, it joins the stalhalia in the south of Bogra district in 24°38′N and 89°29′E. The united stream is known as the Phuljhur and it eventealy finds its way into the Jamuna. The Karatoya bore in ancient times, as we learn from the Purana's, a high character for sanctity and its mermaid goddess, whose image has been found among the reins of Mahasthan, was widely worshipped and this place to even now a favourite place of pilgrimage. The river is mentioned in the Jogin Tantra as the western boundary of the ancient kingdom of Kamarupa, which it separated from Pundra or Paundravardhana, the country of Pods whose capital was Mahasthan. It was along its right bank that Mukhammed-i-Bakhtyar Khilji, the Muhammadan conquerer of Bengal marehed upon his ill fated invasion of Tibet in 1205, and in the narrative of that expedition the Karatoya is described as being three times of the width of the Ganges. It was no doubt the great river crossed by Hiuen Tsiang on his way to Kamarupa in the seventh century and by Ala-ud-din Husain on his invasion of the country in 1498.

(Imperial Gazetteer of India Vol. XV, p. 24)

Brahmi Script: *(An extract from The Origin of Brahmi Script)* "The origin of Brahmi script is one of the most hotly debated questions of ancient Indian history. The Brahmi script are India's own script. Did the Indian of pre-Asokan time know the art of writing? It was presumed that the script which was known to the Indians of the pre-Asokan time was the earlier form of Asokan Brahmi. The question of the antiquity of Brahmi and antiquity of the knowledge of the art of writing in India is important. In the Vedic times Aryans knew the art of writing the script must have been

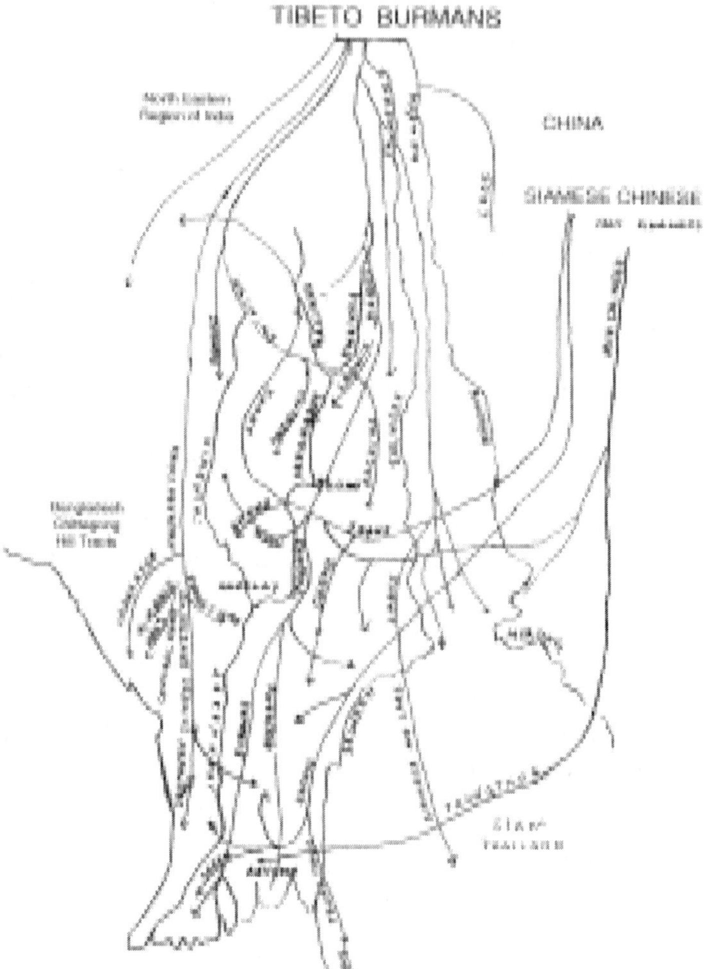

MAP
SHOWING THE COURSE OF
THE MAIN IMMIGRATION OF
TIBETO BURMAN

WAVES INTO MYANMAR, CHT
AND NORTH EAST INDIA

an earlier form of Ashokan Brahmi. But that may not be true. The knowledge of art of writing to only a few can not entitle that society to be called literate. When the art of writing became a matter of social expression a society could be called literate. The Tibetan society was certainly literate in the age preceding the accession of Strong-Tsen-Gampo (first half of the 7th century AD) through, because of their contacts with China and India.

Greek Script: The Tibetans must have been aware of the idea of writing and a few of them might have also learned the script of their neighbours. Such a possibility can't be ruled out in the case of India of the pre-Mauryan and early Mauryan periods also, at least with regard to knowledge of the Greek script. The Indians of Gangetic valley were in close contact with the Greeks and the people of Gandhara, etc. at least since the conquest of Chandragupta Maurya. Now, if Chandragupta Maurya married the daughter of Selucas and Bimbisara was her son Asoka as well as his father might have learned the Greek alphabets from the Greek lady or even from Megasthenes. Therefore theoretically it is quite possible that the message which Bindusara is said to have sent to the contemporary Greek rulers were in Greek language or script. But such instances can not prove the prevalence of Greek language or script among the educated Indians much less in the society in general. But it can not prove the existence of pre-Ashokan form of Brahmi while none of our sources indicate the existence of this particular script in the pre-Ashokan period. We observe that in the Vedic and the early Buddhist period all the religious and non-religious literature including the indices was kept only in memory. That is why Vedas designated as Sruti, the learned were called Bahusutra. Only Mukhastha Vidya was held in esteem and when writing came in to use the manuscripts were designated as Sarasvatimukha. It may also be regarded as significant that in the Vedic religion, which had such a large pantheon, there was no god of writing. Sarasvati was the Goddess of only speech in this period".

Culture, Belief, Society and Social Mind

Being human is becoming individual and we become individual under the guidance of cultural patterns, historically created system of meaning in terms of which we give form, order-point and direction to our lives. The guiding principle of society like lives containing their own interpretation. So, culture is providing some rituals that are coming down historically in a society. As Clifford Geertz writes, culture is generated in the womb of nature as men in the belly of women. In worlds everything is transient - growing and decaying. Everything in this world is relative, change with respect of time and place. So in the holistic world we go through life, we can only see the 'shadow' of truth, the fact figure remain unknown. Human beings are integrated in nature. If he does not use his reason or intelligence for truth and knowledge, he becomes an animal. Going back to history, the finding leads us to believe that the migrants from Central Asia into India are known as Scythian (Indo-Scythian). A group of them is known to be Saka in which Sakyamuni Buddha (Gautama) was born. Chakmas are blood related with Saka. Saka (Chak) in which Burmans (Burmese, Arakanis, Mayanmars) are the blood brothers. According to Friedrich Miller and other German ethnologist Chakmas belong to Lohitic (Tibeto-Burman) group because of their association with Tsangpho (Brahamaputra) River on the bank of which they must have lived at one time in the olden days.

Social Customs

There are still many social customs common of Tai-Shans people like Khamti, Ahoms with Chakmas like marriage solemnized with sacrifices of fowls and pigs called

Chumulong in Chakma and *Chaklong* in Ahoms and Khamtis Tai races. In their social mind they thrieve relationship of people of South Asian region they have believe in *F* (evil sprit) and purifying from such misfortunes through some ceremonies call *Burpara* which is performed by village clergy. In the social cultural festival of Chakmas and Tai-Shans people there is a ceremonial festival call Biju in Chakma and Bihu in Tai-Shans people of Assam. The Biju festival is the biggest culture festivity of Chakmas which is celebrated on the first three days; last day of the year and the first two days of Baisak (new year of Bengali calendar in the month of April every year. It is celebrated with pomp and show by all groups small, young, old men and women. They decorate their houses according to their resourcefulness with scented perfumes in all homely items prepared by them on that occasion. The guests are received with warm welcome. The first day is called Phool-Bizu which dawned with a bath in the river or nearby water source. There is tradition of eating the *Bizu-gula* for children, *i.e.* to lend them to take bath and thereafter children visit door to door with basketful of corns to feed small and big animal. The next day is called *Mool-Bizu*. It is a combining of the ritual of looking after the welfare of elderly people in the community and seeking their blessings. This is most fascinating as women have more important role and the sprit of women lies in it. Apart from rituals mentioned here, other individual rites are also performed. For instance, young women are provided to put on Khadi (breast covering) thus being recognized to have attained full fledged youth. This day is celebrated as non-meat day with various vegetable items called *Pajan-toon*. There would be varieties of preparations of ethnic cakes (*Pithas*). In the olden days the festival was celebrated with a lot of hard liquors (*doo-chuni*) and sweet fermented liquor (*Jagara*). It seems it has passed by.

On the following day which is called *Gocheya-Pocheya-Bizu*, elderly people are given bath by the young and receive their blessings. Normally, all members of the family remain at home and make pujas (prayers) to the Buddha and Bhikkhus in the temples. The pious men and women spend the days and night during the festival in the temples to edify themselves by observing eight precepts (*Asta sila*). In this eightfold path you will develop right understanding that will lead you to samadhi. Chakma women are an entity in itself in their traditional dress/costumes. The hand woven textile making being followed traditionally which symbolizes their culture. Women drape in their own home woven textile dress - the lower part which covers from hip joint (waist) to the bottom of the ankle is called Pinon and the breast covering cloth is called Khadi. Different herbs are used for dying the looms (yarn) with amazing colours. A variegated combination-black (caution and careful), blue (confidence), red (wisdom, emotional view) on the body and body part and at the edge, a potent mixture of five colours (see at the photo at annexure). The tribal weaving system has been written in details by Aratrik Dev Burman, an expert in Fashion technology[1]. Chakma women are fond of ornaments[2] whose list is given below :

1. Nak Phul - Nose ornament
2. Kan Phul - Ear ornament
3. Bala Banguri - Wrist ornament
4. Taj-jur - Arm ornament
5. Thengat Kharu - Ankle ornament
6. Ajali - Neck ornament
7. Tenga-chara - Necklace with silver coins.

These are all made of silver getting depleted in the modern era. The central fact of Chakma culture comes down from Buddhist faith, religious ceremonies, rituals where their identity lies, but women's physical being prevents them at times in joining as women are considered impure in Therovada Buddhism. Their apprehension of culture and behavior is primarily on Buddhist moral ethics of Dhamma with no gender classification. Buddhism has been the ongoing system in Sakyan Chakmas as in Tibetians but in Tibet most significantly the representation is in feminity like Avalokiteshvera, Manjusri and Tara. It has become purely optional in ones own belief according to his contentions. Some Therovadins are practicing Mahyanism and vice versa. This is the historical past of the last two thousand and five hundred fifty years. In the modern era of global society the Chakmas are getting interwoven in different situations in different parts of the world their common properties and common ties are being transformed.

Notes on the Weaving Tradition of North Eastern India

By Aratrik Dev Barman

The hand-woven textile traditions of the north eastern region of India strongly reflect it's culturally distinct tribal identity, and bear more similarity to textiles from South East Asia (in pattern, proportion and technique) than they do to textiles from mainland India.

Mostly wraps (breastcloths, head cloths or sarongs), the cloth is woven on a backstrap loom, one of the earliest loom technologies known to man. The warp is laid out between two bamboo sticks horizontal and parallel to each other. One of these sticks is fastened to a pole, tree or a window grill, while the other is attached to a belt that is worn by the weaver around her back while seated on the ground. The weaver leans back far enough to keep the threads taut, and controls the tension of the warp by bending forwards or backwards while weaving. This loom is also called a body tension loom or a loin loom.

Though primitive, the backstrap loom is significant in this region because it is perfectly suited to the tribal way of life, and is a symbol of the people's efforts to remain self sufficient. It is light, mobile and can be installed anywhere.

Made out of bamboo and wood that is locally available, it costs little and can be rolled and stored away compactly when not in use.

The earliest textiles woven on these looms were made from handspun cotton and were coloured using natural pigments made from plants, minerals and insects found in the environment. They were always woven in strips that ranged from 5 inches to approximately 22 inches, which is a distinctive feature of the loin loom. Larger cloths were achieved by joining two or more strips together. Today, acrylic is the material of preference as it is cheaper, stronger and affords a very bright palette of colours not found in cotton.

Most pieces are clearly structured in composition with carefully proportioned border. Weaving on the backstrap loop results in fabric that tends to be warp dominated and fairly compact. As a result, bold striped patterns running in the direction of the warp are a common feature. These stripes are often interspersed with small motifs or horizontal weft patterns woven using the supplementary weft technique. Inter regional influences have resulted in a great diversity of colour and pattern, and there exists a profusion of motifs including human figures, abstract geometric shapes, flowers, birds, animals and monsters etc. equally beautiful are the plain dyed pieces with very narrow borders in a contrast colour used for everyday clothing.

Examining these textiles closely would reveal their significance in several ways. As bearers of an identity code, each tribe had their own distinct set of colours and motifs which could denote the age or marital status of the wearer. Very often, these textiles assumed roles of heirloom objects that were passed on from one generation to the next. They were given as gifts to consolidate allegiances and social relations. Silk as a material was introduced a means for the nobility to establish their standing in the social hierarchy.

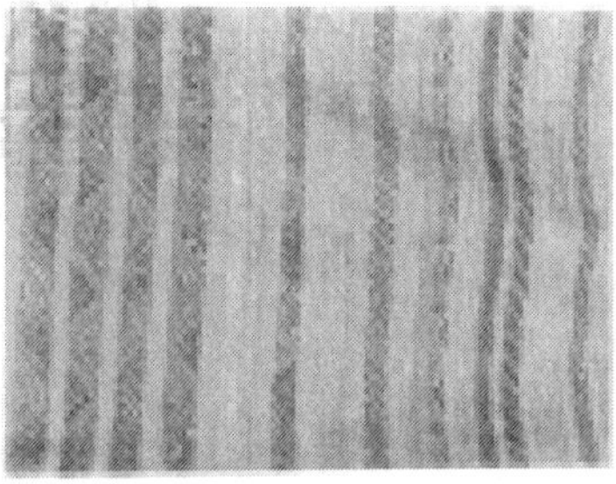

Weaving in tribal societies remains exclusively a woman's activity. Tribal textiles were rarely bartered or sold. The women wove to meet the needs of their families and skills were passed on from mother to daughter. A history of no organized trade perhaps explains why, even today, there is no system that helps weavers reach wider markets.

References

1. Chakma alphabets.
2. Alphabets of the Tai language akinness in curvic style and forms.
3. A note of Suniti Kumar Chatterjee, National Professor of India in Humanities on Chakma Language.
4. A note of Nalinakhsha Dutta on Chakma Language.

5-11. English translation of Bengali poem, lyric Rhyme written by a most estimable Chakma poet

Pran Hari Talukder (*a*) "How Beautiful Our Hill Chatan, (*b*) Power, (*c*) Simply Go Bye, (*d*) A World Peace, (*e*) What is Wisdom and its Shape? (*f*) Rhyme.

Original Bangali hand writing adjoined.

A piece of writing (monograph) in Chakma script by Kamal Mukhi Talukder mother of captain (Dr.) Pramode Bikash Talukder (1880 AD) adjoined.

12. The Hill Men of CHT, Osaka University, 1964.
13. Wearing tradition of N.E. India by Aritrik Dev Arman.

5

The Holocaust of Human Rights

Introduction

On 10 December 1948, the General Assembly of the United Nations adopted and proclaimed the Universal Declaration of Human Rights, the full text of which appears in the following pages. Following this historic act, the Assembly called upon all Member countries to publicize the text of the Declaration and "to cause it to be disseminated, displayed, read and expounded principally in schools and other educational institutions, without distinction based on the political status of countries or territories".

Kofi Annan

SECRETARY-GENERAL

All human beings are born with equal and inalienable rights and fundamental freedoms.

The United Nations is committed to upholding, promoting and protecting the human rights of every individual. This commitment stems from the United Nations Charter, which reaffirms the faith of the peoples of the world in fundamental human rights and in the dignity and worth of the human person.

In the Universal Declaration of Human Rights, the United Nations has stated in clear and simple terms the rights which belong equally to every person.

These rights belong to you.

They are your rights.

Familiarize yourself with them. Help to promote and defend them for yourself as well as for your fellow human beings.

Universal Declaration of Human Rights

Preamble

Whereas recognition of the inherent dignity and of the equal and inalienable rights of all members of the human family is the foundation of freedom, justice and peace in the world,

Whereas disregard and contempt for human rights have resulted in barbarous acts which have outraged the conscience of mankind, and the advent of a world in which human beings shall enjoy freedom of speech and belief and freedom from fear and want has been proclaimed as the highest aspiration of the common people,

Whereas: it is essential, if man is not to be compelled to have recourse, as a last resort, to rebellion against tyranny and oppression, that human rights should be protected by the rule of law,

Whereas it is essential to promote the development of friendly relations between nations,

Whereas the peoples of the United Nations have in the Charter reaffirmed their faith in fundamental human rights, in the dignity and worth of the human person and in the equal rights of men and women and have determined to promote social progress and better standards of life in larger freedom,

Whereas Member States have pledged themselves to achieve, in co-operation with the United Nations, the promotion of universal respect for and observance of human rights and fundamental freedoms,

Whereas a common understanding of these rights and freedoms is of the greatest importance for the full realization of this pledge,

Now, Therefore,

THE GENERAL ASSEMBLY

proclaims

THIS UNIVERSAL DECLARATION OF HUMAN RIGHTS

As a common standard of achievement for all peoples and all nations, to the end that every individual and every organ of society, keeping this Declaration constantly in mind, shall strive by teaching and education to promote respect for these rights and freedoms and by progressive measures, national and international, to secure their universal and effective recognition and observance, both among the peoples of Member States themselves and among the peoples of territories under their jurisdiction.

Article 1

All human beings are born free and equal in dignity and rights. They are endowed with reason and conscience and should act towards one another in a spirit of brotherhood.

Article 2

Everyone is entitled to all the rights and freedoms set forth in this Declaration, without distinction of any kind, such as race, colour, sex, language, religion, political or other opinion, national or social origin, property, birth or other status.

Furthermore, no distinction shall be made on the basis of the political, jurisdictional or international status of the country or territory to which a person belongs, whether it be independent, trust, non-selfgoverning or under any other limitation of sovereignty.

Article 3

Everyone has the right to life, liberty and security of person.

Article 4

No one shall be held in slavery or servitude; slavery and the slave trade shall be prohibited in all their forms.

Article 5

No one shall be subjected to torture or to cruel, inhuman or degrading treatment or punishment.

Article 6

Everyone has the right to recognition everywhere as a person before the law.

Article 7

All are equal before the law and are entitled without any discrimination to equal protection of the law. All are entitled to equal protection against any discrimination in violation of this Declaration and against any incitement to such discrimination.

Article 8

Everyone has the right to an effective remedy by the competent national tribunals for acts violating the fundamental rights granted him by the constitution or by law.

Article 9

No one shall be subjected to arbitrary arrest, detention or exile.

Article 10

Everyone is entitled in full equality to a fair and public hearing by an independent and impartial tribunal, in the determination of his rights and obligations and of any criminal charge against him.

Article 11

(1) Everyone charged with a penal offence has the right to be presumed innocent until proved guilty according to law in a public trial at which he has had all the guarantees necessary for his defence.

(2) No one shall be held guilty of any penal offence on account of any act or omission which did not constitute a penal offence, under national or international law, at the time when it was committed. Nor shall a heavier penalty be imposed than the one that was applicable at the time the penal offence was committed.

Article 12

No one shall be subjected to arbitrary interference with his privacy, family, home or correspondence, nor to attacks upon his honour and reputation. Everyone has the right to the protection of the law against such interference or attacks.

Article 13

(1) Everyone has the right to freedom of movement and residence within the borders of each State.

(2) Everyone has the right to leave any country, including his own, and to return to his country.

Article 14

(1) Everyone has the right to seek and to enjoy in other countries asylum from persecution.

(2) This right may not be invoked in the case of prosecutions genuinely arising from non-political crimes or from acts contrary to the purposes and principles of the United Nations.

Article 15

(1) Everyone has the right to a nationality.

(2) No one shall be arbitrarily deprived of his nationality nor denied the right to change his nationality.

Article 16

(1) Men and women of full age, without any limitation due to race, nationality or religion, have the right to marry and to found a family. They are entitled to equal rights as to marriage, during marriage and at its dissolution.

(2) Marriage shall be entered into only with the free and full consent of the intending spouses.

(3) The family is the natural and fundamental group unit of society and is entitled to protection by society and the State.

Article 17

(1) Everyone has the right to own property alone as well as in association with others.

(2) No one shall be arbitrarily deprived of his property.

Article 18

Everyone has the right to freedom of thought, conscience and religion; this right includes freedom to change his religion or belief, and freedom, either alone or in community with others and in public or private, to manifest his religion or belief in teaching, practice, worship and observance.

Article 19

Everyone has the right to freedom of opinion and expression; this right includes freedom to hold opinions without interference and to seek, receive and impart information and ideas through any media and regardless of frontiers.

Article 20

(1) Everyone has the right to freedom of peaceful assembly and association.

(2) No one may be compelled to belong to an associa-tion.

Article 21

(1) Everyone has the right to take part in the government of his country, directly or through freely chosen representatives.

(2) Everyone has the right of equal access to public service in his country.

(3) The will of the people shall be the basis of the authority of government; this will shall be expressed in periodic and genuine elections which shall be by universal and equal suffrage and shall be held by secret vote or by equivalent free voting procedures.

Article 22

Everyone, as a member of society, has the right to social security and is entitled to realization, through national effort and international co-operation and in accordance with the organization and resources of each State, of the economic, social and cultural rights indispensable for his dignity and the free development of his personality.

Article 23

(1) Everyone has the right to work, to free choice of employment, to just and favourable conditions of work and to protection against unemployment.

(2) Everyone, without any discrimination, has the right to equal pay for equal work.

(3) Everyone who works has the right to just and favourable remuneration ensuring for himself and his family an existence worthy of human dignity, and supplemented, if necessary, by other means of social protection.

(4) Everyone has the right to form and to join trade unions for the protection of his interests.

Article 24

Everyone has the right to rest and leisure, including reasonable limitation of working hours and periodic holidays with pay.

Article 25

(1) Everyone has the right to a standard of living adequate for the health and well-being of himself and of his family, including food, clothing, housing and medical care and necessary social services, and the right to security in the event of unemployment, sickness, disability, widowhood, old age or other lack of livelihood in circumstances beyond his control.

(2) Motherhood and childhood are entitled to special care and assistance. All children, whether born in or out of wedlock, shall enjoy the same social protection.

Article 26

(1) Everyone has the right to education. Education shall be free, at least in the elementary and fundamental stages. Elementary education shall be compulsory. Technical and professional education shall be made generally available and higher education shall be equally accessible to all on the basis of merit.

(2) Education shall be directed to the full development of the human personality and to the strengthening of respect for human rights and fundamental freedoms. It shall promote understanding, tolerance and friendship among all nations, racial or religious groups, and shall further the activities of the United Nations for the maintenance of peace.

(3) Parents have a prior right to choose the kind of education that shall be given to their children.

Article 27

(1) Everyone has the right freely to participate in the cultural life of the community, to enjoy the arts and to share in scientific advancement and its benefits.

(2) Everyone has the right to the protection of the moral and material interests resulting from any scientific, literary or artistic production of which he is the author.

Article 28

Everyone is entitled to a social and international order in which the rights and freedoms set forth in this Declaration can be fully realized.

Article 29

(1) Everyone has duties to the community in which alone the free and full development of his personality is possible.

(2) In the exercise of his rights and freedoms, everyone shall be subject only to such limitations as are determined by law solely for the purpose of securing due recognition and respect for the rights and freedoms of others and of meeting the just requirements of morality, public order and the general welfare in a democratic society.

(3) These rights and freedoms may in no case be exercised contrary to the purposes and principles of the United Nations.

Article 30

Nothing in this Declaration may be interpreted as implying for any State, group or person any right to engage in any activity or to perform any act aimed at the destruction of any of the rights and freedoms set forth herein.

SWARAJ KAUSHAL
MEMBER OF PARLIMANET
RAJYA SABHA

8 Safdarjung Lane
New Delhi-110011
July 15 2003
Shri L.K. Advani
Deputy Prime Minister
Government of India
New Delhi

Respected Advaniji

I am pained to write that Arunachal Pradesh Government has served eviction notices on Chakmas. A report in the Hindustan Times dated 8th July 2003 also confirms this.

Chakma is a long story of sufferings. They are striving for survival of their identity between Islamic fundamentalism and Christian missionaries campaign for conversion. Sir, Chakmas are refugees not by choice. They are victims of partition because our leaders exchanged Chittagong Hill Tract for Ferozpur. While all others have been rehabilitated Chakmas continue to be refugees in their own country.

Today the world has woken up to the Chakma cause. Can we not give them a permanent home in their own country?

Chakmas have struggled for hundreds of years. They fought the British during freedom movement. They stood by the country in our fight against insurgency. This is the least that we can do for them.

Sir, while you ask the Arunachal government to withdraw the eviction notices on the Chakmas, I request the Government of India to undertake a comprehensive programme for rehabilitation of the Chakmas in the country. It is humanitarian cause and our national responsibility.

Profound regards

Swaraj Kaushal MP

swarajkaushal@hotmail.com

Subsequent to the clauses of the NHRC mentioned above a Public Interest Petition was filed by the

NHRC in 1995 details of which follow in the pages ahead.

IN THE SUPREME COURT OF INDIA

ORIGINAL CIVIL JURISDICTION

WRIT PETITION (CIVIL) NO. 720 OF 1995

National Human Rights Commission........Petitioner

Versus

State of Arunachal Pradesh and Anr........Respondents

JUDGMENT

AHMADI, CJI

This public interest petition, being a writ petition under Article 32 of the Constitution, has been filed by the National Human Rights Commission (hereinafter called "NHRC") and seeks to enforce the rights, under Article 21 of the Constitution, of about 65,000 Chakma/Hajong tribals (hereinafter called "Chakmas"). It is alleged that these Chakmas, settled mainly in the State of Arunachal Pradesh, are being persecuted by sections of the citizens of Arunachal Pradesh. The first respondent is the state of Arunachal Pradesh and the second respondent is the Union of India.

The NHRC has been set up under the Protection of Human Rights Act, 1993 (No. 10 of 1994). Section 18 of this Act empowers the NHRC to approach this Court in appropriate cases.

The factual matrix of the case may now be referred to. A large number of Chakmas from erstwhile East Pakistan (now Bangladesh) were displaced by the Kaptai Hydel Power project in 1964. They had taken shelter in Assam and Tripura. Most of them were settled in these States and became Indian citizens in due course of time. Since a large number of refugees had taken shelter in Assam, the State government had expressed its inability to rehabilitate all of them and requested assistance in this regard from certain other States. Thereafter, in consultation with the erstwhile NEFA administration (North East Frontier Agency—now Arunachal Pradesh), about 4,012 Chakmas were settled in parts of NEFA. They were also allotted some land in consultation with local tribals. The Government of India had also sanctioned rehabilitation assistance Rs. 4,200/- per family. The present population of Chakmas in Arunachal Pradesh is estimated to be around 65,000.

The issue of conferring citizenship on the Chakmas was considered by the second respondent from time to time. The Minister of State for Home Affairs has on several occasions expressed the intention of the Arunachal Pradesh Students Union (hereinafter called "AAPSU") had issued "quit notices" to all alleged foreigners, including the Chakmas, to leave the State by September 30, 1995. The AAPSU had threatened to use force if its demand was not acceded to. The matter was treated as a formal complaint by the NHRC and on October 28, 1994, it issued notices to the first and the second respondents calling for their reports on the issue.

On November 22, 1994, the Ministry of Home Affairs sent a note to the petitioner reaffirming its intention of granting citizenship to the Chakmas. It also pointed out that Central Reserve Forces had been deployed in response to the threat of the AAPSU and that the State Administration had been directed to ensure the protection of the Chakmas. On December 7, 1994, the NHRC directed the first and second respondents to appraise it of the steps taken to protect the Chakmas. This direction was ignored till September, 1995 despite the sending of reminders. On September 25, 1995, the first respondent filed an interim reply and asked for time of four weeks' duration to file a supplementary report. The first respondent did not, however, comply with its own deadline.

On October 12, 1995 and again on October 28, 1995 the

CCRC sent urgent petitions to the NHRC alleging immediate threats to the lives of the Chakmas. On October 29, 1995, the NHRC recorded a *prima facie* second respondent in this regard. Groups of Chakmas have represented to the petitioner that they have made representations for the grant of citizenship under Section 5(1)(a) of the Citizenship Act, 1955 (hereinafter called "The Act") before their local Deputy Commissioners but no decision has been communicated to them. In recent years relations between citizens of Arunachal Pradesh and the Chakmas have deteriorated, and the latter have complained that they are being subjected to repressive measures with a view to forcibly expelling them from the State of Arunachal Pradesh.

On September 9, 1994, the People's Union for Civil Liberties, Delhi brought this issue to the attention of the NHRC which issued letters to the Chief Secretary, Arunachal Pradesh and the Home Secretary, Government of India making enquiries in this regard. On September 30, 1994, the Chief Secretary of Arunachal Pradesh faxed a reply stating that the situation was totally under control and adequate police protection had been given to the Chakmas.

On October 15, 1994, the Committee for Citizenship Rights of the Chakmas (hereinafter called "The CCRC") filed a representation with the NHRC complaining of the persecution of the Chakmas. The petition contained a press report carried in "The Telegraph" dated August 20 1994 stating that the All conclusion that the officers of the first respondent were acting in coordination with the AAPSU with a view to expelling the Chakmas from the State of Arunachal Pradesh. The NHRC stated that since the first respondent was delaying the matter, and since it had doubts as to whether its own efforts would be sufficient to sustain the Chakmas in their own habitat, it had decided to approach this court to seek appropriate reliefs.

On November 2, 1995, this Court issued an interim order directing the first respondent to ensure that the Chakmas situated in its territory are not ousted by any coercive action, not in accordance with law.

We may now refer to the stance of the Union of India, the second respondent, on the issue. It has been pointed out that, in 1964, pursuant to extensive discussions between the Government of India and the NEFA administration. It was decided to send the Chakmas for the purposes of their resettlement to the territory of the present day Arunachal Pradesh. The Chakmas have been residing in Arunachal Pradesh for more than three decades, having developed closes social, religious and economic ties. To uproot them at this stage would be both impracticable and inhuman. Our attention has been drawn to a Joint Statement issued by the Prime Ministers of India and Bangladesh at New Delhi in February, 1972, pursuant to which the Union Government has conveyed to all the States concerned, it's decision to confer citizens on the Chakmas, in accordance with Section 5(1) (a) of the Act. The second respondent further states that the children of the Chakmas who were born in India prior to the amendment of the Act in 1987, would have legitimate claims to citizenship. According to the Union of India, the first respondent has been expressing reservations on this account. By not forwarding the applications submitted by the Chakmas along with their reports for grant of citizenship as required by Rule 9 of the Citizenship Rules, 1955, the officers of the first respondent are preventing the Union of India from considering the issue of citizenship of the Chakmas. We are further informed that the Union of India is actively considering the issue of citizenship and has recommended to the first respondent that it take all necessary steps for providing security to the Chakmas. To this end, central para-military forces have been made available for deployment in the strife-ridden areas. The Union Government favours a dialogue between the State Government, the Chakmas and all concerned within the state to amicably resolve the issue or granting citizenship to the Chakmas while also redressing the genuine grievances of the citizens of Arunachal Pradesh.

The first respondent, in its counter to the petition, has contended before us that the allegatations of violation of human rights are incorrect; that it has taken *bona fide* and sincere steps towards providing the Chakmas with basic amenities and has, to the best of its ability, protected their lives and properties. It is further contended that the issue of citizenship of the Chakmas has been conclusively determined by the decision of this Court in *State of Arunachal Pradesh* V. Khudram Chakma (1994 Supp. (1) SCC 615 – hereinafter called *"Khudiram' Chakma's case")*. It is therefore contended that since the Chakmas are foreigners, they are not entitled to the protection of fundamental rights except Article 21. This being so, the authorities may at any time, ask the Chakmas to move. They also have the right to ask the Chakmas to quit the state, if they so desire. According to the first respondent, having lost their case in this Court, the Chakmas have "raised a bogey of violation of human rights."

The first respondent has filed a counter to the stand taken by the Union of India. The first respondent denies that the Union of India had sent the CRPF Battalions of its own accord; according to it, they were sent pursuant to its letter dated 20.9.1994 asking for assistance. It has also denied that certain Chakmas were killed on account of economic blockades effected by the AAPSU; according to it, these casualties were the result of a malarial epidemic. The first respondent reiterates that the *sui generis* Constitutional position of the State debars it from permitting outsiders to be settled within its territory, that it has limited resources and that its economy is mainly dependent on the vagaries of nature; and that it has no financial resources to tend to the needs of the Chakmas having already spent approximately Rs. 100 crores on their upkeep. It has also been stated that the Union of India has refused to share its financial responsibility for the upkeep of the Chakmas.

Referring to the issue of grant of citizenship it is submitted as follows:

> "It is submitted that under the Citizenship Act, 1955 and the Rules made thereunder a specific procedure is provided for forwarding the application for grant of citizenship. According to that after receiving the application, the DC of the area makes necessary enquiries about the antecedents of the applicant and after getting a satisfactory report forwards the case to the State Government which in turn forwards it to the Central Government. It is submitted that on enquiry if the report is adverse the DC would not forward it further. It is submitted that the applications, if any, made in this regard have already been disposed of after necessary enquiry. There is no application pending before the DC."

It may be pointed out that this stand of the first respondent is in direct contravention of the stand adopted by it in the representation dated September 25, 1995, submitted by it to the NHRC where it had stated:

> "The question of grant of citizenship entirely governed by the Citizenship Act, 1955 and the Central Government is the sole authority to grant citizenship. The State Government has no jurisdiction in the matter."

It is further submitted by the first respondent that under the constitution, the State of Arunachal Pradesh enjoys a special status and, bearing in mind its ethnicity, it has been declared that it would be administered under part X of the Constitution. That is the reason why laws and regulations applicable during the British Regime continue to apply even today. The settlement of Chakmas in large numbers in the State would disturb its ethnic balance and destroy its culture and identity. The special provision made in the Constitution would be set at naught if the State's tribal population is allowed to be invaded by people from outside. The tribals, therefore, consider Chakmas as a potential threat to their tradition and culture and are therefore, keen that the latter do not entrench themselves in the State. Besides, the financial resources of the State without Central assistance, which is ordinarily not forthcoming, would throw a heavy burden on the State which it would find well nigh impossible to bear. In the circumstances, contends the first respondent, it is unfair and unconstitutional to throw the burden of such a large number of Chakmas on the State.

We are unable to accept the contention of the first respondent that no threat exists to the life and liberty of the Chakmas guaranteed by Article 21 of the Constitution, and that it has taken adequate steps to ensure the protection of the Chakmas. After handling the present matter for more than a year, the NHRC recorded a *prime facie* finding that the service of quit notices and their admitted enforcement appeared to be supported by the officers of the first respondent. The NHRC further held that the first respondent had, on the one hand, delayed the disposal of the matter by not furnishing the required response and had, on the other hand, sought to enforce the eviction of the Chakmas through its agencies. It is to be noted that, at no time, has the first respondent sought to condemn the activities of the AAPSU. However, the most damning facts against the first respondent are to be found in the counter affidavit of the second respondent. In the assessment of the Union of India, the threat posed by the AAPSU was grave enough to warrant the placing of two additional battalions of CRPF at the disposal of the State Administration. Whether it was done at the behest of the State Government or by the Union on its own is of no consequence; the fact that it had become necessary speaks for itself. The second respondent further notes that after the expiry of the deadline of October 30, 1994, the AAPSU and other tribal student organization continued to agitate and press for the expulsion of all foreigners including the Chakmas. It was reported that the AAPSU had started enforcing of economic blockades *the in refugee* camps, which adversely affected the supply of rations, medical and essential facilities, etc, to the Chakmas. Of course the State Government has denied the allegation, but the independent inquiry of the NHRC shows otherwise. The fact that the Chakmas were dying on account of the blockade for want of medicines is an established fact. After reports regarding lack of medical facilities and the spread of malaria and dysentery in Chakma settlements were received, the Union Government advised the first respondent to ensure normal supplies of essential commodities to the Chakma settlement. On September 20, 1995 the AAPSU, once again, issued an ultimatum citing December 31, 1995 as the fresh deadline for the ousting of Chakmas. This is yet another threat which the first respondent has not indicated how it proposes to counter.

It is, therefore, clear that there exists a clear and present danger to the lives and personal liberty of the Chakmas. In *Louis De Raedt v. Union of India* [(1991) 3 SCC 554] and *Khudiram Chakma's case t*his court, held that foreigners are entitled to the protection of Article 21 of the Constitution.

The contention of the first respondent that the ruling of this court in *Khudiram Chakma's* case foreclosed the consideration of the citizenship of Chakmas is misconceived. The facts of that case reveal that the appellant and 56 families migrated to India in 1965 from erstwhile East Pakistan and were lodged in the Government Refugee Camp at Ledo. They were later shifted to another camp at Miao. In 1966, the State Government drew up the Chakma Resettlement Scheme for refugees and the Chakmas were allotted lands in two villages. The appellant, however, strayed out and secured land in another area by private negotiations. The State questioned the legality of the said transaction since, under the Regulations then in force, no person other than a native of that District could acquire land in it. Since there were complaints against the appellant and others who had settled on this land, the State, by order dated February 15, 1984, directed that they shift to the area earmarked for them. This order was challenged on the ground that Chakmas who had settled there were citizens of India and by seeking their forcible eviction, the State was violating their fundamental rights and, in any case, the order was arbitrary and illegal as violative of the principles of natural justice. On the question of citizenship, they invoked Section 6-A of the Act which, inter alia, provides that all persons of Indiam origin who came before January 1, 1966 to Assam from territories included in Bangladesh immediately before the commencement of the citizenship (Amendment) Act, 1965, and who had been ordinarily resident in Assam since their entry into Assam shall be deemed to be citizens of India as from January 1, 1966. Others who had come to Assam after that date and before March 25, 1971, and had been ordinarily resident in Assam since then and had been detected to be foreigners, could register themselves. It will thus be seen that the appellant and others claimed citizenship under this special provision made pursuant to the Assam Accord. The High Court held that the appellant and others did not fall under the said category as they had stayed in Assam for a short period in 1964 and had strayed away therefrom in the area now within the State of Arunachal Pradesh. On appeal, this Court affirmed that view. It is, therefore, clear that in that case, the Court was required to consider the claim of citizenship based on the language of Section 6-A of the Act. Thus, in *Khudiram Chakma's case,* this court was seized of a matter where 57 Chakma families were seeking to challenge an order requiring them to vacate land bought by them in direct contravention of clause 7 of the Bengal Eastern Frontier Regulation, 1873. The issue of citizenship was raised in a narrower context and was limited to Section 6-A(2) of the Act. The Court observed that the Chakmas in that case, who were resident in Arunachal Pradesh, could not avail of the benefit of section 6A of the Act which is a special provision for the citizenship of persons covered by the Assam Accord. In the present case, Chakmas are seeking to obtain citizenship under Section 6(1)(a) of the Act, where the considerations are entirely different. That section provides for citizenship by registration. It says that the prescribed authority may, on receipt of an application in that behalf, register a person who is not a citizen of India, as a citizen of India if he/she satisfies the conditions set out therein. This provision is of general application and is not limited to persons belonging to a certain group only as in the case of Section 6-A. Section 5, therefore, can be invoked by persons who are not citizens of India but are seeking citizenship by registration. Such applications would have to be in the form prescribed by part II of the Citizenship Rules, 1956 (hereinafter called "The Rules"). Under Rule 7, such application has to be made to the Collector within whose jurisdiction the applicant is ordinarily resident. Rule 8 describes the authority to register a person as a citizens of India under Section 5(1) of the Act. It says that the authority to register a person as a citizen of India shall be an officer not below the rank of a Deputy Secretary to the Government of India in the Ministry of Home Affairs, and also includes such officer as the Central Government may, by a notification in the official Gazette, appoint and in any other case falling under the Rules, any officer not below the Rank of a Joint Secretary to the Government of India in the Ministry of Home Affairs, and also includes such other officer as the Central Government may, by notification in the official Gazette, appoint. Rule 9 next enjoins the collector to transmit every application received by him under Section 5(1)(a) to the Central Government through the State Government or the Union Territory administration, as the case may be, along with a report on matters set out in clauses (a) to (e) thereof. Rule 10 provides for issuance of a certificate to be granted to persons registered as citizens and Rules 11 and 12 provide for maintenance of registers. These are the relevant rules in regard to registration of persons as citizens of India.

From what we have said hereinbefore, there is no doubt that the Chakmas who migrated from East-Pakistan (now Bangladesh) in 1964, first settled down in the State of Assam and then shifted to areas which now fall within the

State of Arunachal Pradesh. They have settled there since the last about two and a half decades and have raised their families in the said State. Their children have married and they too have had children. Thus, a large number of them were born in the State itself. Now it is proposed to uproot them by force. The AAPSU has been giving out threats to forcibly drive them out to the neighbouring State which in turn is unwilling to accept them. The residents of the neighbouring State have also threatened to kill them if they try to enter their State. They are thus sandwiched between two forces, each pushing in opposite direction which can only hurt them. Faced with the prospect of annihilation the NHRC was moved, which, finding it impossible to extend protection to them, moved this court for certain reliefs.

By virtue of their long and prolonged stay in the State the Chakmas who migrated to, and those born in the State, seek citizenship under the Constitution read with Section 5 of the Act. We have already indicated earlier that if a person satisfies the requirements of Section 5 of the Act, he/she can be registered as a citizen of India. The procedure to be followed in processing such requests has been outlined in Part II of the Rules. We have adverted to the relevant rules hereinbefore. According the these rules, the application for registration has to be made in the prescribed form, duly affirmed, to the collector within whose jurisdiction he resides. After the application is so received, the authority to register a person as a citizen of India, is vested in the officer named under Rule 8 of the Rules. Under Rule 9, the Collector is expected to every application under section 5(1)(a) of the Act to transmit the Central Government. On a conjoint reading of Rules 8 and 9. It becomes clear that the Collector has merely to receive the application and forward it to the Central Government. It is only the authority constituted under Rule 8 which is empowered to register a persons as a citizens of India. It follows that only that authority can refuse to entertain an application made under Section 5 of the Act.

Yet it is an admitted fact that after receipt of the application, the Deputy Collector (DC) makes an enquiry and if the report is adverse, the DC refuses to forward the applications; in other words, he rejects the applications at the threshold and does not forward it to the Central Government. The grievance of the Central Government is that since the DC does not forward the applications, it is not in a position to take a decision whether or not to register the person as a citizen of India. That is why it is said that the DC or collector, who receives the application should be directed to forward the same to the Central government to enable it to decide the request on merits. It is abvious that by refusing to forward the applications of the Chakmas to the Central Government, the DC is failing in his duty and is also preventing the Central Government from performing its duty under the Act and the Rules.

We are country governed by the Rule of Law our constitution confers certain rights on every human being and certain other rights on citizens. Every person is entitled to equality before the law and equal protection of the laws. So also, no person can be deprived of his life or personal liberty except according to procedure established by law. Thus the State is bound to protect the life and liberty of every human-being, be he a citizen or otherwise, and it cannot permit any body or group of persons, *e.g.*, the AAPSU, to threaten the Chakmas to leave the State, failing which they would be forced to do so. No State Government worth the name can tolerate such threats by one group of persons to another group of persons; it is duty bound to protect the threatened group from such assaults and if it fails to do so, it will fail to perform its constitutional as well as statutory obligations. Those giving such threats would be liable to be dealt with in accordance with law. The State Government must act impartially and carry out its legal obligations to safeguard the life, health and well-inhibited by local politics. Besides, by refusing to forward their applications, the Chakmas are denied rights, constitutional and statutory, to be considered for being registered as citizens of India.

In view of the above, we allow this petition and direct the first and second respondents, by way of a writ of mandamus, as under:

(1) the first respondent the State of Arunachal Pradesh, shall ensure that the life and personal liberty of each and every Chakma residing within the State shall be protected and any attempt to forcibly evict or drive them out of the State by organized groups, such as the AAPSU, shall be repelled, if necessary by requisitioning the service of para-military or police force, and if additional forces are considered necessary to carry out this direction, the first respondent will request the second respondent, the Union of India, to provide such additional force, and the second respondent shall provide such additional force as in necessary to protect the lives and liberty of the Chakmas;

(2) except in accordance with law, the Chakmas shall not be evicted from their homes and shall not be denied domestic life and comfort therein;

(3) the quit notices and ultimatums issued by the AAPSU and any other groups which tantamount to threats to the life and liberty of each and every Chakma should be dealt with by the first respondent in accordance with law;

(4) the application made for registration as citizen of India by the Chakma or Chakmas under Section 5 of the Act, shall be entered in the register maintained for the purpose and shall be forwarded by the Collector or the DC who receives them under the relevant rule, with or without enquiry, as the case may be, to the Central Government for its consideration in accordance with law; even returned applications shall be called back or fresh ones shall

be obtained from the concerned persons and shall be processed and forwarded to the Central Government for consideration;

(5) while the application of any individual Chakma is pending consideration, the first respondent shall not evict or remove the concerned person from his occupation on the ground that he is not a citizen of India until the competent authority has taken a decision in that behalf; and

(6) the first respondent will pay to the petitioner cost of this petition which we quantify at Rs. 10,000/- within six weeks from today by depositing the same in the office of the NHRC New Delhi.

The petition shall stand so disposed of.

......................................CJI

....J.

(S.C. Sen)

New Delhi;

January 9, 1996

ELECTION COMMISION OF INDIA

No. 23/ARUN/2003 Dated: 03rd March, 2004

ORDER

The Government of India, during the period 1964-69, settled some Chakma refugees from Bangladesh in Arunachal Pradesh. Their population has increased manifold. The Committee for Citizenship Rights of the Chakmas has been demanding conferment of Indian citizenship status and enrolment of their names in the electoral rolls. The said Committee has taken the matter to the National Human Rights Commission and the Supreme Court of India. The Hon'ble Supreme Court vice order dated 09.01.1996 directed the Government of India and the State Government of Arunachal Pradesh to settle the issue imperiously and further directed inter alia that the State Government shall ensure that the life and personal liberty of each and every Chakma residing within the State of Arunachal Pradesh shall be protected and any attempt to forcibly eviction drive them out of the State by any organized group shall be repelled. In the mean time the High Court of Delhi Order dated 28.9.2000 held that such of the Chakmas who were born in India after their settlement in the State of Arunachal Pradesh but before 01-07-1997 became citizens of India by birth under section 3)1) (a) of the Citizenship Act even if their parents were not citizens of the time of their birth.

The Election Commission is concerned with the enrolment as electors purpose Chakmas who have acquired Indian citizenship by birth as aforesaid are who ordinarily resident in Arunachal Pradesh. Under the provisions of Article 325 of the Constitution read with section 19 of the Representation of the People Act, 1950 these Chakmas are constitutionally entitled to be registered as electors in the electoral rolls of the constituencies in which they are ordinanly resident in Arunachal Pradesh. These constituencies are 14 Dolmukh (ST), 46-Chowkham (ST), 49 Bordaamsa Diyam and 50 Miao (ST) assembly constituencies.

THE STATESMAN

Published Simultaneously from CALCUTTA and DELHI

JUNE 12, 1989

Vol. CXXIII No. 257680

VICTIMS OF PARTITION

Ironically, the first attempt made by the Bangladesh Government to grant a measure of autonomy to the Chakmas and other tribes of the Chittagong Hill Tracts has led to a worsening of the situation, with thousands of refugees once again pouring into India to escape persecution in their own homeland. The fresh influx has started in the wake of yet another round of killings and retaliatory attacks in which the Buddhist tribals and Bangladeshi settlers, who are Muslims,have been involved. The latest outbreak started with the murder of a settler who was chairman of a local committee, as well as seven others, said to be businessmen, in the Rangamati area. Blaming the underground tribal organization, the Shanti Bahini, for the attack, the settlers went on the rampage, killing seven tribals and injuring more than 50 others. Savage clashes of this kind have been a feature of the area ever since leaders like Sheikh Mujibur Rahman and General Ziaur Rahman encouraged Bangladeshis to move into the area so as to relieve the pressure on land erstwhile in the country and also, perhaps, to counter the threat of recession by tribals who had opted for India in 1947 and were pushed into erstwhile East Pakistan against their will.

Unlike its predecessors, the Ershad Government seems to have realized that the policy of harassing the Chakmas has to be changed, presumably because of the bad name Dhaka has been earning internationally because of the unending flow of refugees over the border. Apparently taking a leaf from India's Constitutional provision for setting up autonomous councils for ethnic minorities, the Bangladesh government prepared legislation to establish three such councils in the Chittagong Hill Tracts. But although the date for holding elections is drawing near there is no sign that the Chakmas have agreed to the government's plan. Even Dhaka's offer of amnesty to the Shanti Bahini does not seem to have been accepted.

Clearly, the long years of repression have made the Chakmas so bitter and mistrustful of the government that they are unwilling to believe that it may have undergone a change of heart. The recent bloodshed—the latest in a series of killings of tribals—must also have strengthened their misgivings. Nor, perhaps, are the tribals fully convinced that the proposed councils will protect their interests, given the Government's earlier blatant policy of persecution. Their fear apparently is that no matter what the law may prescribe, the gradual infiltration of people from elsewhere in the country will continue, and not only will their land be taken away from them but their distinctive way of life will also be under severe pressure. As it is, with more than 50,000 Chakmas living in refugee camps in Tripura, the future of the entire community on both sides of the border looks bleak, especially when a revival of the Hill Tract Regulations of 1900, which prohibited the entry of outsiders into the area, is now thought to be out of the question. For the hapless Buddhist tribals, caught in the cross-fire between two larger religious communities, the trauma of partition seems to be never-ending.

This was delivered by Sakya Talukdar at the annual conference, Amida Trust in London on April, 2003. The plight of the Chakmas a healing community.

INTRODUCTORY REMARKS

Distinguished participants and guests,

First of all, I must express my deep indebtedness to the Amida Community for their best efforts to bring me up at this workshop, without which I would not have been here in the midst of you. It gives me an abounding feeling of friendship of happiness to be with you all here. I thank you all for taking interest in this workshop.

The purpose of my coming over here is to present a picture of the present setting of the ardent ethnic Chakma Bhuddhist, in the North-East India in the background of their sanguinary disposition at their homeland, Chittagong Hill Tracts, since the partition of the Indian subcontinent in 1947. The continuous Govt. sponsored migration of plain Muslims to the Hill Tracts changed the demographic profile of CHT with 98% ethnic Buddhists to 50% at present. This was the origin of the history of their displacement and migration to India and their present condition/situation is still a very complex and precarious one. A paper 'The Plight of the Chakmas' is already in your hand. The truncated faltering history of Chakmas need no further elaboration.

The uprooted Chakmas are still struggling hard to stay afloat in life. There might come some opportune time/ moment for reviving them for greater cause in the future. The transience of everything is underlying core message in Buddhism. They hope to overcome this critical and crucial period sooner or later.

So, as with the time, there are people who have come up with various welfare programmes for improving the condition of the Chakmas who are badly off. The peoples group working on it is called "Friendly Society" with its headquarters at Guwahati, the gateway of the North-East India. Similarly, there is an organization by name "The Chakma Buddhist Foundation" with its headquarter at Bodhgaya, the world heritage centre, I know precisely, they are the parts of the whole who have initiated various welfare projects for the hapless ethnic Buddhists.

India's population (Religion wise)

Sl.No.	*Name*	*Percen-tage*	*In Million*	*In crore*
1.	Hindu	82%	820	82
2.	Muslim	12%	120	12
3.	Christian	2.5%	25	2.5
4.	Sikh	2.0%	20	2.0
5.	Buddhist+Jain+Others	1.5%	15	1.5
	Total	100%	1000	100

Note: The ethnic tribal Buddhist population (excluding Tibetan) in India is 0.5 million only.

The list of papers:

1. The plight of the Chakmas.
2. The other writings - 18 nos.
3. Friendly Society's present work

I hope this workshop will be worth of your notice. I thank you all from the core of my heart for having come to this workshop.

Sakya Talukdar

Annual conference (Amida Trust), April, 03, London.

The Plight of the Chakmas A healing community

By Sakya Talukdar

The Racial Name

In the 18th century, the British Colonial rule for the first time described the indigenous hill people in the Chittagong hill tracts by the term *'Chakma'*. But they (the indigenous hill people) keep calling themselves as *"Changma"*. The variant spelling (Chakma) has become the officially accepted term referring to the hill people of CHT and since then they have become well known by this term.

Where they Come From

Chittagong Hill Tracts (CHT) had provided a safe heaven to Chakmas by its own geography and natural set up. As knowledge goes, they were the earliest setters here.

Genealogically, they claim their origin from *"Sakya"* ancestry in which Gautam Buddha was born, in the kingdom called *"Champak Nagar"*. It has remained unidentified because there is more than one place by the name Champak Nagar both in India and Mayanmar. So the issue of their origin remained epigrammatic and it is wanting more in details. History has recorded that the *Sakya* clan was internally and externally displaced and uprooted from their original kingdom (Kipalavastu) and as well as their other kingdoms in the course of history. They took to eastward journey and established kingdoms one after another till reaching at Dinnyawadi and Babootong in Arakan Yoma bordering with CHT where Chakmas live. The English spelling of Chakma has different phonetics spelling in Myanmar language which is as *Tsakma* (*ts* is pronounced as *ch*). It is similar to the river spelling *Tsangpo* in Tibet which is known as Brahmaputra in India. A very akin group of people of Chakmas is living in Myanmar which is known to be *Doingnak* and *Tungjaingya*. According to some historian there are two groups of Chakmas one *Annakya* (those who had migrated to CHT from Myanmar) and two *Rowyangya* (those who remained in Arakan).

For many centuries the inhospitable mountain tracks from CHT to Arakan Yoma remained untraversed and remained unexposed and unknown to people. At that time people swamped along the mountain streams and reached the river *Matamuri* and established a kingdom at *Alikandam,* which is now in the Chittagong Division outside the Jurisdiction of CHT, bordering with *Arakan*. Under the pressure of the colonial British rule the Chakma Chief had to shift his head quarters at *Rangamati* inside CHT in 1860 AD. In their trail of long journey their knowledge of education became almost erased (their scripts are now a 'piece of item's for the museums!). In the absence of any written transcription, there is no knowledge of the ancient past. The Chakma's *Gengkhuli* singers (ballad singers) alight the glorious past of theirs through the songs, which are very popular among them.

The Chakmas are divided into 10 (ten) groups:

1. *"Phwa-ho"*
2. *"Tai-yo"*
3. *"Ang-ngu"*
4. *"Bor-ua"*
5. *"Bung-ngu"*
6. *"Zotia"*
7. *"Bu-se-ke"*
8. *"Undu"*
9. *"Talao"*
10. *"Ang-ngu"*

They are further divided into forty (40) sub-clans (*gajas*).

Present Habitation

CHT emerged as a majority Chakma inhabited land, the rest were also Mongoloid races of very akin tribe till the mid of 20th century. But they had sunk into deep despair after the Indian sub-continent got independence from the British in 1947. In the process of the creation of the separate nations for the Muslims and Hindus, the control over CHT got transferred to the Muslims. In the throes of this process many had fled or were driven away from CHT, and now many of them had taken shelter in the adjoining countries in India and Myanmar. The Chakmas, therefore, are bisected into three countries viz. Bangladesh, Myanmar and India which are religiously Islamic, Buddhist, and secular respectively. The Chakmas in India are committed to pluralism.

Racial Mark

It is worthy to note that a "Mongolian spot" (a deeply pigmented patch, commonly present in the sacral region) is noticed in the babies (on birth) of Chakma parents. The mark gradually disappears with age. They possess most of the characteristic marks associated with Mongoloids viz. a short medium size in structure with hairs often straight and yellowish in colour.

According to some historian, the Sakya clan belonged to the Mongolian race and presently a number of Mongolian groups in Nepal, Myanmar, Bangladesh and India claim to be from the Sakya clan. A research study is being carried out on the origin of human relationship among those who claim common heritage with the Sakya race. This hypothesis is being studied using genetic variation on Y-chromosome by the University College of London/University College London Hospital Committees on the ethics of Human Research

(Study number 99/0196).

Dress

The distinguished art of weaving on loin loom is an established Chakma woman's home learning skill. A woman is not seen to be suitable for a bride till she becomes skillful in weaving. In the rural Chakma society, the women exhibit lot of interested in weaving. Chakmas harvest cotton abundantly in their "*Jhums*" (primitive slash and burning method of cultivation), which help in a way to make them self reliant in their attires and other clothing viz. towels, bed sheets etc. The women dress is known by the name of "*Khadi*" and "*Penon*". It is the testifying evidence of the Chakma community which is artful with six colours (black, white, red, yellow, blue and green). A set of women's dress consists of three pieces viz. khadi (adult normal size 56 inch × 40 inch) for wrapping waist to the bottom of the toes. The name of their headgear is "*Khobong*", but it is no more in use.

Language

The Chakma alphabets (scripts) signify the imprint mark of its origin which is akin to Myanmar–Thai scripts. It seems there is no written literature in the Chakma language. The language was not standardized with syntax, phonology, grammar etc, until now. So it has been on its own is a Linguafranca. There are many intrinsic characters of words in the Chakma language which remained unexplained and unknown. The Chakmas had to forgo their language and script in favour of Bengali language which was at the time the court language under the British colonial rule.

They are now in the puzzling diversity of languages. The community which did not have any script before the coming of the British rule is now having the opportunity to take pride of their written languages mainly because of the earlier Christian missionaries. Thanks to the change of political fortunes of the Chakmas.

Women

Women are strong and equal partners to males in the Chakma society. They offer help to their male members in all indoor and outdoor household works, in tilling lands and rearing the domesticated animals. They are fond of wearing jewelry and ornaments. They are also decorative by nature. Out of superstition they do not eat together with the male members of the family. They feel it is their prerogative to see that male members are fed first before the women take their meal. The men have to pay price to the bride at the time of marriage.

Now talking about Chakma women, I remember an amazing Chinese philosophy : "yin and yang" (yin is the female principle, characterized as dark and negative, while yang the male principle, being light and positive). Such superstitions are prevalent among the women in the Chakma society and because of this they are not admitted in the monasticism. It seems *Theroveda Buddhist* in India has not yet admitted women in monkhood *as yet*. Therefore, though the Chakma women have yearning for the religious Buddhist life–on the path of Nirvana, they only get initiations to become a devotee with 8 fold path (precepts). They become bald headed and wear seamless white dress or yellow coloured dress and keep living in the monastery, if they wish to. But as the society (women world) is now pushing for greater opportunity for women, many hurdles of the past would perhaps soon be over in the case of Chakma women. Women are being treated equal to men even in spirituality.

Original Dwelling House

The Chakma houses are squarely built with bamboo with a "*machan*", a bamboo woven platform some six feet above the ground. They are usually built on the bend of a river near the streams or on the mountain valleys or hills slopes where there is abundance of water. The water networks used to be the life line for their movement from one house to another or from one village to another. The normal Chakma house is divided into compartments and the requirements of the married members of the family are the first to be attended to. In the event of several families living together the rooms are apportioned in order of seniority. For instance, in a family of in which three members are married, the house will be divided by mat walls into four compartments. The outer one is reserved for the unmarried male members or for the use of visitor and is called "*Pinagudi*", the next apartment will go to the eldest male representative of the family with his wife, and the third room will be given to the youngest married member. Each room averages fifteen feet in length, including the "*ochalen*" (back verandah), which is from five to seven feet in breadth. When laying out the compartments, the house is divided breadth wise, taking the center or ridge of pole of the front of the house is a "*verandah*" (alley way) which is divided into two by a mat partition for the use of the males and females respectively. In front of it, the bamboo "*machan*" (raised platform) used for various household purposes of domestic use. One has to climb up through a "sang–u" (steps dug out on a wooden log) on the "*ejor*" and then through alley way to the apartments.

Elders

The old age is also the golden age for the older Chakmas in the society. All the older ones in the family are either old 'dear dad' or 'grand dad'. All the family activities are pivoting to the old ones. The respectability to the old ones is an important part in the social system. A spending Indian new year celebration is called "*Biju*" in Chakma, where in a traditional way the old ones are respected with various offerings. They become the custodian of the customary social laws and settle all social disputes. They also devote their time in homework.

Children

Earlier the children used to spend their energy and enthusiasm in the field works with the elders. In the present generation they are attending schools. But the education they are undergoing is substandard when compared to the town schools. So they are not able to get the fruit of their education. They are also getting distanced from the nature of working in the rural forest areas and this is leading them into frustration. Despite all these setbacks, they have in them an inner desire for learning.

Society

The Chakma society orignated in the geographical condition of CHT. With the movement of its people it has spread over to different area. With their mutual help and co-operation, strong togetherness, they have managed to pursue their language and their common way of life. The Chakma society, therefore, is an organization of individuals in a particular geographical area/condition in the present time. But in general, in respect of involvement from bottom in the birth and growth till death it undergoes through the traditional social structural laws relating to marriage, birth, death, religious ceremonies, social offences and other religious festivals which are not being discussed here fully. To give some idea of their distinctiveness of their traditional characteristics a few social laws are being drawn below:

1. Traditionally, their minds have become conditioned to live freely and not to carry out any menial job of others like the carrying of shoes of others. They are averse in doing lower jobs like sweeper, barber, cobbler etc.

2. Beating of drums in public is prohibited (except the war drums).

3. The social punishments are as follows:

(a) "*Jarimana*": Cash fine

(b) "*Muchilika*": Bond agreement

(c) "*Marpeet*" : Physical punishment

(d) "*Jendhera*": In this the offender's hair on the head are cut into three parts and fowl is hung on the neck and a bamboo is kept on their head

(e) "*Vandala*" : In this, the offender is to offer food with reverence to all village elders.

By tradition, a temporary hut is made outside the house whenever a pregnant woman is to deliver a baby. Before getting into the house the mother and the baby are to be purified through some rituals.

The Post Partition Grimness

For providing independence to the Hindu and Muslims of the Indian sub-continent the colonial British rule divided India for the creation of Hindustan and Pakistan on the basis of areas dominated by Hindus and Muslims, but it unwittingly added CHT with 98 p.c ethnic Buddhists to Pakistan arbitrarily, violating the partition rule. The Muslim political power wanted CHT for its strategic geographical importance but did not want its non-Muslim people, as they feared insecure with them. So nothing satisfied them till the Muslims outnumbered the locals. The ethnic tribal Buddhist had no inklings what was in store for them with the Muslim political power/Muslim country. The Pakistani government began to take away all their land rights and also systematically planned to uproot them from CHT. The government actions began as follows:

(1) Withdrawal of the CHT regulations of 1900 AD to make way to outsiders to move into it;

(2) The destruction of forest natural resources and changing of ecology, which was the supporting tribal economy;

(3) Construction of a dam of hydro-electric project in

CHT, that uprooted a large number of Chakmas from their ancestral homes:

(4) Fundamentalist powerful Islamic organizations began their activities to bring the Buddhists into the fold of Islam;

(5) The security forces and terror crazed Muslims were let loose in CHT and they began to rough on to the Buddhists.

What shall they do? What can they do? The government was not at all satisfying with all their moves to live happily in harmony with the majority Muslims. They made several attempts to strive out a deal with the successive governments to clear all the fears of the government, but yielded no results.

As a result, an insurgency movement broke out in CHT and many began floundering in the intimidating darkness. The Buddhists began to live under the shadow of insecurity and unhappiness due to large number of killing, missing of people, physical torture, human violation of all ages of both male and female (see the annexure at page "A"). The Buddhists are now having a narrow existence of living.

In comparison to the Chakmas in Bangladesh, the Chakmas in India are not confronting any such adversities, but they are yet to walk a very long way to before getting settled in India. Even after being born in India, many of them are being denied with citizenship right. Therefore, a great fear runs through them especially those who are in *Arunachal Pradesh* (a province in the north-east India). On the whole many of them had already established themselves in India, but a vast group of them in Assam could not stand up on their feet as they were living in the remote areas in the distant hills.

Natural Philosophy and Religion

From the very early time, the most regarded divine worshiping ceremony performed by Chakmas is called "*Burpara*" which signifies cleansing and purifying from all evils, sprits, curses, illness, misfortunes, and all kind of odds. It is performed by "*ooza*" (village clergy), on the belief that whatever happens in life it is influenced by the cosmic forces from the universe. From the very earliest time, religion was regarded as divine power (*Shakti*) which signifies protectivity or destructivity. They feel that it is the most beneficent act which is practiced by them.

How they have been connected with Buddhism? According to Dr. Farchammer, "There are old Buddhist tradition among the *Talaings* and *Arakanese,* traditions which could not have originated with the southern Buddhist school, but are the remnants of the old Northern Buddhism which reached Arakan from the Ganges when India was mainly Buddhist; they form a substratum cropping up here and there apparently without any connection; its centre is the *Mahamuni* pagoda, the most important remains of ancient Buddhism in Burma, antedating in this province both Brahmanism and the Buddhism of the southern school."

The ancient religious book of Chakmas is called "*Agartara*" which has 28 parts viz. *Agartara, Malem Tara, Sadenggiri Tara, Annicha Tara, Sree Mangal Tara, Dosa Paramai Tara, Bora Kuruk Tara, Trikundu Tara, Talik Shastra Tara, Aristama Tara, Raken Ful Tara, Sahes Ful Tara, Jyon Dharam Tara, Anjna Tara, Pudum Ful Tara, Angra Sutra Tara, Fakira Tara, Sakya Tara, Suba Dijiya Tara, Sarak Dham Tara, Raja Hora Tara, Sak Suttam Tara, Buddha Ful Tara, Chaneng Ful Tara and Arinama Tara.*

These Taras are not transcripted in their language, so it is no more found in them. But they still carry it from mouth to mouth as their old religious books. The Taras were the hand of '*Roul* or *Ari*' the earlier Buddhist monks in the distant hills. Some disreputably call them as corrupt monks. In the *Mahayana Tara* is a personification of Nirvana, which identifies with 'shakti' or female principle. In otherwise, Tara is a manifestation of the wisdom, compassion, love and in particular, the skill activity of all enlightened beings.

Around 12 AD Theravada Buddhism made an edge over the Mahayana in this region and now the Chakmas whose religious emancipation shaped from Theroveda Buddhism from last many centuries. History records that around 272 BC, a Prince U. Cancha Uparaja from *magadha* came and lived in Arakan as a monk. The Chakmas claim their relationship with the rulers of Kapilavstu.

Healing Community

Buddhism postulates that human life in 'Samsara' (worldly life) begins in 'dukka' (suffering), and it starts a reversible journey towards death, at the very moment when it is conceived in mother's womb. In Buddhism, it is the '*upadana*' (attachment) that leads to becoming (rebirth). No attachment is permanent—impermanence is '*dukkha*'. The Buddha taught and preached the way to combat this "*dukkha*" (illness); healing. The Buddhist healing means keeping the body and mind in blissfulness and pure through all our actions that results the cause and effect. Healing is always discharged through "*health care*" and "*mental care*". In Buddhist healing, mind has an overriding power to combat and restoring health.

Now, want to pick up the subject that left of earlier in (The plight of Chakmas) part one. It passes belief, how 98 percent ethnic majority Buddhist land (CHT) that could turn into Muslim majority in the last half a century. Imagine the unusual frightening way the ethnic Buddhist people had to pass on to escape from killing and cruelty! Many of them had to flee away from their ancestral homes. Till now, a number of them are yet a dejected band of people moving around in distant mountains in many provinces in the north-east region. Many of them could not sustain life and had to pass away in the cruel hands of the mighty. It reminds me of the historic event, when the king Bimbasra of *Magadha* was imprisoned and left to die without food by his own son Ajatasatru, the queen Veidehi made entreaty to Buddha. It was in response to her entreaties that Buddha Sakyamuni preached the meditation sutra, which teaches a series of sixteen visualization (of *Amitava Buddha*, the pure land) leading to re-birth her in the land of ultimate bliss.

In the second place, I would like to cite the following teaching of non-violence and abstention from killing, some students and staff of *ven*. Thich Nhat Hanh uttered at a function their commitments, in this way:

"Now once again, we solemnly promise never to hate those who kill us, above all never to use violence to answer violence, even if the antagonists see us as enemies and kill until they annihilate us. We re-call our pledge that people, no matter what their origins, never are enemies—Help us to keep steadily this non-violent mind in our social work by love that asks nothing in return."

Buddha has propounded the doctrine of non-violence, that is the beginning of letting peace into practice in mind, that results in healing of suffering in mind-body, which comprises of four viz earth element (skin, hair, nail, teeth, bone and flesh, etc), liquid element (blood saliva, urine etc), fire element (body heat), and wind element (breathing movement). The four elements composed together is "sankara" (body). The body has six sense organs viz eyes, nose, tongue, body and mind. The interaction of all these senses is the central power of Buddhist healing. This also benefits the physical health. It is being universally accepted in all researches.

Heart is the hollow muscular organ of mind which by its rhythmic contraction and relaxation drives the blood round the vascular system. The conditioning of mind results in heart especially love and anger (positive and negative). The positivity comes with the compassion of Buddha (in

Theroveda). In Mahayana it is emanation of the *Amitava* Buddha and a co-resident of the western paradise "*Avolokiteshvara*" – the Bodhisattava of compassion—the lord who looks down with loving care for humanity. Below is quoted from his Holiness,The Dalai Lama:

> "Whether one believes in religion or not,
> and whether one believes in re-birth or not,
> there is not anyone who does not appreciate,
> Kindness and compassion."

Due to its long existence in the indigenous Chakma community, Buddhism has been an indispensable and inseparable part in their life from time immemorial. In every village whether small or big there would at least be one monastery for daily services to Buddha. It is maintained with the support of the villagers themselves without any assistance from outside. The monastery is usually left under the care of a *Bikkhu* who is selected by the villagers for a certain spell of time on a yearly basis. In the rural areas, the monks are usually lacking in higher education, which is not financially affordable to them. They are also lacking in opportunities to gain spiritual training from learned monk teachers. Many young monks are very keen to get higher religious education, so that they could participate in the bigger religious ceremonies and discussions. The profound Buddhist knowledge is the central path of healing in Buddhism.

I would now like to mention a great Chakma Buddhist *Bhikkhu* who has become widely known by the name "BANA BHANTE" (forest monk). He seems to have attained *Arahathood* according to the devotees. His original name is Sadhana Nanda. He was born in a poor family and did not

Appendix 1

Incidents / Massacres	*Killed*	*Injured/raped*
		[illegible]
		[illegible]

Incidents / Massacres	Killed	Injured / raped	Missing	Perpetrators
Panchari/Dighinali and Bara Merung 8 December 1971	10	20	2	Mukti Force
Panchari/Kalanal 19 December 1971	47	7	-	Do
Khagrachari/Khabongparia Mohajanpara 13 April 1977	-	279	1	BD Military
Matiranga/Guimara/Manikchari/ Laxmichari 13 May 1977	73	14	20	BD Military
Rangamati and adjacent area 24 December 1977	-	45	-	Do
Khagrachari/Kukichari 30 December 1977	12	10	-	Do
Ruma/Dumdummya Bandarban, December, 78 and January, 79	-	35	-	Do
Rangamati/Subalong 9 January, 79	1	5	-	Do
Khagrachari/Gargajjyachari 5 March 1979	-	1	15	Do

Panchari/kanungupara 2 April 1979	-	-	-	Do
Rangamati 9 April 1979	-	14	-	Do
Rangamati/kalampati 25 March 1980	300	175	13	Military and Settlers
Matiranga/Belchari 25 June 1981	261	234	7	Do
Rangamati/Bushanchara	62	6	5	26 EBR, 17 Battalion BDR & Settless
Choto Horina 31 May 1984				Battalion BDR and Settlers
Mahalchari/khularampara 1 July 1985	-	2	-	13 EBR
Longadu/Tintillya 22 July 1985	-	Raped 4+7=11	-	Led by Lt. Mohasin
Mahalchari/Chandra Kumar Karbaripara 2 August 1985		2 raped and converted	-	Settlers

Incidents / Massacres	*Killed*	*Injured / raped*	*Missing*	*Perpetrators*
Panchari/Matiranga 30 April-1 May 1986	51	5	5	Military/BDR/VDP
Matiranga	42	8	-	BDR/VDP/Settlers

18 May 1986				
Merung/Changrachari 19 December 1986	1	16	-	41 EBR/VDP/ Settlers
Hirachar/Sharbuatuli Choto Haria	36	21	26	Military/VDP/ Settlers
8-10 August 1988				
Langadu/Malya	32	11	-	VDP/Settlers
4 May 1989				
Malya, 2nd Feb, 1992	30	-	-	BSF and BMIs
Logang, 10th April 1992	Children and women where burnt alive in their houses			BSF and BMIs
Naniachara, 17th Nov, 1993	100	500	-	BSF and BMIs
Rangamati, 11th Jun, 1996	Miss Kalpana Chakma, student leader kidnapped and believed to be killed by BSF and BMIs			

Incidents / Massacres	*Killed*	*Injured / raped*	*Missing*	*Perpetrators*
Bandarban, 15th Mar, 1995	Inhuman physical torture not even sparing monks			BSF and BMIs
Babuchara Bazaar, 16th Oct, 1999		100 men and women were		BSF and BMIs

		tortured		
Ramgarh	12	-	-	BSF and BMI's
Dighinala, 18th, May, 2001	Inhuman physical torture			BSF and BMIs

Note: BSF = Bangladesh Security Forces
BMIs = Bangladesh Muslim Infiltrators

receive any school education. But since his childhood he was driven by a burning desire to take on the Buddhist path of enlightenment. So he retreated to the forest and started meditation. Having gained great wisdom and spiritual awareness, he became known as BANA BHATE. On the fervent appeal of a large number of devotees, he returned to a monastery in Rangamati of CHT,

Bangladesh. A great number of people gather daily to hear his sermons and benefit from the fruits of his enlightenment.

In essence, healing in Buddhism comes by way of self discipline and spiritual knowledge.

"I vow that when my life approaching its end

All obstructions will be swept away:

I will see Amitava Buddha,

And be born in his land of Ultimate Bliss.

When reborn in the Western Land.
I will perfect and completely fulfill
Without exception these Great Vows,
To delight and benefit all beings."

—Avatamsaka Sutra

ETHNIC BUDDHISTS IN ASSAM

Last June, I was asked to go early on a Sunday morning to Heathrow to meet an Amida visitor from Assam, in north east India. His plane arrived even earlier and I wondered how on earth we would find each other, when he did not even know I existed, never mind that I was due to meet him! Near the Information Desk we saw each other, and somehow, perhaps the questioning looks on our faces, we knew. This was Sakya Talukdar, who had come across David Brazier and the Amida Trust via the Internet.

I came to know Sakya as a friend over the next six weeks as he stayed with me several times. The aim had been for him to go to Amida France, but the visa requirements defeated everyone. In the meantime, Sakya met quite a few Amida members in London and in Newcastle, and spent a week at Throssle monastery.

Sakya was keen to come to Europe to meet Amida members because of his project to help the "*ethnic Buddhists*" in his part of the world. The foothills of the

Himalayas and the mountain river valleys are today inhabited by numerous tribes in different countries—India, Bangladesh and Myanmar. They trace their ancestry from Sakya clan in which it is thought Buddha was born more than 2500 years ago. They are the earliest Buddhists ever known in the history of South East Asia.

Over the centuries there has been a lot of movement of peoples and tribes, and in this century the changed status and boundaries of India, Pakistan and Bangladesh have added tension and conflict to the area. This has particularly affected tribes with Buddhist culture as they do not fit into the dominant Hindu, Muslim or Christian area, and they are becoming dispossessed peoples. Some of those who have settled in Guwahati, the capital of Assam, have formed *The Friendly Society*, a not-for-profit social organization, to help to strengthen their sense of culture and identity.

One of their projects is to see if they can throw light on their ancestral history with the help of modern genetic anthropological studies. It so happens that I have a strong interest in this area of work because of my own research into the nature of humanity as a species and as a complex evolving organism. I was able to find a contact in University College London (UCL), Dr. Mark Thomas, who on being introduced to Sakya, immediately recruited him as the first sample for a research project covering the "ethnic" Buddhist tribes! Sakya went home armed with 100 sample kits, and instruction on how to record the correct anthropological information for the samples. I am a go-between now in this research project and will be meeting Dr. Thomas and his colleagues soon.

Little did I know what would emerge from this unexpected request to meet a visitor at Heathrow! Anyone who is interested in understanding more about this fascinating area of human genetic research could look at the very readable book *The Language of Genetics* by Steve Jones. He was the author of some excellent TV programmes a few years ago on the same subject (which is what drew my attention to it all), and the head of the UCL department where Dr. Thomas works. I would be glad to hear from any other Amida member with an interest in this subject and Sakya's project.

This was written for Living Buddhism the Amida Trust journal in the summer of 1999 by Eileen Conn.

Epilogue Conclusion

The Contemporary World

According to Joan Halifax Roshi, Head Teacher, Upaya Zen Center, Santa Fe, New Mexico "Today, more than any other time in human history we are living in a king of intimacy that can destroy or liberate. Our weapons can find their targets within minutes, our diseases can spread like a wild fire in a dry forest, and our delusions can contaminate the minds of millions instantaneously through the media". We are living in the word of nervous nuclear arms race, injustice, violence, racial intolerance, hatred, greed, corruptions and delusions. We are just being the victims of all these intolerances and overbearing nervousness. They is why we are unable to live in harmony with our fellow beings and therefore no happiness. Our mind and thoughts are full of agony when we come to know how our leaders are creating unrest and troubles for their self interest. Humanity in the modern world is living in hard shell in the heart of those in worlds super power (internationally powerful);

1. China and India super power in human resources;
2. G–7 countries, worlds most economically developed super powers;
3. Nuclear power developed countries;
4. The 3rd world (Developing countries);
5. The 4th world (indigenous people of the world).

1. Tenzin Gyatso (b. 1935) was recognized extraordinary spiritual leader since the age of two, His Holiness Dalai Lama in Tibet, now in exile in India.
2. Raja Tridiv Roy (b. 1933) Chakma chief now in self exile (by choice) in Pakistan.

As gleaned from history they descend from the same ethnic line – the Scything: indigenous people of Tibet and Hill Tracts of Chittagong in Bangladesh. Their subjects faced holocaust turning their peace living area into a terror ridden region. They rise to the occasion to alleviate suffering of the natives, but having no effect. His Holiness the Dalai Lama was awarded the 'Noble Prize for peace' in 1989. The Chakma chief, Tridiv Roy was awarded 'Stalwarts of Pakistan award' in 1999. both of them worked hard assiduously to convince the world leaders to understand the sensibility of the situation but in the objective world the earning was loving kindness and compassion with some dole. But the grip of their suffering was not relaxed. The infliction of pain continued unending. The suffering people are trying to resist occasionally which is being highlighted in the media coverage and propaganda compaign. However, their suffering remains undiminished. Both Tibetans and Chakmas had to flee away from their homeland and became landless. The Tibetan received treatment as protectorate from India, but Chakma are not treated in alliance to redress their sufferings. The Tibetans are able to gain publicity of would media for their fullness of Bodhisattva ideology universally, while Chakmas are yet to step up on this. No doubt they are getting set to those ideas, as there seems to be no political willingness to stop infliction of pain to indigenous people Undoubtedly, the indigenous people are the victims of exploit by the majority by breaking up their home and sub-dividing them. They are faced with major threat in all respects of progress and not being elevated at equal level of the majority. They are being left wayside. As for example, the availability of natural water has become obsolete. Mineral water has replaced the natural water in developed countries and modern cities. Similarly, people in the developed society are consuming organic food only, whereas in the 4th world (indigenous people) live on the chemical product of food any they do not have a loud voice and political clout. There is no hesitation to utilize the maximum of nature's wealth for the developed human society. The exclusion of indigenous people on the resources of nature against the law of holistic system, which results in disintegration and devastation in the phenomena of nature. The worst victims in this unholy race are the indigenous people who are completely or partly deprived of their right to the home territory and its wealth, making gross discrimination, dependency and despondency on the rich and powerful resulting holocaust. All living beings are indispensably dependent on the Pandoras box of the world (store). Those knowing how to get over their need for luxurious living are known to be advanced people, and the indigenous people are those who are dependent on the mercy and doles. It is the onus duty of the world's intellectual society, leaders (elected members in the Parliament) of the different countries to ensure the welfare of the indigenous people.

Here is the extraction from the Parliamentary debated (House of Lords) U.K Vol 672 No. 21 Thursday 23rd June, 2005. "Several noble Lords mentioned the Chittagong Hill Tracts. There have been internal tensions since the 1960's' between the Bengali settlers and the tribal inhabitants there. The Bangladesh government initiated discussions with representatives of the tribal inhabitants in December 1996 which, understandily resulted in a peace accord being signed in December 1997. But there has been little progress on implementing it or on setting the land disputes that re at the heart of many of the tensions between, tribal inhabitants and Bengali settlers. "There are writings on the walls, there are fascists pretending to be humanitarians. The most important factor is that the implementation of the peace accord would drag on unless a democratic voice is built up in the world for peace with fair justice and equal share of countries wealth. Here are a people who have been discriminated and victimized economically, and still struggle to be recognized internationally and to have their own power. But, ironically, their homeland has turned into a sanctuary for terrorism – the worst of its kind, and hits the world right now. They beg the question to the world leaders: is there any other way to get off from man- made genocide disaster holocaust, miseries within limit of boundaries of human existence? In the ever changing world there are sings of the times: Join hands together to protect world's indigenous people. Genilaizaiton of their idealisim freely without any warp from those who are deflecting them Let not it remain a visionary, mistic idea alone.

Anton Chekhov writes in three sisters (a one Act play) "one longs for life! O my God! Time will pass, and we shall go away for ever, and we shall be forgotten, our faces will be forgotten, our voices, and how many there were of us; but our sufferings will pass into joy for those who will live after us, happiness and peace will be established upon earth, and they will remember kindly and bless those who have lived before".

Bibliography

1. *The Buddha and his Religion* by J. Barthelemy Saint Hilaire translated by Laura Ensor. Published by George Routledge and Sons Ltd. U.K.
2. *The Great Tang Dynasty* Record of western region by Li Rongxi, USA.
3. *The Historical Buddha* by H.W. Schumann, London, 1989.
4. *Daily life in Ancient India from 200 BC to 700 AD* by A. Auboyer, London 1965.
5. *The Wonder that was India* by A.L. Basham, Bombay, 1963.
6. *Society at the Time of Buddha* by N. Wagle, London 1963.
7. *The Magadhas in Ancient India* by B.C. Law, Delhi, 1976.
8. *An Early History of Vaisali* by Y. Mishra 1962.
9. *Everyday Life in Early India* by M. Edwards, London, 1969.
10. *Ancient India* by D.D. Kosambi.
11. *A History of South-East Asia* by D.G.E. Hall.
12. *The Social Organization in South-East India in Buddha's Time* by Richard Fick.
13. *Indian Culture in the days of Buddha* by A.P. Dezoysa, London.
14. *The People of Asia* by Gordon T. Bowles (1977).
15. *Sakya or Buddhist Origin* by Mrs. Rhys Davids, 1978.

16. *Journal and proceedings of the Asiatic Society of Bengal* (The social and religious ceremonies of the Cakmas) by P.C. Basu (1931).
17. *Britis Burma and its people* by Cpt. CJFS Forbes (1878), London.
18. *Burma Past and Present* by Lt. Gen. Albert Fytche (1878).
19. *The Tribal culture in India* by L.P. Vidyathi and B.K. Rai.
20. *Tai – Ahom Religion and Custom* by Dr. Padmeswa Gogoi (1976).
21. *The Raiders of Arakkan* by C.E. Lucas Phillip (1971).
22. *The Hill Tracts of Arakkan* by William Gwynne Rangoon (1881).
23. *The Monograph on Arakan Antiquities* by Dr. Forchhammer.
24. *Hand Books for the Indian Army Races of Burma* by Maj. C.M. Enriquez.
25. *Burma from the Earliest Time to the Present Day* by Sir J.G. Scott (1924).
26. *Historical and Statistical Sketch of Arakan* by Br. Charlespaton Esq.
27. *Thve Tai Khamti* by Lila Gogoi.
28. *Account of the Kookies or Lunctas* by John Mavnare (1808).
29. *The Wild Tribes of India by Horatio Bickerstaffe Rowney,* Reprinted B.R. Publishing Corporation, Delhi.
30. *Topography of Assam by John M'Cosh 1837 Reprinted* by K.M. Mittal, Delhi, 1975.
31. *The Tribes of Brahamputra Valley* by L.A. Waddel.
32. *The Hill Tracts between Assam and Burma on the Upper Brahamaputra* by Lt. R. Wilcox (1825).

33. *Bangladesh Genocide in the Chittagong Hill Tracts,* Survival International, 1985.
34. *Eastern Bengal District Gazetteers Chittagong* by L.S.S. O'Malley, 1908.
35. *Tribes of Burma* by Lowis C.C.
36. *Report on the Eastern Frontier of British India* by Capt. R. Boileau Pemberton.
37. *Buddha and Buddhism* – Burma by Bigandet (P.A.).
38. *Cultural Heritage of Tibet* by David Macdonald.
39. *The Illustrated History of the British Empire in India* by E.H. Naton, 1987.
40. *The Cambridge History of South-East Asia* by Nicolas Tarling.
41. *Census of India 1901 Vol. XII (Burma)* by C.C. Lowis.
42. *Linguistic Survey of India.*
43. *The History of Hindosthan* (translated from Parsian) by Alexander dow, 1770. Reprinted Today and Tomorrow's Printer and Publisher, New Delhi, 1973.
44. *Caste and Races in India* by G.S. Ghurye.
45. *A Descriptive Account of Assam* by William Robinson.
46. *A Political Life in Assam during 19th Century* by B.B. Hazarika.
47. *The Life of the Buddha* by A. Faucher.
48. *The Age of Vinaya,* New Delhi 1972 by G.S.P. Mishra.
49. *The Buddha of Infinite Light* by D.T. Sazuki.
50. *Society at the Time of Buddha* by N. Wagle, Bombay, 1963.
51. *Buddha and Buddhists by law* B.C. Amsterdam, 1937.
52. *Buddha and Buddhism – India* by Liang (Trevor Os Land).

Index